REINVENTING
THE RETAIL BANK

Cross-Marketing
Investment Products
to Create
the Full-Service
Financial Center

LAWRENCE E. HARB
SARAH E. SLEIGHT

A BANKLINE PUBLICATION

PROBUS PUBLISHING COMPANY
Chicago, Illinois
Cambridge, England

BANK LINE ™

This publication is designed to provide accurate and authoritative information in regard to the subject matter covered. It is sold with the understanding that the author and the publisher are not engaged in rendering legal, accounting, or other professional service.

Authorization to photocopy items for internal or personal use, or the internal or personal use of specific clients, is granted by PROBUS PUBLISHING COMPANY, provided that the U.S. $7.00 per page fee is paid directly to Copyright Clearance Center, 222 Rosewood Drive, Danvers, MA 01923, USA; Phone: 1-508-750-8400. For those organizations that have been granted a photocopy license by CCC, a separate system of payment has been arranged. The fee code for users of the Transactional Reporting Service is 1-55738-386-3/94/$00.00 + $7.00.

ISBN 1-55738-386-3

Printed in the United States of America

BB

1 2 3 4 5 6 7 8 9 0

To Pam and Pete

Contents

Preface

Alternative investment products have become one of the hottest topics in banking circles these days as banks have looked for new ways to service their customers and increase fee income. What products do customers need; what new products can a financial institution properly offer its customers? Bankers who are thinking hard about these issues find themselves forced to confront the question about what businesses banks should be in today, and how banks will best survive and thrive through the turn of the century.

The needs of banking customers are changing and there is no going back. Even if interest rates were to shoot up again, consumers have changed their ideas about saving and are starting to focus on investing. Although higher interest rates could certainly cause a certain amount of funds to be reallocated out of mutual funds and annuities and back into CDs or other fixed-income products, there have been structural changes to the economy over the past ten years that cannot be undone; an educational process has been put in motion. The "savers" of the last generation are starting to give way to the more financially educated "investors."

The younger generation is watching the older generation deal with providing for the exorbitant cost of medical care during a retirement that is likely to last for one-third of most people's adult lives, in the face of a social security system that most of this generation doubt will survive. This situation has forced citizens to take it upon themselves to start saving and investing for their own retirements; this is a consumer need that is not going to change, regardless of interest rates. And financial institutions are the most attractive choice of financial intermediaries to help educate these new investors and assist them in meeting their needs. Consumers approach their banks with trust, expecting to receive conscientious investment advice with their own best interests in mind. This is the key to the banking franchise. *If banks ever lose this trust, they will have lost their franchise.*

We are most emphatic in believing that alternative investment products belong in financial institutions. We have written this book to provide the reader with a guide to these new products and how they fit into the retail bank of the future. (The future is now.) We want the reader to understand what the products are, how they are delivered, and how they best fit into the structure of the financial institution. We want to talk about how marketing, referral, compensation and compliance systems are structured within the overall retail investment services program, and how regulation and legislation affect a program. Above all, we want to impart an understanding of how best to integrate a retail investment services program into the structure and life of *your* financial institution.

Whether you are a bank of whatever size, a third-party provider, or a registered rep, there will be information to make this book meaningful to you. Chapters are meant to stand on their own; one reader might want to read this book from beginning to end, another will be able to consult specific chapters on selected topics. The book is also meant to function as a reference guide: you can use the index to find the subject matter you need. Whether you are trying to figure out what questions to ask as you begin to think about starting a program, or seeking specialized information to help you refine some aspect of an existing program, there is information in this book for you. (However, we do caution you that the law is constantly changing, and it is important to consult with legal counsel.)

Between us, we have more than 32 years of experience in the banking and brokerage industry. We have both worked in very large institutions; we have also worked in a very small business, as we built our own broker/dealer and third-party provider into a thriving concern. Our work as consultants brings another entire realm of experience to this book. We have worked with banks and brokerage units of every size, and with every possible permutation of customer base.

What we have learned as consultants is that there are a myriad of approaches that work, sometimes in surprising ways. We are humbled by the experience of learning something from almost everyone we have talked to. We see that this industry is evolving quickly, and one company or individual cannot know it all. This book incorporates the experiences and ideas of dozens of individuals and programs, and has allowed us to extend well beyond the experience gained from our own efforts.

What we have found is that serving the investment needs of individuals is much more gratifying than working with institutions. With individuals you have to take into consideration the whole of a person's constraints, needs, goals, and dreams, to design an investment program that works. The goal of the retail investment services program is to institutionalize the servicing and satisfaction of such needs. It is the love of this industry that inspires us, for it is a constant challenge to design programs that work for both the individual and the institution.

We must first extend grateful thanks to our co-workers at LCL Investments and Lasalle Consultants, who both helped with the book and picked up the slack when we were working on the book. This book would not exist without them. Each contributed in his or her own way: some read chapters and made suggestions, others typed manuscripts or helped prepare materials. We would like to thank all of them; particular thanks have to go to the other members of our management team: Bob (our most faithful reader), Sharon, Liz, Dave, and Andrew.

We have nothing but gratitude for the many individuals who shared their experiences with us, trusting that we would use that information judiciously. We have been surprised and touched by the generosity of the individuals and institutions that have helped us, many of them preferring to remain anonymous. The list of resources at the back of the book lists the names and addresses of some of the people who made significant contributions to the book, all of whom have particular knowledge or expertise about one or many facets of this business. We would like to thank the many sources that gave us permission to use their statistics or copyrighted material, or whose ideas provided us with inspiration.

There are two individuals we would like to thank by name. Ronald R. Glancz, a partner in Venable, Baetjer, Howard & Civiletti, helped us make our way through the maze of legislation and regulation. We don't know what we would have done without him. He graciously gave us permission to use his previously published material, and even more graciously assisted us with writing additional information. We would also like to thank Richard A. Ayotte, of American Brokerage Consultants, Inc., who is well known in the bank-brokerage industry. He shared his statistics with us, and allowed us to adapt some of the information from his published articles.

Finally, we are deeply indebted to the forbearance of our long-suffering spouses, without whose tolerance we could never have finished this project.

1

Why Sell Alternative Investment Products

Alternative investment products (AIP) have become part of the financial agenda of this country. Many banks have entered this business enthusiastically. "About 91% of banks with over $1 billion in assets offer mutual funds, according to a survey by Alliance Capital Management, New York." [1] Richard A. Ayotte of American Brokerage Consultants, Inc., has done a thorough census of financial institutions (including both banks and savings and loans) ranging in size from $50 million to $10 billion; he estimates that there are 7,700 financial institutions in this group. Overall, 39% of these financial institutions are involved with providing brokerage services. However, of the largest institutions in his survey, $1 billion to $10 billion, 69% offer brokerage services. Table 1.1 shows how the categories break out by size.

Look at the statistics: The Investment Company Institute says that there is now $1.9 trillion invested in mutual funds, with 68 million owners. Over $1 billion pours into mutual funds every day, and mutual funds are only one of the many different alternative investment products. Total mutual fund sales in 1992 were $362 billion, with approximately 14% sold through bank programs.

The annuity market is smaller than the mutual fund market but is growing fast. The American Council of Life Insurance reports that $48.8 billion in total annuity sales (including both fixed and variable) was sold to individuals in 1992,[2] and LIMRA reports that total considerations (sales) in the first half of

---

1 Penny Lunt, "How Are Mutual Funds Changing Banks?" *ABA Banking Journal,* June 1993, p. 31.
2 American Council of Life Insurance, *1993 Insurance Fact Book Update,* p. 37.

Table 1.1 Financial Institutions Offering Brokerage Services

Total Assets	Number of Institutions	Percentage Offering Brokerage	Percentage Offering Brokerage, in the Business Five Years or More
$1-10 billion	590	60%	60%
$500 million-$1 billion	436	46%	54%
$250-500 million	844	48%	51%
$100-250 million	2,546	41%	42%
$50-100 million	3,278	30%	40%
Total	7,694	39%	48%

Source: Bank-Brokerage Census, American Brokerage Consultants, Inc., 1992.

1993 were up 10% over the same period of 1992.[3] *Bank Investment Marketing* magazine reports that, according to Ken Kehrer, president of Kenneth Kehrer Associates, in 1992 "banks sold some $12.2 billion in annuities . . . . That market share has been on the upswing, and Kehrer estimates that if all banks entered the business, they could sell about $26 billion in annuities, from which they would reap as much as $6.5 billion in profits."[4]

How Investing Has Changed

Only a few years ago, the largest investment an ordinary consumer made in his or her lifetime was the the purchase of a home. Furthermore, most people didn't have to worry a great deal about retirement, because they didn't live long enough for it to be an issue. Social Security provided a cushion for those who did live some years into retirement. Coupled with the shorter life span was a different family structure, where older people routinely lived with their adult children.

All of these factors have changed dramatically. Corporate downsizing and restructuring over the last decade have altered the way people look at employment. Lifetime employment with a single employer who accepts responsibility for funding retirement (including medical benefits) for the individual is a thing of the past. Lifetime employment itself is gone forever. Medical benefits for retirees are disappearing rapidly. Pensions have changed from generous, fixed-benefit programs to 401(k) plans that put the onus on the individual to save. The amount available at retirement depends on how much the individual was able to contribute and how well he or she chose investment options. Individuals have grave doubts about the social security system: even if it doesn't collapse completely, how much will it provide?

---

3   Printed with the permission of the Life Insurance Marketing and Research Association.
4   Linda Corman,"Stormy Weather," *Bank Investment Marketing*, November/December 1993, p.28.

Furthermore, as individuals change jobs more often, they are far more likely to receive pension payouts and 401(k) payouts periodically during their working life. They then have to invest those proceeds themselves. Demographic data tell us that a woman who was born in 1950 and reaches the age of 65 is projected to live to age 87, and a man to age 81.[5] If that woman retires at age 62, she can expect to provide for a full 25 years of retirement. Finally, fewer parents can expect their children to take care of them; those children will be struggling to provide for themselves and their children.

These factors are all well known. What they mean to us is that now the largest investment most individuals will make is funding their own retirement. Our experience has shown consistently that most individuals lack the education to do this effectively.

Managing assets was easy for unsophisticated investors in the 1980s. Consumers became accustomed to the high rates of interest on bank certificates of deposit (CDs) that resulted in rapid asset growth, regardless of the inflation rate that eroded the value of those assets as they accumulated. IRAs were introduced when interest rates were at 16%. The return to lower rates that are, historically speaking, more realistic, is forcing retail depositors to find products that yield higher rates of return. The other factor that has changed is that CDs do not have a positive real rate of return. With an inflation rate of 2.8% and a CD yield of 2.9% (on which taxes must be paid), savers do not keep up with the rate of inflation. They lose purchasing power by investing in CDs.

Furthermore, many investors, particularly those on fixed incomes, must receive a certain threshold rate of return to maintain their lifestyles. As interest rates dropped from 16% to 12% to 8%, many savers were still able to meet their threshold. CD rates below 8% presented a problem to many individuals, who were forced to look around for other investments. The first choice would be to lower quality, such as an A-rated bond rather than AAA. When the rates on A bonds dropped below 8%, investors had to seek other kinds of investments, bearing a different kind of risk from bank CDs. (In our view, the risk of losing principal isn't nearly as serious as the risk of not having one's funds grow in real terms.) Memories of the Depression and the 1929 stock market crash have kept many investors from taking part in the great bull market that has been going on for essentially all of their lives. Low CD rates have changed that view, and some investors are now willing to be educated.

The role of banks is being challenged on all sides by other financial intermediaries. Money market mutual funds were one of the earliest competitors for bank deposits. Now you can get an account that looks very like a checking

---

5 "Retirement Savings in America," *The Fifth Annual Merrill Lynch Retirement Planning Survey,* Merrill Lynch, June 1993; quoting NCHS, Middle Mortality Projections, 1990.

account from Merrill Lynch, which will also supply a loan or a credit card. The larger wire houses offer jumbo mortgages. If you want to buy a car, you can get a loan from a credit agency run by the car manufacturer (such as GMAC).

A recent *Wall Street Journal* article quoted Federal Reserve statistics on the decline of banking: "In the past 20 years, commercial banks' share of U.S. financial assets has declined to 24.5% from nearly 40% . . . At current trends, total investments in mutual funds soon will eclipse the $2 trillion in savings and time deposits at banks and thrift institutions."[6] At some point banks are going to have to start fighting back, to keep the customers that are proving so convenient for other institutions to access.

Benefits to the Bank

Satisfying a Customer Need

There is a genuine consumer need that banks can satisfy. The challenge of investing in the 1990s presents banks with a real opportunity. Because customers are unfamiliar with the alternative investment products they are now forced to consider, they are turning to the banks they trust. The banking industry has traditionally had a unique relationship with its customers, a relationship built on trust, safety, and high ethical standards. All the problems banks have had have not changed the fact that customers still trust them. This factor plays a key role in how bankers and their customers deal with each other; it is something that bankers and customers refer to constantly.

Banks will be able to service their customers by expanding beyond banking's traditional role of providing loans and trust department services. Customers of community banks will bring in large amounts of money to a bank investment program because they know the bank. These same individuals might be reluctant to initiate a relationship with a Wall Street brokerage house.

Keeping the Customer Relationship

Lower rates have magnified the difference between the return on CDs and on AIPs and consumers have enthusiastically embraced mutual funds and annuities. As market rates drop, consumers become willing to accept greater risk in order to maintain yield. As customers struggle to maintain the yield they need, they became aware—maybe for the first time—that there are investment alternatives to traditional savings products. Customers are buying these products,

---

6   Kenneth H. Bacon, "Banks' Declining Role in Economy Worries Fed, May Hurt Firms," *Wall Street Journal*, July 9, 1993, p. 1.

whether at the bank or at a brokerage house: if the bank doesn't educate them about these products, someone else will. A retail investment services program provides many benefits to the bank, but the major benefit is the opportunity to strengthen the customer relationship, not lose it.

There's a widely quoted statistic in the banking community that if a customer has a one-product relationship with a bank, the bank has a 17% chance of keeping that customer in the long term. If a customer has a two-product relationship, the percentage is 50%; three-product, 75%; and if a financial institution has a four-product relationship with a customer, that institution has a 90% chance of keeping that relationship for the long term. Whether the statistics are precisely right is not important; the point is to understand that the more services you provide, the stronger the relationship becomes. A customer tends to develop a comprehensive banking relationship with one institution, and it's going to be the institution that offers that customer the most services he or she needs.

Your competition is also gearing up to offer these products and serve this customer need, using the same methods we recommend you use. One of the most powerful tools for forging a strong bond between customer and institution is a financial plan. In providing the information the rep needs to put together a financial plan, the customer will mention assets and investments he or she would not otherwise reveal to an investment counselor, especially in the beginning. This puts your institution in the position of controlling assets and asking the customer about maturing CDs at other institutions, rather than letting the competition's reps ask about the customer's CDs with your institution.

Generating Fee Income

"Our mutual fund activity is more profitable in many ways than some of our banks are," said Steven Settles, director of corporate planning at Barnett Banks, Inc. Settles was quoted in the *ABA Banking Journal* as saying, "Probably our mutual funds are more profitable than a quarter to a third of our banks. There's less fixed cost and less fixed assets involved."[7]

As banks see a decline in their traditional businesses, they are looking for ways to replace the old spread income. Fee-based services banks now provide include such things as trust services and mortgages, but retail investment services have the potential to become one of the most lucrative. Savings and loans were some of the first institutions to recognize that alternative investment products had the capacity to generate fee income. Many of them embraced annuity sales in the 1980s, and have well-established programs by now. Most of the money center regional banks are not far behind.

---

7   Lunt, "Mutual Funds Changing," p. 36.

One thing that financial institutions need to remember is that a defensive program, or only discount brokerage, will not generate the level of fee income they may be looking for. Many smaller institutions offer brokerage programs as a customer accommodation only and hope the program will break even, when the real revenue-earning potential is vastly greater. A well-run, proactive program can significantly increase bank earnings.

Bringing in New Customers

With the exception of loans, few banking products have the potential to bring new customer relationships to a bank. Alternative investment products have that potential because they appeal to depositors who might not otherwise be in the bank. We consider reaching out beyond the bank's customer base to be an important part of marketing a new retail investment services program. These customers could run the gamut from sophisticated investors who have carried brokerage accounts with Wall Street firms to new graduates who are starting an investment program. The seminar-selling approach we advocate offers different types of investors an opportunity to learn and window shop at little risk, to see for themselves what AIPs are about. Seminars are a valuable service offered for free, which appeals to many members of the public, and also benefits a bank in its standing with the community.

Stimulating Cross-Sales Opportunities

A retail investment services program will bring in new customer relationships to the financial institution; as a corollary, that program will stimulate cross-sales opportunities within the bank. The registered rep is one more person who will be looking for opportunities to send customers to the customer service reps (CSRs), and other banking personnel will enjoy being able to refer their customers to the the rep.

Meeting Complete Financial Needs

Despite the banking-type services offered by various other organizations, a bank still has the greatest potential to meet customers' total financial needs. Even a customer whose investment profile is long term and aggressively growth oriented needs the foundation of the investment pyramid, which starts with a checking account and a certain amount of short-term, liquid reserves for emergencies in a savings account.

In addition to mortgages, personal loans, trust services, safe deposit boxes, savings accounts, checking accounts, credit cards, etc., a bank can now offer the customer a diversified investment portfolio as well as complete financial planning services (in many programs). Many retail investment services programs offer investment-type insurance products (annuities), and some offer life and other insurance as well. The more services the bank program can offer, the stronger the relationship between the customer and the bank, and the greater the chance that the customer relationship will remain with the bank. An array of services reduces the chance that the customer will go somewhere else to satisfy one particular need and end up moving the entire relationship.

Introducing a Sales Culture

The reason bankers are just beginning to learn about sales orientation has to do with the history of banking. Until recently, bankers had a product everyone wanted—money, in the form of loans. If consumers wanted that product, they got it from a bank, on the bank's terms. But a fundamental change to the U.S. economy has been that banks are no longer the primary lender. Banks are not always the lowest-cost provider of funds or the most accessible source of money. Later in this chapter we discuss these issues at greater length.

Banks are now competing with other sources to provide their primary product (loans). With the introduction of fee-based services such as retail investment services, banks are competing with other organizations to get consumers to invest their dollars. In other words, the bankers are asking for money! This is a whole new world for bankers, and they are learning to redefine issues such as marketing.

In our view, many bankers need a wake-up call, and that's part of what this book is about. The sales culture that characterizes much of the securities industry will have nothing but benefits for traditional banking. Customers have to be drawn in to your institution, and then relationships have to be built and nourished. This is done through proactive marketing and consultative selling; incentives also play an important role.

Many bankers have a horror of the sales orientation. They imagine that the securities industry has a very aggressive sales culture that will ruin banking as they know it. It is true that there can be a product-pushing orientation to securities sales that has no place in a bank retail investment services program (or in the brokerage industry, for that matter). What should be paramount is the needs-based selling, the relationship building, that characterizes the securities industry at its best. If you and your customer build a financial plan together that helps the solve his or her financial problems, you are well on your way to a solid, lifetime relationship with that customer.

Disintermediation

In terms of retail investment services, disintermediation is the process by which customers move their funds from savings and other deposit accounts with the bank and place them in alternative investment products. The funds are therefore removed from the financial intermediation previously supplied by the financial institution. This legitimate concern of bankers is still the reason most often cited by the uneducated banker for not offering alternative investment products. Many bankers, especially those in smaller or more traditional institutions, have spent their careers trying to build deposits. Now you are telling them that they should actively embrace a program that they think will gouge those deposits. This is a major leap of faith!

In our view, the shift in priorities has come about because banking and consumer needs have changed; we are not implying that bankers have spent their careers in pursuit of the wrong product. However, for many bankers this is almost a personal issue. For them, the securities industry by itself often represents culture shock and seems to insinuate that banking's traditional goals have been misguided.

Many bankers think that they fight this trend by not offering these products themselves. Some of those who perceive the erosion of bank deposits say that at least they won't contribute to the problem by offering AIPs in their own institutions. The shadow of disintermediation won't go away even after the decision to offer alternative investment products has been made. A number of program managers tell us that the issue is still present, although unspoken, in institutions with successful programs.

Jack Shea, senior vice president, Northern Trust, described his institution's experience.

> It is very apparent that there has been a major shift of deposits from savings, checking, and CDs into packaged products. This is happening industry-wide. I do not think this is reversible. Banks have the FDIC cost hanging around their necks and can't be competitive. Savings rates are not and will not be competitive.

> In the retail market, we have documented the fact that more dollars come into Northern Trust as a result of securities transactions than go out for securities transactions, and that is because those funds are being drawn from other institutions. However, the funds do not stay; they are in transition and going into securities.

> The Northern Trust has made a decision to grow its fee income, and the securities business not only generates fee income but satisfies a growing customer need and strengthens customer relationships.

This quote goes to the heart of disintermediation. It is happening, and it is happening for identifiable reasons on a national scale. The current interest-rate environment has resulted in a process of disintermediation that has made sharp inroads into banks' traditional core deposits. The causes are not going to go away, whether or not your institution offers alternative investment products. In fact, in our experience, the best way to fight disintermediation is to enter enthusiastically into a retail investment services program.

There are four main points about disintermediation:

1. Disintermediation is a fact; consumer funds are pouring into alternative investment products and bank deposits are dropping.
2. Those institutions that offer AIPs can not only stop the flow of funds out of their institution but attract funds from the competition.
3. What you risk in not offering AIPs is not disintermediation of customer deposits but disintermediation of the entire customer relationship.
4. What you gain from offering AIPs is an enhanced and strengthened customer relationship.

Disintermediation Is a Reality

Disintermediation statistics are not easy to collect. It is possible to determine overall levels of bank deposits and liabilities, but it takes a judgment call to ascertain what factors are causing changes. For example, we have worked with a community bank that is growing so fast that the disintermediation occurring as a result of its new retail investment services program is insignificant in comparison to its overall growth as an institution. The best way to determine the real disintermediation effect of any given program is to track every single investment. For every annuity or mutual fund bought, where did the funds come from? Although many bank programs and third-party providers have obtained this information on their own programs, it is hard to find sources who will share it, let alone allow it to be published. Our discussions with community bankers lead us to estimate that programs might draw 60% to 70% of their funds from outside the institution.

The *ABA Banking Journal* notes, "Bank certificates of deposit dropped by $191 billion last year, a loss of 18%. At the same time, passbook and money market deposit account balances grew 15% ($158 billion). So while overall deposits have decreased only 1%, CDs—the less liquid money—have certainly taken a hit. Some observers, including George M. Salem, an analyst at Prudential Securities, believe the savings accounts are `hot money' that is going to shift to higher-interest-rate alternatives such as mutual funds."[8] CD amounts have

---

8 Lunt, "Mutual Funds Changing," p. 36.

dropped for another reason as well: savings accounts are paying rates similar to those paid on CDs, so consumers allow CDs to run off and leave those funds in their savings accounts.

Liberty Financial, a well-known third-party provider, to mostly larger institutions has given us some statistics. It compiled figures on the financial institutions for which it provided brokerage and insurance products. The average net disintermediation in 1991 was 3.9%, with a range of 44% net *intermediation* (deposits grew rather than fell) to 59% disintermediation. The 1990 numbers showed net intermediation of 6.8%, with a range of 271% net intermediation to 44% disintermediation. Alan Blank, vice chairman of Liberty Financial, says that 1992 statistics show net disintermediation of 7.3%. This is no surprise, since the continuing decline in interest rates means that investors continue to seek alternative investments.

Joy P. Montgomery, a nationally recognized expert in bank mutual funds who is known as the grandmother of the bank mutual fund industry, distinguishes between initial disintermediation and net disintermediation. The first mutual fund or annuity sales made by a new retail investment services program will often come straight out of a customer's checking account at the bank. Based on a number of sources, she estimates that initial disintermediation is around 40% to 60%. That is, 40% to 60% of the funds for a customer's first purchase of an AIP were funds internal to the financial institution.[9] However, this is the classic case of "is the glass half-empty or half-full?" because 40% to 60% comes from outside the bank. No source we have ever encountered has tried to claim that 100% of the funds flowing into a financial institution's AIPs are domestic or internal funds. Bank programs always draw in funds from outside sources (foreign funds).[10]

But the initial disintermediation doesn't begin to tell the story. Montgomery points out that three major factors combine to mitigate the initial number.

- Replenished deposits: The customer writes the first check on the savings or checking account. Typically those funds are replenished within 12 to 24 months.
- Saved funds: These funds would have left the financial institution anyway, on their way to an investment outside the bank (e.g., a brokerage account or nonbank-affiliated mutual fund). If they stay with your investment program, these funds still go into a mutual fund rather than a savings account, but they stay within your institution and you strengthen the relationship.

9   Joy P. Montgomery, "The Myth of Disintermediation—Where Does the Money Come From?" presentation made to the 1991 Bank Securities Association National Mutual Funds Conference, Nov. 3-5, 1991.

10 Banks refer to funds that come from within the bank (already on deposit with it in some fashion) as *domestic* funds. Funds that come into the bank from outside are called *foreign* funds.

- New deposits: Often the bank retail investment services program will cross-sell deposit products. The registered rep will bring in new business, which will result in new deposits. This process can be accelerated if the rep's incentive compensation system is designed properly.

A financial institution does not have to be a hapless bystander to disintermediation. You can structure a retail investment services program to counter it. For instance, as a result of the last two factors mentioned above, one Liberty Financial program in 1990 resulted in a 271% increase in bank deposits for a financial institution. Some registered rep really knew how to sell deposit products!

Program Effects

In collecting evidence about disintermediation, we have consulted a number of different sources, some of them previously published.

"The investment program at Farmers [State Bank, in Willman, Minn.] now brings in about 80% outside money, although that was not the case when the program first started," according to Jay Gravley, investment executive with PrimeVest at Farmers State Bank.[11]

"T. Charles Bruere, CEO of First State Bank, St. Charles, Mo., says mutual funds and other brokerage products provide significant income for his $90 million-assets bank, and that 85% of the money going into brokerage services overall is coming from outside the bank."[12]

Stephen R. Green, president of the $105 million-assets New Era Bank, Fredericktown, Mo., "is not worried about cannibalizing deposits[13] at present because the bank is only 36% loaned up."[14]

The *ABA Banking Journal* notes, "Most banks that have made a solid commitment to mutual funds have found the threat of disintermediation worse than the reality. Indeed, the underlying rationale for those banks has been the risk of deposit erosion by failing to meet customers' needs for a broader range of product alternatives and financial services. It appears that while some disintermediation is experienced by a bank shortly after its proprietary fund commences operations, deposits are typically replaced within a three to five month period."[15]

---

11 Gina A. Lauer, "Small Investment Programs Shine," *Bank Investment Representative*, April 1993, p. 16.

12 Lunt, "Mutual Funds Changing," p. 34.

13 What the marketing gurus will tell you is that in most cases a company is better off cannibalizing its own business to some extent, because otherwise the competition will do it, and do it better.

14 Lunt, "Mutual Funds Changing," p. 34.

15 Peter Meenan, "Are Mutual Funds in Your Future?" *ABA Banking Journal*, p. 51.

Richard S. White Jr., executive vice president of Premier Bank, said that bank management quickly got over one of the major hurdles when starting an investment program—disintermediation. He said their statistics have ultimately revealed that disintermediation was slight when compared to the amount of money brought in from competitors and new money brought into the bank in the form of CDs. "If you take a look at sources, we get approximately half coming in from other financial institutions," said Charles A. Beard, senior vice president for Premier Bank. [16]

John W. Logan, executive vice president at First American National Bank in Nashville, shared with us his bank's experience with disintermediation: "First American has not experienced disintermediation with those products that the public thinks of as still competitive: money market accounts, NOW accounts, the accounts everyone needs. As long as the public thinks you're being fair, there will be growth in those accounts. We have experienced a runoff of small CDs, particularly in the six-month area, but the runoff was happening before we made any effort to sell investment products. Now that we are selling mutual funds and annuities, the run off is about the same as before the program. The public will buy products they think of as competitive and they won't buy others. This would happen no matter what. There are still a few isolated communities that have not yet experienced disintermediation at all. They're out of the way; there's no broker in town. Bankers in such communities don't want to precipitate disintermediation by offering an alternative products program."

Montgomery cites the experience of several different organizations. A large west coast bank found that 95% of checks drawn on the bank to fund annuities were really from somewhere else. A medium-sized midwestern bank found that mutual funds were purchased with 80% outside funds and annuities with 30%. A large northwest thrift said that its maturing CDs were rolled into its investment products and maturing CDs from other organizations were rolled into its CDs. [17] When Montgomery started the Chase Manhattan proprietary mutual funds in 1984 (now the Vista funds), she monitored the source of all fund purchases to address senior management's concerns about disintermediation. She found that initial disintermediation was less than 5% and that most of the money came from brokerage, CMA-type accounts. She credits the extremely low level of disintermediation to judicious product design (initially just tax-exempt mutual funds).

---

16 Gina A. Lauer, "Customer Service Southern Style," *Bank Investment Representative*, May 1993, p. 10.

17 Joy P. Montgomery, ""The Myth of Disintermediation—Where Does the Money Come From?" presentation made to the 1992 Community Asset Management Annual Weekend Conference, June 12-14, 1992.

Is Disintermediation a Threat?

Our statistics show that disintermediation experience varies significantly across institutions, with the average experience either being wholly positive or not significantly negative. Another way to look at this issue is to ask how important these deposits are to begin with. A program manager at one very large money center bank told us that the financial institution would be just as happy if most of the CD portfolio ran off. His bank generates more profit from the trailer or service fees paid by mutual funds than from CDs. Kenneth Kehrer, a well-known consultant to the bank securities industry, analyzes CD profitability and concludes that only long-term CDs or CDs offered by banks in uncompetitive markets are more profitable than an annuity or mutual fund commission. He also states that since "the net interest margins on most CDs are less than a bank's target rate of return on assets, [i]f the CDs would just go away, the bank's ROA would increase."[18] The effect of alternative investment products on ROA is all R (return) with no A (use of bank assets and capital).

Banks' need for deposits is also down due to a decline in bank lending. The disintermediation of deposits is only one of the kinds of disintermediation experienced by banks. The high-quality companies that used to constitute some of banks' best customers now go directly to the commercial paper market to satisfy short-term funding needs. The economic slowdown of the past few years has also contributed to the decline in bank lending. Many banks now securitize a portion of loans made, and securitized loans don't have to be funded with deposits. This has become another source of fee income for the bank. Although only larger banks securitize commercial loans, financial institutions are contributing to the trend by selling most mortgages into the secondary mortgage market.

Disintermediation of the Customer Relationship

Bank Investment Representative magazine has run a number of stories about the increasing competitive pressures facing community banks at the moment. "If you don't take care of your customer base, they will go elsewhere," said Paul Vollan, president of the $34-million Farmers State Bank in Willman, Minn. "Bob Harris, CEO with a $75-million First National Bank of Detroit Lakes (Minn.) . . . also commented on the need to keep up with the competition—but not necessarily from bank competitors. `We saw intense competition from non-bank-

---

18 Kenneth Kehrer, "The 'D' Word: Fears Fade over Cannibalization of Deposits," *Bank Investment Representative,* June 1993, p. 19.

related firms,' Harris said. Bill Lowe, first vice president and cashier at National Exchange, one of the largest independent banks in Wisconsin, concurred. `We were beginning to see many of our customers using brokerage firms for money markets and savings vehicles,' he said."[19]

The worst disintermediation a banker can imagine is the customer leaving the financial institution altogether, whether the customer shifted the total relationship to a brokerage house or to another bank. Retail investment services programs allow a banker to attract customers back into the bank. Here is what Alan Leach, senior vice president of Deposit Guaranty National Bank in Jackson, Miss., says about his institution's program: "In my opinion, the only way to get the customer what he or she really needs and the only way to really scare the Wall Street brokerage houses is to sell securities with the same level of professionalism and quality of service you would get in a Wall Street firm. We are poised for success, if we can just get it right. If I worked for the local Wall Street broker, I would be scared to death to see banks going into this business. Banks have the money and the customers. As a bank-based brokerage, I would hate to say later on that we had the bullet but didn't know what gun to put it in. Deposit Guaranty is already the second-largest brokerage house in the state and will probably be the largest next year. We can do the same thing as a brokerage house, but in a more ethical, open-air environment."

Banking has changed, and it is not possible for banks to continue as they were. They will either have to change with the times or die a slow (or possibly not so slow) death. Alternative investment products offer banks the greatest possibility of retaining and strengthening the customer relationship. Keeping the status quo is not an alternative. The alternative to offering these products is losing your customer base to the competition.

Who Should Not Offer Alternative Investment Products

There are those who feel that investment products have no place in banks. Bankers are, on the whole, a very conservative group. Many bankers feel that these products carry a level of risk and uncertainty that is inappropriate in a banking product. They don't want to have to watch the securities markets to try to determine whether or not the bank will have a satisfied customer. Professionals in the securities industry are concerned that the current bull market has carried along a generation of registered reps, and their customers, who have never experienced the undertow of a bear market. Bankers don't want to enter the securities business just in time to watch the market collapse. If the

---

19 Lauer, "Investment Programs Shine," p. 13.

market did collapse, all the arguments about strengthening the customer relationship by increasing the number of bank/customer ties would backfire, leaving a very dissatisfied customer ready to sever all ties with the bank.

Bankers are reluctant to allow outsiders in their lobbies. The brokerage professional is worse than simply an outsider: the brokerage/securities culture is in many cases an active sales culture that is unwelcome. Bankers worry that registered reps will entice customers into unsuitable investments and then leave the bank holding the bag. Bankers never stop worrying about lending their customer base to any outsider, no matter how benign the intention or how seemingly secure the contract. There can be unpleasant surprises resulting from allowing an outside vendor access to the bank's customer list.

Especially in areas outside affluent metropolitan or suburban locations, bankers claim that customers are not in fact asking for alternative investment products. They have not offered those products in the past and do not want to start now. They are being asked to shift from offering a guaranteed, insured product to offering one that carries considerable risk and uncertainty, and they feel that has no place in banks.

One final concern expressed by bankers, particularly in rural areas, is not wanting to upset the local broker or insurance salesperson, who may have established a friendly and/or mutually beneficial relationship with the bank. While a metropolitan banker would easily dismiss this consideration (given the heavy competition in urban practices), this is not something the rural banker takes lightly.

What does a banker do if faced by a customer complaint or threatened lawsuit? But what does a banker do under any circumstances when faced by a liability suit? Bankers are skittish about possible liability from selling these new products because they don't know enough about the products or the programs to know how to defend themselves. They think that these products are somehow more dangerous than other bank products, which we do not believe to be the case.

These are the reasons given by bankers who are worried about changing the focus of banking and shifting to products and programs that are unfamiliar to them. In a way, this whole book deals with those concerns. For any kind of banking or investment product, you build a program based on sound management principles; you staff it with conscientious, well-trained employees; and you educate employees, customers, and management as thoroughly as possible. By the time you have done that, you will have integrated that program and its personnel into the life of your institution—and reinvigorated the institution as well.

As a banker, what do you advise your customer who wants to invest IRA money for retirement, when all you have to offer is CDs? In today's economic environment, can you honestly say that a CD is appropriate for that type of investment? The principal is guaranteed to be returned at maturity, but the rate of inflation versus the rate earned on the investment means the principal will decline in real terms.

We hope we have raised enough of the questions and concerns that are on the minds of many people, including bankers, to interest you in learning more about alternative investment products and their role in the retail bank. In our view, introducing these products will do more than satisfy customer needs, strengthen customer relationships, and contribute fee income. These products will help bankers reinvent retail banking so that it will thrive in the next century!

2

Senior Management Support

We cannot overemphasize the importance of management support to the success of a retail investment services program. There are three key ingredients in building an investment program: its overall structure, the personnel involved (most particularly the registered rep), and—probably most important of all—senior management support of the program. We talk about choosing an appropriate structure and about personnel issues such as hiring, training, and compensation in other chapters.

One of the best ways to demonstrate the importance of management support is to offer some examples of programs that did and did not have that support, and how those programs developed.

Case One

Our first example concerns a savings bank located in the Midwest. Out of seven financial institutions in the area, this was the only one not offering alternative investment products. The president of the institution liked the idea of having a retail investment services program, so he instructed the CFO to do the necessary research on how to implement a program. He mentioned what he was doing to the chairperson of the board, in passing. All was well.

This financial institution has about $160 million in total assets, so hiring a third-party provider (TPP)[1] seemed like the most reasonable way to structure the program. The bank interviewed a number of different providers and finally settled on one. The recruiting process was started. As luck would have it, the third-party provider was able to hire an experienced registered rep from a competitor's program. The implementation process began: desk location was chosen, phones were ordered, training was started. Signs were placed in the main lobby and in all branch locations. Everything was going well. A referral program was put into place and the employees were doing a great job of identifying prospects. This looked to be a very successful program for all concerned, until it came time to implement the marketing program. Surprise . . . Actually, the institution knew all along what was expected. In fact, it even brought in outside marketing consultants to work with the third-party provider's marketing group to launch the new program—which is when the problems started. When the board of directors heard that the institution was going to help the third-party provider market these products to the institution's customer base, they acted as if they had been struck by lightning. The board could live with the third-party provider being in the institution but could not stand the idea of it being proactive and doing any marketing.

The board and the bank president got into a heated discussion. The outcome was that the president was forced to terminate the lease agreement with the TPP. The chairperson of the board told the president that it was "a good move for him personally."

Obviously this organization has a few internal problems to work out, but the moral of the story is that senior management support doesn't mean just the president or his or her direct reports; it means all of senior management, from the chairperson of the board on down. The politics of institutions are such that it is impossible to predict who might kill a program. Furthermore, there is a multiplier effect for every member of senior management who does not support the program. The higher the level of the person opposed to the program, the greater the multiplier effect.

This program had all the ingredients of success and was providing a needed service to customers. It was well on its way to being profitable. However, today this institution has no program, due to a lack of senior management "buy-in" caused by a lack of communication. It will probably not have a program until the current board retires.

---

1   A third-party provider (also called a third-party marketer) is an entity that contracts with a financial institution to sell brokerage and/or insurance products to the institution's customers. Because the TPP is not a bank, it is not subject to the various banking regulations that make offering these products expensive, difficult or impossible for a bank. TPPs differ greatly in size, structure and program features. See Chapter 5 for more information.

Case Two

The next story concerns a $90 million family-owned bank that was having earnings problems. Management was looking for ways to increase fee income, so one of the board members invited a TPP to a special meeting to discuss setting up an AIP program. The bank has a five-member board comprising four family members and a president; the meeting was attended by the four family members and the commercial development officer. The president was busy with a transaction and was unable to attend. Things went well; the board decided to use this TPP and start providing products as soon as possible. It took about six days to get going, with all decisions made by consensus.

Once the TPP had identified the registered rep and was ready to make an offer to this person, it invited the bank to interview the rep. The president said, "We don't need to interview him, he is your employee." The TPP took this as a sign of confidence in its ability and continued to move ahead.

The program appeared to be off to a good start. Surprise . . . The sign of confidence wasn't that at all. The president was insulating himself from the program and had started putting up little roadblocks. When it came time to train employees, they were always busy. The invitation for the grand opening went out late, and employees were excluded. When the TPP asked what had happened, it was told that the president did not approve the invitation in time and did not think it necessary for employees to attend the grand opening. All of the marketing that was originally planned and agreed to by the head of marketing was not implemented or was implemented off schedule. The reason was always the same: other bank projects took priority.

It soon became clear to the third-party provider that there was a problem. The implementation would have been much smoother and the program would have achieved greater success if everyone had bought in to the program. Management had bought in. What was the problem?

As it turned out, this institution was losing deposits and the president saw this program as one more thing competing for customer deposits; therefore, he did not really buy in. Since he had missed the initial presentation, he did not understand the long-term benefits of the program. He focused only on the short term and his lack of support rippled throughout the organization. None of his direct reports saw this program as a priority.

We later learned that part of the president's compensation was tied directly to the cost of funding the bank. Apparently the president saw this program as a direct threat to sources of funding for the bank and to his personal compensation. Once this conflict surfaced, the president's compensation plan was changed to adjust for the sale of AIPs.

Today this program is doing extremely well. The employees find time in their busy schedules to be trained and the bank's earnings have improved. The outward flow of deposits has stopped and the bank is growing. In fact, the bank has just opened a new branch and has requested the TPP to set up a retail investment services program in the new location. The moral to this story is that people always do things for reasons, but the reasons aren't always obvious.

Case Three

The third story is about a bank that asked us to review its retail investment services program. It was using a TPP but was unhappy with the results. The president of the bank expressed management's unhappiness with the results of their program. The TPP was an individual who owned a franchise of a national broker/dealer. This individual had established five different locations and he personally worked in the largest one. The location in the bank in question used a full-time dual employee. This registered rep was originally the marketing support person in the bank who ordered brochures, customer premiums, etc.

This program was not reaching anywhere near its potential. One problem was that the bank was using an individual as its TPP instead of an organization. The TPP in this case was a burned-out broker with no management experience who thought it would be easier to sell products through a bank than to cold-call clients.

Our research disclosed that the TPP was very happy. He was making more money than he had made as a broker with a wire house firm. His other four locations were dual-employee programs. The bank covered all expenses, and the TPP was paid an override on the gross production. Life could not get better as far as he was concerned. He was happy and making money. Surprise . . . His banks were not happy, nor were they making money. They were all underproducing substantially.

The program we were consulting to was in a $140 million institution that paid the dual employee an annual base salary of $22,000 plus a commission on all products sold. The bank had data equipment that cost about $1,400 per month, and there were marketing expenses that varied from month to month. The bank was probably spending $3,000 to $5,000 per month, and gross production was averaging about the same. The TPP was happy because he received his percentage override on the gross, so as long as the program had any production at all he made his override.

The TPP did not have the right incentives to make the program successful, so the institution suffered. However, this was only half the story. As we interviewed senior management, it became clear that this institution wanted a proactive program. It wanted this program to be profitable and was willing to make it an important part of the strategic plan. Senior management believed it was truly committed to making this program successful, to the extent of project-ing and budgeting revenue. To further prove the point, it was willing to bring in consultants (us) to make it work. Surprise again . . . We found that manage-ment was saying one thing and doing another.

As good consultants, we always do a little preliminary research before we accept an assignment. (This is like the due diligence that we stress registered reps should do on their potential customers.) Doing your homework ahead of time is wise no matter what product you are marketing. We found that while senior management did support the program, it did not support the registered rep. "What do you think, is she any good? Do you think she knows products? Can you evaluate her selling skills?" The questions never stopped, and they came from all members of senior management.

As we began to realize what the real problem was, we asked senior manage-ment a few questions of our own. "Where do you do your investing? How many customers have you recommended to the registered rep? What do your customers say about her? How do the other employees feel about her skills?" The responses confirmed our suspicions. While management believed in the program, they did not believe in the rep. They questioned her skills and ability to handle customers. They saw her in the marketing support position she used to have, with little if any knowledge about investments. As one manager put it, "I would not trust her with my money." And he didn't. Nor would he trust her with his customers' money, so he did not refer any of his customers. This atti-tude percolated through the institution from the president on down.

None of the customers knew her as the marketing support person, so as far as they were concerned she didn't carry the baggage that senior management thought she carried. Some of them knew that she had worked at the bank for a long time, but they weren't really sure what she had done before. Furthermore, the first-line staff (customer service reps and tellers) believed she was doing a good job. Their customers liked her and were very comfortable with the service she was performing.

To the rep's credit, she was more than willing to tell her customers about the fact that she did have a college degree, had passed the NASD's Series 7 and 63 licensing requirements, and was taking additional financial planning courses in the evening (which the bank wasn't paying for because the courses didn't meet its requirements for tuition reimbursement). Senior management supported the program but not the rep, so she was left out in the cold. The moral to this story is that management buy-in means supporting the entire program, including the TPP and the registered rep (which is sometimes easier said than done). In this classic case, management truly believed that they supported the entire program; unfortunately, they did not.

Case Four

We have one last story to share with you, and this one is different. This is the story of an institution that bought in too much.

The institution is located in a little town in middle America with a population of 20,000. As in most smaller towns, the major employers have come and gone. The industrial base has changed to what is now a health-care and service-based economy. The competition among financial institutions is tough. A number of independently owned and operated institutions have been bought by larger regional banks. Every institution in town is now offering alternative investment products; most are larger institutions that have their own in-house programs and proprietary products. However, one mutual savings bank is the lone survivor.

This savings bank realized that it needed to offer AIPs to its customers to stay competitive with the larger institutions. This $120-million bank interviewed TPPs and chose the one it thought would do the best job for its customers and the organization.

Implementation unfolded smoothly. The board approved the program, the president supported it and all of the bank's employees were trained, starting with the senior officers. The president sent out the typical president's letter letting customers know that the bank was now offering this service. A grand opening reception was planned with catered food. Everyone was invited, including the mayor and the local newspaper. The TPP provided gifts for everyone who attended.

Full-page ads were placed in the local newspaper announcing that the TPP was located in the bank's lobby and would be offering AIPs to customers. Announcements were sent out to each household in a five-mile radius of the bank. The bank placed the message on a number of billboards around town. It mailed statement stuffers announcing the new program to its customers. Lobby handouts were also used. This bank did not miss a marketing opportunity to get the word out to its customers and the community.

The key to all this marketing was that the chairperson of the board was responsible for the bank's marketing programs. He understood how important it is for the program to be marketed not only to the bank's customer base but also to the community. The marketing program was well thought out and well executed. Surprise . . . All of management's efforts and support could not substitute for the time it takes to get a program going; management support by itself cannot bring revenue in the door. The first two months started out very strong and revenue came in nicely, but then the easy transactions were done and production slowed—and management became nervous. Management supported this program and everything was done right. But management had forgotten that it takes time to educate customers and employees in the features and benefits of a new product.

The moral of this story is don't get discouraged. Selling alternative investment products is new for most banks. Banks are used to the traditional situation, where they have the money and customers ask to borrow it. Banks are accustomed to having control of the situation. With a retail investment services program, the customer has the money and the bank or the TPP is asking to invest it. Traditional bank products have never claimed to be the highest-yielding products in the marketplace, but they do guarantee repayment of principal and interest. Alternative investment products have no guarantees; in fact, the principal and interest can fluctuate. If the institution is doing its job correctly, it is educating its customers about these products and their differences. Banks have traditionally sold against these products, and now they are enthusiastically embracing them; it will take time for everyone to move up the learning curve.

Program structure and the right registered rep are key ingredients for a successful retail investment services program. But in our experience, management support is truly the essential ingredient. Programs that lack management support will limp along, without ever reaching their maximum potential. As one TPP put it, trying to run a program without management support is like trying to walk a dead dog.

3

Basic Definitions

W e know a number of our readers want to offer alternative investment products (AIPs) through their financial institution but do not have a very clear understanding of the mechanics of these instruments and markets. This chapter will provide some of the background information necessary to understand how the brokerage and insurance industries function. We discuss the securities industry first and the insurance industry second. The next chapter includes basic information about the products themselves. Chapter 12 discusses the regulatory institutions and their mandates.

What Is a Broker/Dealer?

A broker is an intermediary who brings together buyers and sellers of securities or commodities, executes their orders, and receives a fee for so doing. The broker acts as agent, effecting a transaction between the buyer and the seller without ever owning the security.

A dealer has the legal status of a principal in relations with customers and buys and sells for its own account. The dealer buys from the seller and sells to the buyer, and owns the security between the two transactions. The dealer tries to resell the security at a price higher than the price at which it was originally purchased, thereby creating the dealer's profit.

For example, suppose I am a broker/dealer. My customer is Mr. Smith, who wants to buy a corporate bond, and Jones Securities Inc. has a $100,000 bond that meets Smith's investment needs. As agent for Smith, I will buy the bond from Jones Securities and sell it to Smith at the same price, charging Smith a fee for executing and clearing this transaction for him. The confirmation will state that the transaction was completed on an agency basis, and the fee will be disclosed. I might make a $200 agency fee on the transaction, paid to me by the buyer, and the security is sold at the same price at which it was purchased. In this case, I acted as a broker.

If I effect the transaction as a dealer, I might buy the bonds on a riskless principal basis at 99-1/2 (paying $99,500) and resell them to Smith at par or 100 ($100,000), thereby making $500 profit.[1] I call this a riskless principal transaction because Smith has agreed to the transaction before I purchased the bonds. The securities were purchased at one price, marked up, and sold to the customer at a higher price than the one I paid to purchase them, thereby creating a profit for the dealer.

If this same transaction were completed on a normal principal basis, the dealer would have purchased these bonds some time before receiving Smith's order. By purchasing the securities in anticipation of a customer order, the dealer is risking capital because owning them means the dealer is subject to market fluctuations. In this case, the dealer could sell the bonds at an even higher price, like 101, and earn $1,500 in profit. On the other hand, the market might go down, and a fair market price for Smith would mean the dealer had to sell at a loss (a price less than the 99-1/2 the dealer paid for the securities). Although the transaction actually consists of two transactions (when the dealer bought from Jones Securities Inc. and when the dealer sold to Smith), Smith will see only the confirm between the dealer and him.

Many dealers prefer to work on a principal basis or on a riskless principal basis because they don't have to disclose their markup or profit to the customer. When a transaction is done on an agency basis, the fee must be disclosed.

Members of the National Association of Securities Dealers (NASD) are called broker/dealers because the member may act either as a broker or as a dealer on different transactions, depending on the market, the customer, and the particular transaction. (An introducing broker/dealer might easily do stock transactions as agent but execute mutual fund transactions as principal.) The NASD regulates brokers and dealers, and all brokers and dealers must be members in order to do business with each other. The NASD is registered with the Securities and Exchange Commission as a self-regulatory organization (SRO) and has legal status for its own markets equivalent to that of other SROs, such

---

1   The price of a bond is expressed as a percentage of par. If I buy a bond at par, I buy at 100. A price of less than 100 indicates a discount bond; a price over 100 indicates a premium.

as the New York Stock Exchange, the Municipal Securities Rulemaking Board (MSRB), and the Chicago Board Options Exchange (CBOE).

There are several different levels of membership with the NASD. Each level requires a certain amount of capital and each level has authority to carry out certain activities within the market, based on capital. The greater the risk levels of the market activities a broker/dealer wishes to take part in, the greater the capital requirements. This makes sense because the more risk a firm takes, the more capital it should have. At the highest levels of capital, a firm might be underwriting new issues, trading stocks as principal, and holding extensive inventory positions.

An introducing broker/dealer has minimum risk and requires a minimum level of capital. Currently, an introducing broker/dealer must hold at least $5,000 in net capital, although there is a proposal pending with the SEC to raise this amount to $25,000. An introducing broker/dealer does not clear securities trades itself nor does it have custody of client funds or securities.

There are also broker/dealers that sell only mutual funds and variable annuities. At the moment, they have the lowest required net capital, $2,500. This kind of broker/dealer has even further restrictions as far as handling customer funds.

Clearing Transactions

A bank-affiliated broker/dealer or third-party provider (TPP) can be an introducing broker/dealer and still process customer transactions as necessary. An introducing broker/dealer hires the services of a clearing member or clearing broker/dealer on a fully disclosed basis. That is, the name, positions, and complete customer activity of each individual customer of the introducing broker/dealer are fully disclosed to the clearing firm. Account statements are produced by the clearing firm, and the name of the clearing firm must be disclosed to the customer.

The clearing member is also a general securities firm (although not all general securities firms are clearing members). It maintains a minimum of $250,000 in net capital and settles or clears trades, holds customer cash and securities, maintains customer ledger accounts, and provides all other back-office support services. The clearing member might be called the clearing firm, the clearing agent, or the clearing broker/dealer.

An introducing broker/dealer depends on a clearing member to provide almost all of its required clearing services. An introducing broker/dealer focuses its attention on the marketing and sales aspects of the securities business, and pays a clearing member to provide payment and delivery services (also called clearing services).

The clearance and delivery process is sometimes referred to as the back office, a term used industry-wide to refer to the employees who process the transactions and their functions. Back-office employees transform the customer's agreement to do a transaction into an accounting reality.

Each kind of instrument, whether mutual funds, equities, bonds, or other, has its own market characteristics and rules, and each is cleared in a different fashion. To those just entering the securities industry, it might seem like a nightmare of financial quirks. Each separate instrument's history helps to explain why it trades and clears the way it does. The book-entry technology used today has actually resulted in far more efficient operations than ever before available. In simple terms, clearing an instrument means the buyer takes possession of the security in some fashion and the seller gets the money. Precisely how this happens depends on the instrument.

The process was easier to understand when physical securities were used more widely. The seller would deliver a negotiable instrument to wherever the buyer wanted it delivered. An individual investor would typically have a safekeeping account with the financial institution or brokerage house that sold him or her the investment. The instrument would be put in the bank vault, the customer's account would be charged for the amount of the investment, and the security would be kept secure until maturity or until the investor instructed it to be sold. These transactions were processed by pieces of paper changing hands, including physical securities, checks, and bank debit and credit slips. Now all that processing is handled electronically and the investment itself is often "book entry," meaning that a record is kept in both the customer's account and the accounts of the clearinghouse for that instrument.

The clearing agent opens an account for the customer. The customer writes a check, which is either sent directly to the clearing agent or deposited by the introducing broker/dealer into an account that belongs to the clearing agent. An introducing broker/dealer may not receive or handle securities for any reason, even if they are forwarded to the clearing agent immediately. The introducing broker/dealer may receive checks made out to the clearing agent as long as they are forwarded promptly to the clearing agent or deposited in the clearing agent's account.

The introducing broker can also use what is called an omnibus account, which increases the minimum net capital requirement. A broker/dealer using an omnibus account provides its own customer accounting, including posting positions to customer accounts and producing customer statements. All of the broker/dealer's transactions are put into the one omnibus account and cleared through the clearing member in the name of the introducing broker/dealer only. The clearing firm will not know the names of individual customers. The advantage of the omnibus account is cost: the clearing firm might charge the introducing broker/dealer only half as much for clearing on a fully disclosed basis.

For example, say that I am a broker/dealer named Green Securities and my customers are individuals named Smith, Jones, and Doe, and my clearing agent is named ClearsAll Securities. On one day, Smith bought 100 shares of IBM and sold 50 shares of Procter & Gamble; Jones bought 150 shares of IBM and 200 shares of Exxon, and sold 100 shares of Procter & Gamble; Doe bought 500 shares of Exxon and sold 200 shares of IBM. If I am a fully disclosed (introducing) broker/dealer, then ClearsAll Securities will record on its books each of those separate transactions. ClearsAll will send confirmation to each individual customer (although Green Securities will also be referenced on the confirm).

However, if Green Securities is using an omnibus account, it will issue the customer confirm and statement. Green Securities will record all customer transactions in its omnibus account and tell ClearsAll Securities that Green Securities is buying 250 shares of IBM, selling 200 shares of IBM, buying 700 shares of Exxon, and selling 150 shares of Procter & Gamble. ClearsAll Securities has no idea which of Green Securities' customers are buying or selling. ClearsAll then takes all the orders from Green Securities' omnibus account, combines them with all the orders from all the other broker/dealers it clears for, and tells the clearinghouse for these stocks the totals for buys and sells for all its customers together (totaling perhaps millions of shares). Each entity in the clearing hierarchy maintains its own level of accounting information and balances against the next level.

Most instruments utilize a clearinghouse of some sort. The clearinghouse keeps electronic records of all transactions, and the clearing member balances every night against the clearinghouse. Rather than each separate transaction taking place between two customers, the transaction in effect takes place between the customer and the clearing agent, and the clearing agent processes all of its transactions at the same time with the clearinghouse. For example, the Depository Trust Company (DTC) is one of the major clearinghouses for both listed and unlisted equities and many different bonds. FundServ is the clearinghouse for mutual funds. Every clearing member totals up its entire position for all its customers at the end of the day and balances as a firm against the appropriate clearinghouse.

In one sense, a broker/dealer's clearing arrangement should not make a great deal of difference to a customer as long as certain standards are met. Clearing agents' services differ according to proprietary technology and software, but there are regulatory requirements that all must meet. We recommend that a clearing agent have the systems and capacity to service all its customers in all market environments, as the market learned in the crash of October, 1987. There are packaged systems available to a broker/dealer who wants to self-clear; these systems can help the broker/dealer provide as high a level of service as the largest clearing agents. However, if the clearing agent is the custodian for your customers' securities, it is important to make sure that it is financially sound and well managed.

Safekeeping Agents/Custody Services

Many banks offer safekeeping or custody services to their customers. The customers turn over to the bank whatever negotiable securities they have, including bank CDs. However, an enormous percentage of the negotiable securities of the United States change hands in New York, and smaller banks tend to have a contractual connection to larger banks that use the largest New York banks as their safekeeping agents. It is likely that a negotiable security bought by an individual would never be sent physically to that individual's bank, but instead would be safekept where it was bought, in an account for that individual's benefit in New York.

New York Stock Exchange and the OTC Market

A stock transaction for an individual can be executed only through a member of the exchange where the stock is listed, whether the New York Stock Exchange or one of the others. Any stock traded on one of the exchanges is called a listed stock; stock traded over the counter (OTC) is called unlisted. If a broker/dealer sells stocks, then either it or its clearing agent is a member of the exchange. It doesn't matter to the customer which party holds the membership. If the broker/dealer or its clearing agent is part of an automated system, small stock orders are sent by computerized order routing systems and filled automatically. If the broker/dealer is not part of an automated system, it may call orders to the floor of the exchange, where they will be filled. There are two different kinds of OTC securities. Approximately 4,300 stocks are listed on the automated system run by the NASD, the Nasdaq Stock Market^{SM}. There are another 12,000 OTC securities traded in the interdealer market, which represent some 600 securities dealers across the country.

Once the order has been filled for the customer's account, the clearing process starts. The order is recorded in both the customer's account (the purchaser) and the account of the counterparty (the seller). The clearing process ensures that the stock moves from the seller to the buyer and the funds move from the buyer to the seller.

Bonds and Other Securities

Corporate and municipal bonds used to clear through a physical delivery process that was very easy to understand but inefficient to operate. Although most bonds are now book entry, there are still a few older issues that require physical delivery, as we describe it elsewhere in this chapter: a messenger brings the physical bonds to a custodian in New York, and the custodian receives the bonds and pays for them. Book-entry bonds clear through the National Securities Clearing Corp. (NSCC) or DTC in the same way other securities clear through their clearinghouses. Each individual member of the clearinghouse passes its entries to the clearinghouse and clears against it. The clearinghouse matches the buys and the sells. Anything that doesn't match must be researched individually.

The Federal Reserve Wire System

For our purposes, the "Fed wire" is the means by which billions of dollars of U.S. government securities change hands daily. When a customer buys a Treasury security, it is delivered to a Federal Reserve member as a notation on a computer that the securities have been delivered. Payment is also sent electronically via Fed wire. Once delivery has been effected, the securities are allocated to the appropriate account according to the safekeeping arrangements. For example, the clearing agent for an introducing broker/dealer might have an account with a money center bank that is a Federal Reserve member. This member would receive the Treasury securities and allocate them to the clearing agent's account. The clearing agent would keep the securities on its books in the name of the introducing broker/dealer and its customer.

Forms of Securities

Only a few years ago, most securities came in physical (bearer) form, because that was what worked best in a manual age. A true physical security was a negotiable instrument, like cash. These hardly exist any more. Using physical securities was a costly and cumbersome process.

Registered securities are securities that have been recorded in the customer's name on the books of the transfer agent. Most registered securities can be registered as to both principal and interest, which means that principal and interest payments can be made directly to the registered holder of a security. A physical certificate can be issued to the customer, although this is a not a bearer or negotiable certificate. Corporate bonds, stocks, or municipal bonds can be delivered to the customer in this fashion.

Now, however, securities are increasingly issued in book-entry form only, which means they exist as ledger entries in the transfer agent's accounting system. This provides much greater protection for the customer and has streamlined the clearing process.

Mutual Funds

Direct Mutual Fund Trades

Many broker/dealers process mutual fund trades directly with the mutual fund companies. The broker/dealer has the customer fill out the customer application contained in the prospectus and sends the application directly to the mutual fund. Procedures must be devised for ensuring that all customer funds have been accounted for and that each investment made is accounted for. However, typically the mutual fund does not charge for making this kind of investment and charges perhaps $10 annually for an individual retirement account (IRA) fee. The customer will receive a separate statement for each mutual fund company he or she invests in.

The broker/dealer must have systems for tracking and processing the fee income from mutual funds that are sold directly. Mutual fund companies vary considerably in the amount of information they provide in the accounting statements that accompany fee-income checks.

Processing Mutual Funds Through a Brokerage Account

Mutual fund transactions can also be cleared through a brokerage account in the same way any other securities transactions are cleared. The major advantage to processing through a brokerage account is that the customer receives a consolidated statement of total holdings. The major disadvantage is cost. Each additional deposit to the mutual fund incurs the normal transaction cost.

General Rules About Trade Execution

A trade is executed when an order has been filled on an exchange, a customer has accepted an offer of a bond, or a mutual fund order has been entered into the processing system. The day the trade is executed is called the trade date. The settlement date is the day the customer owns the security and starts earning interest on the investment. Standard settlement for retail customers is five business days for mutual funds, equities, municipal bonds, and corporate bonds. Standard settlement for U.S. government securities—bills, notes, and bonds—is one business day.

Five business days from trade date to settlement date allows the paperwork necessary to settle trades. This custom originated many years ago, when all operations were manual and transactions were entered by hand into ledgers. Soon this process will be shortened to three business days.

Money center banks, clearing firms, and industry participants in general are talking about industry attempts to move to "T+3," meaning standard settlement of transactions on trade date plus three days. The industry is developing technology as fast as possible to cope with this change. It means that customer funds will have to be received promptly, and securities firms will be even more reluctant to deal with registered securities. This will contribute to the trend away from registered securities and hasten the arrival of only book-entry investing.

Explaining Some Terminology

Dollar Cost Averaging

Dollar cost averaging is a way of saying the customer is investing the same amount periodically over time, say $200 per month, year in and year out. One could simply call this periodic investing, but the industry prefers the term "dollar cost averaging." That same $200 might buy 20 shares of a mutual fund this month, 19.5 shares next month if share value increases, and 20.7 shares the month after next if share values decline. When share prices are lower, the customer takes advantage of the lower price and gets more shares; when share prices are higher, the customer buys fewer shares. This dampens cyclical price fluctuations and allows the customer to reduce the average cost of the shares he or she is buying.

Wirehouse Rep

A wirehouse is a brokerage firm. The term has increased in usage because people need a term to distinguish between bank broker/dealers, third-party providers in banks, and traditional brokerage houses. Since brokerage could refer to either bank or nonbank brokerage, "wirehouse" has come to designate nonbank brokerage.

12b-1 Fees

There has been much commentary recently over 12b-1 fees, also called service
fees or trailers. (12b-1 refers to the section of the regulation that allows this kind
of fee to be charged.) This is a fee paid by a mutual fund to the broker/dealer
who maintains the customer account with the mutual fund. The amount is typically an annual 15 to 30 basis points[2] of the assets under management, paid
quarterly. Some mutual fund companies have cut front-end loads and increased
continuing fees.[3]

If the registered reps of a broker/dealer have customer accounts in a given
mutual fund totaling $10 million, then the broker/dealer will receive $25,000
annually, typically in quarterly checks. Even a new registered rep can expect to
sell $1 million in mutual funds in a year although that amount may be spread
out over 10 to 100 different funds. New broker/dealers do not build up threshold balances overnight. Sometimes the mutual fund company won't pay the
fees at all until the broker/dealer has had a selling agreement with it for some
period of time, such as a year.

Mutual fund companies pay these amounts to compensate the broker/dealer
for maintaining ongoing contact with customers, answering questions, and
sending account statements. It is a way to garner loyalty from all parties concerned. Many third-party providers simply add these amounts to gross monthly commissions and then split the commissions in the usual way. Other third-
party providers keep the whole amount for themselves. This topic is discussed
further in Chapter 6.

Insurance Companies

There are three different ways insurance agents can be organized. In a captive
system, an agent works for only one insurance company. The agent cannot by
contract sell the insurance of any other company, at risk of termination.
Property and casualty companies are typically organized in this fashion.

An insurance company might use an agency force, whose agents are not captive. The insurance company might supply office space, a secretary, marketing
and sales support, and medical and retirement benefits to its agency force.
However, to keep all these benefits, each agent has to produce a certain amount

---

2   One basis point (bp) equals one one-hundredth of a percentage point; therefore 10 bp equal one-
    tenth of a percentage point and 100 bp equal one percentage point.
3   In general, where a front-end load fund will have a 25 basis point trailer, a back-end load fund will
    charge 75 basis points. In either situation, the broker/dealer receives 25 basis points. For a back-
    end load, the mutual fund company retails the additional 50 basis points as compensation for pay-
    ing the broker/dealer a commission on a purchase and not charging the customer an up-front fee.

of business annually for the insurance company. Such agents can sell policies from other companies as long as they produce the required amount for the one company.

The third kind of agent is a broker. Independent brokers can license themselves with a number of different insurance companies and sell their products. An insurance company that uses independent brokers will typically pay higher commissions than one that uses an agency force, because independent brokers don't receive any noncash benefits from the insurance company.

Insurance companies are organized like a totem pole, with a hierarchy of agents in the distribution system. Different companies use different names to refer to the levels in the hierarchy. Some of the names used are general agent, special agent, master general agent, and managing general agent. The terms have no standard meaning in themselves; you have to look at the structure of each individual company. The usual structure is that the more premium dollars an individual produces, the higher the percentage commission will be and the higher the insurance company will put the person in its hierarchy.

Insurance companies give exclusives to various underagents. Some insurance companies don't want to get involved in the kind of sales support necessary at that level; they want to limit their contact with individual agents. An individual agent or new insurance agency that called one of these insurance companies would be referred to the master agent or managing general agent (or whatever it uses) for the geographic area.

When a financial institution wants to offer insurance products, the first consideration is what it can legally do. Even if a bank can act as an independent insurance agency in its state, using a third-party provider might be beneficial because the third-party provider might already sell enough insurance to earn a much higher place in the hierarchy than the financial institution could. Even after the third-party provider has taken its cut of the commission, the financial institution might have more left over than it would have earned if it had contracted directly with the insurance company. If a bank does contract directly with an insurance company, it needs to ask whether it can have territory protection or exclusivity or whether everyone else who wants to sell those products will have equal access to the insurance company's products.

4

What Are Alternative Investment Products?

To those of us who have spent our careers working in the securities markets, alternative investment products are as much a part of our life as checking accounts are for other people. We sometimes find it hard to understand why friends and prospective customers ask us for precise definitions of these products. This chapter gives an overview of alternative investment products. We name them and describe briefly what they are, how they are traded and priced, and how a customer buys them. We discuss who issues them and who rates them and mention some of their risks. We consider whether these products are appropriate for a bank and how you determine if they are suitable for your customer.

However, since this book is about offering products, not about the products themselves, we do not provide an in-depth study of their underlying financial characteristics. Any registered rep should have a much broader understanding of how these products work than is presented here. After reading this chapter, however, we hope that bankers who are considering offering alternative investment products will have a better understanding of them and the financial markets in which they operate.

Kinds of Risk

Almost every instrument we are going to talk about here is subject to credit risk and interest-rate or market risk. Credit risk is the risk that the entity that issued the security might not be able to stand behind or repay the security at maturity or when the investor wishes to redeem it. Credit risk on a bond is the risk that the issuer might not be able to repay principal at the bond's maturity; credit risk on a stock is that the issuer might go bankrupt and the stock would be worthless. All financial markets evaluate credit risk through the mechanism of price. If the market's evaluation is that a certain company represents an increasing financial risk, then the price of both its bonds and its equities will fall. (The bond will therefore have a higher yield.) The rating agencies will downgrade a company in trouble. A lower rating is one of the signals the market responds to in evaluating credit risk.

Market risk, or interest-rate risk, is the risk that interest rates in the market will fluctuate, causing changes in the price of the financial instrument. Changes in interest rates have a direct, immediate, and measurable effect on bonds or any other interest-bearing instrument. Changes in interest rates have a much more indirect effect on stocks, depending on the particular stock (the business it is in, the industry it is part of, lending conditions, and other factors). The rule is that the longer the maturity of the debt instrument, the more sensitive its price will be to changes in interest rates. This is all part of basic finance, so we won't stop to give a lesson on the subject.

Packaged Products

Packaged products have come to represent alternative investment products in the minds of many people. These investments are "packaged" because an investment company has taken underlying securities or investments of some sort and bundled them into a different security having certain characteristics.

Mutual Funds

A mutual fund is issued by an investment company, which sells redeemable securities representing an undivided interest in the assets held by the fund. Mutual fund assets generally include stocks, bonds, and government securities. The main advantages to the individual investor are that a mutual fund by itself represents a diversified investment and that investment is professionally managed.

A mutual fund can be open-end or closed-end. An open-end fund, the more common kind, offers new shares continuously to investors and guarantees redemption at net asset value per share. The most popular mutual funds are open end, so we are going to discuss them at length, but first we will cover closed-end funds.

Closed-end funds

A fixed number of shares are issued for a closed-end fund, and the management company does not issue or redeem shares on demand. If an investor holding shares of a closed-end fund wishes to sell them, he or she must sell those shares in the open market to an investor who wishes to buy them. Because this purchase is completed in the marketplace, the price the seller receives may or may not equal the value of the underlying securities in the fund. There are some real values to be had in closed-end funds for those who understand these funds in depth. Although you might get a bargain when you purchase such funds, you might have to give someone else the bargain when you need to sell them. This is not an area that bank programs emphasize. Buying or selling shares of closed-end funds in the secondary market is like buying or selling a bond. There are a limited number of shares issued. Therefore, supply and demand play a role in the pricing and liquidity of a closed-end fund. The underwriting cost on a newly issued, closed-end fund can be as high as 8%.

Open-end funds

There are several main categories of mutual funds:

- Growth and aggressive growth fund: Funds seeking to maximize capital appreciation.
- Income fund: The primary objective is current income. Investments are mostly bonds and stocks that pay dividends.
- Balanced fund: Balanced funds use a portfolio mix of bonds, preferred stocks, and common stocks. The objective is to conserve initial principal, pay current income, and achieve long-term growth of both principal and income. The managers of this kind of fund vary amounts invested in each sector of the market depending on market conditions and outlook.
- Bond fund: A bond fund by definition invests in one or more segments of the bond market, whether U.S. Treasury and agency securities, corporate bonds, or municipal bonds. A bond fund provides many of the characteristics of the underlying security but also provides liquidity to the individual investor. There are several kinds of bond funds.
  - U.S. government bond fund: Invests in U.S. government securities and those issued by U.S. government agencies.
  - Corporate bond fund: Invests in bonds issued by corporations.
  - High-yield bond fund: Invests in bonds with less than investment-grade ratings, also known as junk bonds.

- Global bond fund: Invests in securities traded worldwide.
- Mortgage-backed bond fund: Invests in securities backed by pools of mortgages, including those issued by GNMA, FNMA, and FHLMC.
- Municipal bond fund: Invests in tax-free bonds issued by state and municipal subdivisions.
- Growth and income fund: A fund seeking both capital growth and current income.
- International fund: A fund specializing in the securities of particular geographic regions outside the United States. Buying shares of such a fund allows an individual investor to participate in the economic growth of another part of the world.
- Specialty fund: A fund specializing in one sector of the market, such as medical or financial stocks.

Load versus no-load

A load is a sales charge that is subtracted from the initial mutual fund investment. Typical loads average around 4%. A no-load fund does not have this charge, although other fees or service charges may be buried in its cost structure. It used to be that the commission was simply charged up front. Salespeople will tell you that a mutual fund is a long-term investment, and the sales charge should be considered one percentage point a year for four or five years. This is the cost structure on Class A shares.

Some investors prefer to have the sales charge levied on the back end as a contingent deferred sales charge (the load is charged when the investor redeems shares in the fund). Mutual fund companies started offering Class B shares, which have a contingent deferred sales charge that constitutes a back-end load as well as 12b-1 trailer fees. An investor who redeemed shares in the first year he or she owned them would pay a 5% sales charge. The amount would drop by an equal amount each year, until after six years the shares would be redeemed without further charge. Class C shares have various definitions, such as B shares that pay no trailer after six years. They may have no up-front fee, possibly a 1% deferred sales charge in Year 1 (sometimes longer), and high annual expenses (up to 1% per year). A level load is also sometimes used in conjunction with C shares; it includes a 1% contingent deferred sales charge and a 1% trailer fee for as long as the fund is held.

Buying a no-load mutual fund is like doing your own electrical work; you can save money if you know what you're doing, but if you don't have the required time and expertise, you can make a serious mistake. Paying a load on a mutual fund compensates the registered rep for his or her knowledge, service, and experience. The other important fact to remember about no-load funds is that you have to call the 800 number of the mutual fund company if you have a question about your account. The person who answers the phone is an employee of the mutual fund and may give you biased advice. The customer of the retail investment services program should always be able to call the registered rep with a question and get an unbiased reply.

The qualified registered rep does more than simply select a couple of mutual funds for a customer. Even when the rep does not use software to outline a formal financial plan, he or she should still build what is essentially a financial plan, taking into account both the short- and long-term needs, concerns, and objectives of the customer. There are investors who can do this for themselves: people who are truly devoted to learning about financial matters, follow financial news, and read enough to keep themselves well informed. Investors who do not match this description would be well advised to seek professional guidance for their investments.

The chapter on due diligence talks about ways to evaluate funds, but here are some of the properties and qualities to consider when choosing a mutual fund.

Return history: Look at the total return of a fund over the short and long term. Return data are evaluated in three ways: in an absolute sense, relative to an appropriate index, and relative to the performance of other funds in the given category (e.g., equity growth). For example, in the case of an equity fund, what has the rate of return been over the entire history of the fund; how does it compare to an index such as the S&P 500; how well have other equity funds done in comparison? Obviously you want to select the fund that does the best in all three senses.

Risk history: The riskiness of an investment can be expressed as both volatility risk and market risk.

- Volatility risk is a measure of the variability of a fund's returns over time. That is, how stable have the fund's returns been from year to year? A number of outstanding aggressive growth funds have returned more than 15% per year, on average, over more than 15 years. However, if you look at the returns broken down by year, you will see stomach-lurching volatility. A year with a 70% increase may be followed by a year with a 6% decrease. To find out how well a particular fund performs in an adverse market, look at what it returned in 1987 (the year of the stock market crash). In the current low-interest-rate environment, investors are worried about putting money into a bond fund and immediately losing principal as rates start to increase. Those investors should look for a fund that has had stable principal over many years, including years of interest-rate increases. Standard deviation is the usual measure of volatility risk.

- Market risk is the sensitivity of a fund to factors independent of the securities in the fund. Such factors include changes in the business cycle, inflation, unemployment, war, and political events. Market risk is borne by all securities, does not comprise events unique to an individual entity, and cannot be diversified away. To measure market risk of a particular fund, compare the returns of that fund with the returns on a broad-based indicator of market activity. For example, the returns on equity funds are often compared to the returns on the S&P 500. This measure is called beta. The beta for the market is 1; all other betas are compared to this. A fund with a beta of 1 has average market risk. A fund with a beta of 2 has twice the risk of the market as a whole. If the market goes up, that fund will go up twice as much as the market; if the market falls, that fund will fall twice as much. A fund with a beta of 0.5 has half the risk of the overall market.

Most bank customers are more concerned that their fund choices outperform the return on a riskless asset, such as a CD. But understanding market risk is important to the asset manager in making recommendations to customers.

Each risk measure is evaluated both on an absolute basis and relative to the risk characteristics of other funds in a given category. All else being equal, only those funds with relatively low-risk profiles should be given further consideration.

Expenses and fees. The annual expense ratio of a fund indicates the percentage of fund assets withdrawn each year to pay the costs of operation. It is calculated by dividing the expenses of a fund (management fees, administrative costs, transaction expenses, and service fees) by its assets at the end of the year. Expense ratio data is evaluated both in an absolute sense and relative to other funds in a given category. Very small or new funds tend to have higher expense ratios than larger funds, because there is a smaller asset base over which to spread the total expenses of the fund. All else being equal, only those funds with relatively low expense ratios should be given further consideration.

Consistency of purpose. Has the objective of the fund been stable over the life of the fund?

Consistency of holdings. Occasionally a fund may hold securities that are not consistent with its objective. Only funds that consistently hold securities appropriate to the objective should be given further consideration.

Consistency of portfolio statistics. Portfolio financial ratios such as price to earnings (P/E), price to book value (P/B), earnings growth, and dividend yield must be consistent with the fund's objectives. This requires a thorough understanding of the fund's investment style. For example, growth funds can be run as either value or high-growth style. A value fund will have relatively low P/E and P/B ratios and a relatively high dividend yield. A high-growth style will have relatively high P/E and P/B ratios and low dividend payouts. Only funds that exhibit this consistency should be given further consideration.

Fund management. In this electronic age (thanks partly to Louis Rukeyser), investors are far more familiar with certain money managers than in previous times. But however often one may have seen Peter Lynch on TV, there is no substitute for hardcore financial analysis in evaluating fund performance.

Unit Investment Trust

A unit investment trust (UIT) is also issued by an investment company, but the portfolio of bonds or notes in the trust is fixed when the trust is issued. The unit investment trust issues redeemable securities that represent an undivided interest in a unit of the specified securities. The bonds in the trust are not bought and sold during the life of the trust. There are as many kinds of UITs as there are bonds: corporate, government, and municipal bonds, in all maturities.

Since the UIT is not managed but the assets are fixed, you can evaluate the UIT by looking at the securities that are in it. Evaluate the possibilities of credit and market risk carefully, because there is no manager to protect against credit deterioration in any of the bonds composing the UIT. As long as the investor plans to hold the UIT to maturity, there is little interest-rate risk. That risk would come into play if an investor had to sell his or her shares prior to maturity. The coupon is fixed, so a fixed amount of interest is paid monthly (at least until the first bonds mature), yet the investor still gets diversification. There is no management fee.

The advantage of a UIT is that, since it has a maturity date, its price rises towards par as the fund nears maturity. This could make UITs attractive to investors who want to be sure principal will be paid back in full but who do not have sufficient funds to buy a diversified portfolio of bonds. The sponsoring firm and the trustee maintain surveillance over the bonds in the trust until they are redeemed or called. The trustee provides a monthly report on the trust's activity.

Secondary UITs are bought and sold like bonds. The dealer can sell them to the customer either as agent or as principal. Markups are similar to those of bonds. When an investor buys a UIT at issuance, the price includes a sales charge, which can range from 3.5% to 5% of the total public offering price. As with a mutual fund, this sales charge is significant, so the investor should plan to hold the UIT for a number of years to average it out. There is no annual management fee.

Fixed-Rate Annuities

There is a certain amount of confusion about how to classify an annuity. By definition it is an insurance product; it is offered by an insurance company, and the rep selling a fixed-rate annuity must have an insurance producer's license, not a security license. However, when bankers think about alternative investment products as a whole, they usually think first of mutual funds and annuities. Like a mutual fund, an annuity is a product that has many different securities underlying it and a number of different features associated with it, so in that sense it is packaged. The Comptroller of the Currency has chosen to allow national banks to sell annuities in certain circumstances where other insurance products cannot be sold because it classifies annuities as investments, not as insurance. Also, an annuity requires no medical underwriting, so we talk about annuities under the heading of packaged products, not under insurance.

An annuity contract is an insurance policy issued by an insurance company based on fixed or variable payments with the purpose of paying investment returns on those deposits. An annuity can be further defined by its two phases, the accumulation phase, when the funds are paid in and build on a tax-deferred basis, and the payout phase, when the funds are distributed.

The process of buying an annuity is different from buying a security. The applicant fills out an application, writes a check to the insurance company, and mails the application and check to the insurance company (or maybe to the general agent, who forwards it to the insurance company). The policy is delivered to the general agent or the insurance producer (salesperson) within two weeks, and the salesperson delivers it to the customer. It is a good idea for the rep to meet with the customer in person when he or she delivers the policy, because insurance laws allow the customer a "free look," which is at least a ten-day period during which the customer can rescind the policy. If the policy is delivered in person, the salesperson can answer any new questions the customer might have. Some insurance companies offer lobby-issue policies that have the application attached to the policy. The application is completed and removed, and the customer leaves with the policy in hand. The advantage of a lobby-issue annuity is that it looks more like a security or a bank transaction and it goes into effect immediately.

A fixed annuity can be either single premium or flexible premium. A single premium annuity requires an initial lump sum deposit (generally a minimum of $1,000 to $5,000) and does not accept any future contributions. Flexible premium annuities can accept future contributions and often require a smaller initial deposit.

One advantage to the buyer of an annuity is that the funds accumulate tax-deferred: the owner doesn't pay taxes on the annuity's interest until the funds are paid out. If the owner takes funds from the annuity before age 59 1/2, there will be a 10% IRS penalty on those funds in addition to the other taxes owed. This is the reason fixed annuity customers tend to be in their 50s. They are not worried about needing funds before retirement, and they are trying to accumulate as much money as possible on a tax-deferred basis.

There are no front-end charges (loads) to the customer for purchasing an annuity. The customer's entire investment amount goes into the policy and begins earning interest. There are, however, back-end surrender charges for early withdrawals from the policy. These charges and the length of time they apply to the policy vary widely across the industry. The average policy probably has a 7% to 8% first-year charge that declines one percentage point per year. Most products also have a 10% annual free withdrawal provision that gives the customer access to 10% of the annuity value annually without paying any surrender charges. Any distributions above 10% annually are subject to the surrender charges.

An annuity is a very safe investment. Industry surveys show that the primary reason investors buy annuities is for safety not rate. (However, salespeople tend to sell them on rate.) The policies are guaranteed by the issuing insurance company, which makes the strength of the company an important consideration. Annuity rates are based on the rates on bonds, including intermediate and longer-term Treasuries, agencies, and corporate bonds. The surrender charges give the insurance company some comfort about how long the money will stay invested and therefore some flexibility about investing it.

Although the insurance company might pay out total commissions (including everyone in its distribution hierarchy) of 1% to 7%, depending on the product, every dollar the customer invests goes into the annuity, and the commissions are paid separately by the insurance company. Again, it is the longer-term nature of the instrument that allows the company to pay these charges without using a direct sales charge to the customer. However, it takes the company some time to generate the profit to cover those charges.

If the annuity owner dies during the accumulation period, the total value of the account (including interest earned), passes to the beneficiary, free of probate costs. The beneficiary has settlement options but must take receipt of the money and is subject to taxes on the growth. A spouse is the only beneficiary who can continue the contract in his or her name and is not required to take receipt of the proceeds.

The prime prospect for an annuity is a person who is beginning to think about retirement. It usually earns a higher rate than a CD, it does not have the interest-rate risk like bonds, and is tax-deferred. It also provides additional benefits, like avoiding probate. However, as we mentioned, like an IRA there are IRS tax penalties for withdrawing funds before age 59 1/2.

Selecting Insurance Products

Beyond the due diligence performed on the insurance company, the banker needs to be aware of how annuities are structured. Some of the annuity characteristics to be analyzed and compared include the following: initial interest rate, interest-rate guarantee, bailout rate, surrender charges, withdrawal provisions, commissions, and renewal rate history. To compare products, prepare a grid with all of the features listed for each product.

Initial interest rate. This is the most obvious way to get the customer's attention. Beware of rates that seem too good to be true. What risks is the company taking to obtain rates higher than anything else in the market? Are they "buying" business with an excessively high bonus rate that they can't support?

Interest-rate guarantee. It is guaranteed that the renewal rate will never fall below a particular level. Typical policies today have a 4% to 5% guarantee.

Bailout rate. This feature is offered on some annuities and allows the customer to surrender the annuity with no penalty if the interest rate falls below a certain floor.

Surrender charges. How long does a customer have to hold an annuity before surrender charges disappear? What are those charges?

Withdrawal provisions. Does the policy have a 10% free withdrawal provision? Is that provision cumulative? In other words, if the customer doesn't use the 10% for the first year, can he or she get 20% free the next year?

Commissions. What is the commission? Does the insurance company take commissions back (called charge-backs) in the event of the customer's early surrender of the policy?

Renewal rate history. The company should be able to supply you with a copy of their renewal rates, to see how their rates have held after the initial rate guarantee period.

Variable Annuities

Variable annuities are a popular product at the moment. Many bank programs report considerable success with them. *United States Banker* reported: "Banks and thrifts sold $1.35 billion worth of variable annuities in 1992, more than double that of the year before, says annuity consultant Kenneth Kehrer in Princeton, NJ. And interest is building. A survey by Liberty Financial last fall found that 36% of 201 surveyed banks and thrifts were selling variables, and another 16% planned to."[1]

A variable annuity is a life insurance investment contract that invests customer funds in a variety of mutual funds or separate accounts managed by the insurance company. In effect, it allows a customer to invest in mutual funds within the tax-advantaged structure of an annuity. It is offered by an insurance company and may be purchased with either a lump-sum payment or a number of installment payments. Unlike a fixed-rate annuity, where the insurance company determines how to invest the funds, the investor can choose his or her own investments. A variable annuity offers a number of different investment options that are much like mutual fund categories, including stocks, bonds, and balanced funds. These investments may be managed by a mutual fund company or by the insurance company.

Variable annuities have additional features that pure mutual-fund investing does not. If the annuitant dies, the value of the death benefit is the greater of the amount originally invested in the contract or the annuity's account value. The death benefit is guaranteed never to be lower than the amount invested in the annuity.

You should perform the due diligence necessary to make sure the insurance company is sound and has good products. A variable annuity's inherent load is much heavier than that of a mutual fund because the investor is not only paying the management expenses and fees on the underlying mutual fund but also paying risk and mortality expenses plus $20 to $30 annually for a contract fee. Most variable annuities have back-end surrender charges like fixed annuities, but there are some that carry a front-end load instead. The typical total annual expense for management fees and mortality expenses is on the order of 1.5% to 3.0%.

A fixed-rate annuity is a good investment for an investor who is thinking about retiring in a few years, because it is essentially a fixed-income instrument with a certain interest rate and no fluctuation in principal. A variable annuity offers a vehicle for a young person to accumulate wealth in equities on a tax-deferred basis. A variable annuity is generally more appropriate for investors with longer time horizons, to allow a substantial accumulation of wealth through equity investments on a tax-deferred basis. We are not optimistic that tax rates are going to decrease any time soon, and the higher the tax rate, the more attractive the opportunity to accumulate wealth on a tax-deferred basis. You have seen the analyses showing how much more quickly tax-deferred

---

1   Jeffrey Marshall, "Variable Annuities: Hope or Hype?" *United States Banker,* June 1993, p. 25.

wealth grows, even when the tax must ultimately be paid, and this is the major justification for buying a variable annuity.

A variable annuity is considered both an investment and an insurance product. The person selling the variable annuity must have both an insurance license and a securities license (either a Series 6 or a Series 7).

Fixed-Income Products

Money Market Instruments

Many high net-worth individuals used to be able to take care of all their fixed-income investment needs under the auspices of a bank bond department. Such a department sold U.S. government bills, notes, and bonds, as well as various money market instruments. Many of us remember selling bankers' acceptances or holding company commercial paper at double digit rates. With rates like that, who needed to take equity risk? Times have changed so dramatically that the entire money market is now moribund, and real interest rates are so low that even institutional investors who need the liquidity of the money markets are exploring all alternative methods of enhancing yield.

Money market instruments are by definition debt securities that have a maturity of less than one year. They include bank (brokered) CDs, commercial paper, bankers' acceptances (BAs), and Treasury bills.

We will discuss these instruments very briefly; for all practical purposes, most individuals stopped investing directly in them when money market mutual funds started to become popular in the early 1980s. These funds come into the institutional market shopping for $100 million of securities at one time and command the highest interest rates available anywhere in the market. The differential between the rate an individual could get for investing even $100,000 and what the institutional investor will receive might be as much as 50 basis points. Furthermore, funds in a money market mutual fund are liquid, are available by check or wire transfer to the individual, and provide account statements and tax reporting.

Technically, many money market instruments (including commercial paper, bankers' acceptances, and Treasury bills) do not pay interest. Instead they are discounted instruments, issued at a discount from the face amount and redeemed at maturity for the full face amount.

Brokered CDs

When interest rates were higher, sometimes an individual would buy a brokered CD from a registered rep. The rep would offer a CD for less than $100,000 from an institution that needed to raise deposits. The interest is paid monthly. This is attractive to individuals because the entire amount is FDIC-insured. There is less demand for these CDs now that interest rates are so low.

Commercial paper

This is not a generic term; it refers to a short-term promissory note issued by a corporation for a specific amount and with a specified maturity date. Commercial paper is usually issued at a discount, with the full face amount payable at maturity. Most commercial paper is rated by the rating agencies. The size and depth of this market have contributed to one kind of disintermediation: a sound corporation has easy direct access to institutional investors and no longer needs to borrow on bank lines for short-term funds.

Bankers' acceptances

This is a security created to facilitate commercial trade transactions. The bank "accepts" ultimate responsibility to repay a loan to its holder. By the time the security arrives in the money market, it looks and acts like a discounted money market instrument except that it is often issued in very odd amounts. The BA carries the credit risk of the bank issuing it, but it is also backed by the underlying trade transaction and is therefore considered to have a slightly lower risk than commercial paper, resulting in a slightly lower rate.

Treasury bills

These are short-term IOUs issued by the U.S. Treasury. T-bills with maturities of three or six months are auctioned by the Treasury every Monday and one-year bills are auctioned once a month. Market analysts study these auctions for indications of market trends. Treasury bills are the most popular money market instrument. Like all U.S. government debt, they are considered to be riskless; that is, to have no credit risk. Any security issued directly by the U.S. government is considered AAA-rated and free of default risk. The rate of return on direct obligations of U.S. government securities of all kinds constitutes the risk-free rate, and the rates of return on all other securities in the market are measured as spreads over it. The larger the spread, the riskier the investment.

The secondary Treasury bill market is the largest and most efficient market for any money market instrument, and Treasury bills are highly liquid. There is no central exchange for Treasury bills the way there is for listed stock. Each individual dealer that sells Treasury bills will provide an offer (the rate at which the dealer will sell bills) or a bid (the rate at which the dealer will buy bills) depending on market conditions and on his or her individual position (that is, on whether the dealer owns the bills already or has to buy them from someone else in order to resell them). Dealers sell bills as principal, meaning they buy and sell them from their own position, and adjust the price to build in their profit.

Individuals can buy Treasury bills directly from the government through the Federal Reserve system to eliminate all transaction charges and receive the same yield as institutional investors. The investor can apply to one of 37 servicing offices. This is an efficient operation, with interest payments and maturing principal mailed directly to the account specified and all investments consolidated into one account. Customers who use this option will not have much use for a bank investment program. However, with the direct method, the customer usually must pay a fee to liquidate a T-bill.

Trust departments and fiduciaries have traditionally bought large quantities of Treasury bills because they are so safe, but in today's market environment, bills barely keep investors even with taxes and inflation. Treasury bills are appropriate investments for investors looking for safety of principal with little market risk.

An individual buying less than $100,000 of bills generally will either pay 10 to 50 basis points in yield (that is, if the bills can be bought in the market at 3%, the individual will be able to buy them at 2.9% to 2.5%) or will be charged a $50 to $100 transaction fee, making this an altogether unprofitable investment for an individual. A customer may also have to pay a safekeeping fee. While bills are a very safe investment, they are also a very costly one. Treasury bills are free of credit risk, but their nominal rate is about equal to the inflation rate. Once you have subtracted fees from the all-in rate of return, in today's interest-rate environment you are probably losing purchasing power with this investment.

Debt Instruments

There are three main categories of debt issuers: the U.S. government or one of its agencies, corporations, and municipalities. While these three types have some different characteristics, they share some basic structures. Mortgage-backed securities are different from traditional bonds and therefore we will discuss them separately. When you buy a bond, you in effect lend your money to the issuer of the bond. The issuer agrees to make periodic interest payments to the investor who holds the bond and to repay the original sum (the principal) in full on a certain date, which is known as the bond's maturity date.

When should an individual buy a bond rather than a mutual fund? The facile answer is that you will encounter customers who refuse to buy mutual funds, for whatever reason. You will also find customers with inheritance issues or family gifts in mind who would like to buy a $10,000 bond for each grandchild, for instance. There are better reasons: very short bonds (two to five years) held to maturity have very low market risk, and credit risk is less than on longer bonds because you don't have to look as far into the future to see if the issuer will remain sound. As long as the customer does not plan to sell the bond, interest rates can soar and the customer will still be repaid the entire principal at maturity. Interest payments are certain, and there will be no volatility with the investment. Even a mutual fund with quite stable NAV will be affected to some extent by changes in interest rates.

More importantly, the owner of individual bonds has much greater control of both cash flow and tax consequences. The investor controls when to take profits and losses based on what is in his or her best interests. If it matters to an investor whether a tax gain is taken in December or January, a bond can allow that choice. In addition, by buying specific maturities and coupon payment dates, the individual investor controls cash flow as well as return of principal.

Comparing individual bonds to mutual funds, an individual investor with less than $50,000 to invest in bonds is probably better off in mutual funds (or UITs), with their diversification and professional management. As we discussed earlier, mutual funds have other advantages: any institutional investor buys bonds more cheaply than an individual, and the bonds in a mutual fund have all been bought at the institutional price. The institutional investor pays a minuscule portion of total price in transaction costs, whereas transaction costs can be significant for an individual—and it gets worse if the individual has to pay for safekeeping the securities. (On the other hand, the mutual fund pays a management fee that might equal in yield the transaction cost the individual would pay.) The mutual fund pays dividends monthly since it owns bonds with so many different payment dates, whereas individual bonds pay out only semiannually.

The following is information the investor should know about a bond before purchase. When you buy a bond, you must know the following about it:

- security description: type of bond, purpose of the bond, and the issuer
- rating: for example, A or AA
- trade date: date the bond is purchased in the market
- settlement date: the date the purchaser pays for the bond and interest starts accruing.

- maturity date: the date you will be repaid the principal and last interest payment
- interest payment dates: dates interest payments are made, usually semiannually
- coupon: fixed annual interest rate (interest income) stated on the bond
- price: dollar price paid for the bond. (An offer price is the price at which the individual investor buys the bond; the bid price is the price at which the individual can sell the bond)
- current yield: the coupon divided by price, giving a rough approximation of cash flow
- yield to maturity: measure of total return on the bond, including reinvestment of coupon payments and any capital gains or loss of principal.
- par amount: face amount of the bonds
- accrued interest: the amount of interest income (coupon income) earned from the date of the last coupon payment to settlement date; all bonds trade plus accrued interest
- whether the bond uses a 360-day or 365-day basis to calculate interest payments
- special features: features specific to a bond that can affect value, trading characteristics, etc
- form: book entry, registered, or physical

Buying a bond is a somewhat different process from buying stocks or mutual funds, because only a certain dollar amount of each bond is issued and that amount is almost certainly much smaller than the amount of equity issued. Large companies have millions of shares of stock outstanding, and all shares of common stock are the same. To buy a bond, the customer can't just consult the *Wall Street Journal,* pick a bond, and place an order. Buying a bond means finding the someone (such as an institutional trading desk) who owns the bond that meets the customer's needs.

The main form of market risk, or interest-rate risk, for a bond is the risk of interest rates changing once the customer buys it. If market interest rates go up, the bond loses principal value; if market rates go down, the bond gains principal value. The longer the term of the bond, the more the price will be affected by changes in interest rates. Whether the bond is issued by the U.S. government, a corporation, or a municipality, the market risk is similar.

Credit risk is what gives the bond market its diversity. We will discuss credit risk separately under each separate kind of bond.

Bonds are also subject to call risk, the risk that the bond issuer will choose to redeem (call) the bond before the maturity date. The call provisions must be stated in the prospectus, along with other special features—but prospectuses can be hard to understand.

U.S. Government Notes and Bonds

The U.S. government issues both treasury notes (maturities of two to ten years) and bonds (maturities over ten years). U.S. government securities are considered to have no credit risk, and their rates of return are the benchmark all other rates of return in the market are compared to.

U.S. government securities are auctioned by the government on a regular quarterly schedule. The ability of the capital markets of the United States to absorb and distribute these notes and bonds is essential to the government and its deficit financing. U.S. government notes and bonds are exempt from state and local taxes.

In a normal yield-curve environment, U.S. government notes typically have yields 50 to 250 basis points higher than those on T-bills and the same spread lower than a U.S. government bond. Notes are the most likely investment for an individual investor because of the maturity range. The 30-year bond is actively traded by institutional investors and traders.

U.S. Agency Securities

A number of agencies of the U.S. government sell bonds. Notes and bonds issued by the agencies look and act much like those issued by the government, except they are considered to have a very small amount of credit risk. The U.S. government has a legal obligation to repay securities it issues directly; it has only a moral obligation to repay securities issued by agencies. Agency securities therefore trade at a spread 5 to 150 basis points higher than instruments of similar maturity issued directly by the Treasury. Many investors like agency securities because they are almost riskless debt but carry slightly higher yields than the corresponding Treasuries.

Zero Coupons

Zero coupon securities are also known as strips, because they are U.S. government bonds whose interest payments have been stripped off, probably by an investment bank that has repackaged the securities. The investor in a zero does not receive any interest payments and is therefore not subject to coupon reinvestment risk. The investor buys the bond at a deep discount from face value and receives the full face value at maturity.

Zero coupons can have a number of disadvantages for individual investors. Since they are a manufactured product and not highly liquid, buying small amounts can subject an investor to a high markup in price. Zero coupons are extremely volatile in price. Furthermore, tax treatment makes them unsuitable for many investors. Although investors receive no interest payments for the years they hold the instrument, they must pay tax every year on the imputed interest (the interest that is assumed to have accrued on the investment). Investors therefore pay taxes on funds they have not yet received.

Zeros are most suitable for tax-deferred investing in an IRA or other pension vehicle. The high volatility of zeros means the individual investor should be certain he or she can hold them to maturity.

Corporate Bonds

Corporate bonds are bonds issued by corporations of every size and credit quality, from the very best blue-chip companies to small companies with low ratings. The first thing to learn about a bond is its credit rating, which is supplied by one of the large rating agencies. Any institutional trader will tell you the spread at which it is currently trading, the difference in yield between the bond and the U.S. Treasury note or bond of comparable maturity (it may be 20 to 200 basis points). These spreads vary over time. When markets are quiet and consumer confidence is high, spreads tend to be narrow. When the market is roiled by news of bankruptcies or worry about the economic health of the nation, spreads widen, as investors demand a higher yield for putting money into riskier investments. (All investments are riskier than government debt.)

Corporate bonds are not easy to evaluate, especially in the longer maturities, when call provisions may apply and the credit outlook is less certain. Many investors simply choose to stay in shorter maturities or with extremely sound companies, such as utilities. Corporate bonds may be backed by collateral. They are fully taxable at the federal, state, and local level.

All market participants use the ratings services to evaluate particular companies or bonds, but the economic outlook is such that today's blue-chip company could be tomorrow's fallen angel (a company once highly rated but now with a rating lower than investment grade). In the 1980s, corporate bonds were subject to "event risk," which refers to the takeovers, leveraged buyouts, and restructurings that took place during that time. Companies and their attendant credit risk could change radically overnight. As a result, investment bankers began to add new features to bonds either to make them more attractive or to prevent takeovers. Such features can make it more difficult to compare bonds, especially for the individual investor.

However, in our experience, there is no substitute for a medium-term (two to seven years) plain vanilla corporate bond with an investment-grade rating, a recognizable name, and a price around par. The investment is very safe and the yield is higher than that available on a CD or government-issued or insured debt. The coupon is fixed and return of principal is guaranteed by the issuer if the investor holds until maturity. If the investor sells the bond prior to maturity, the bond will be subject to market fluctuation. Investors who want to be able to check the prices of their bonds in the newspaper might want to buy listed bonds, preferably those listed on the New York Stock Exchange.

Keep in mind that the fully taxable nature of corporate bonds (as opposed to municipals or Treasuries) has an effect on yield. When buying a AAA-rated corporate bond, you are buying a security that has more risk than a U.S. government bond. For the risk you are taking, you should receive an additional 25 to 50 basis points in yield. For bonds with lower ratings, the spread should be even greater.

Municipal Bonds

Municipal bonds, or munis, are issued by city, county, and state governments, as well as by political subdivisions that serve the public interest, such as utilities, universities, and hospitals. Municipal bonds are exempt from federal income taxes. In some states, they are also exempt from state and local income taxes for residents. Municipal bonds are truly federal tax exempt, not just tax deferred. That means no federal income tax is owed on the interest income earned from municipals. The muni tax exemption will only get more valuable if tax rates increase. However, buying bonds at a discount results in capital gains, which are taxable.

The municipal bond market is large and confusing. The NYSE lists 2,089 common stocks and the Nasdaq lists 4,900 issues. But there are over 1.5 million different municipal bond issues.[2] Almost all trading is done in the over the counter markets. Learning your way through this market is not simple, and there are many pitfalls for uninformed investors. This is one market where UITs or mutual funds are essential for investors who don't want to do their homework. We can only outline some of the issues involved and urge you to acquire the information you need before you decide to invest.

There are two different kinds of municipal bonds, general obligation (GO) bonds and revenue bonds. Interest payments on the bonds are made from either taxes or user fees. GOs are issued to raise money for general-purpose

---

2 Suzanne Wooley, "Munis 101: Basic Self-Defense," *Business Week,* Sept. 6, 1993, p. 55.

projects. The issuing municipality pledges the bonds are backed by its "full faith and credit and *ad valorem* taxing power." Revenue bonds are issued by different entities that perform public functions—electric utilities, toll roads, airports, hospitals, universities, and the like. The enterprise itself generates the funds needed to pay interest to bondholders. Bonds that are backed by the revenues of the project as well as by the *ad valorem* taxing power of the issuer are called double-barreled bonds.

Information about issues and issuers is available through official statements, offering circulars, or prospectuses. Ask your dealer for details. Municipal bonds are rated by the rating companies, but ratings alone don't always tell the whole story. GOs have traditionally been considered safer than revenue bonds because they are backed by the supposedly unlimited taxing power of the issuer. However, the power to tax is limited by practical considerations. Size alone can cause a small municipality to get no higher than an A rating, or a very strong community might issue so little debt it has no rating (n.r.). Just because a bond is unrated doesn't necessarily mean it is a poor or bad credit. Ratings for revenue bonds are determined primarily by the debt service coverage ratio: the amount of money specifically available for payment of debt service divided by the amount of debt service to be paid. The coverage ratio on a revenue bond should be above two to one.

Bond insurance has become popular recently because it provides comfort to individuals buying the bonds. The three major bond insurance firms are the Municipal Bond Insurance Association (MBIA), Financial Guaranty Insurance Company (FGIC), and American Municipal Bond Assurance Co. (AMBAC). Bond insurance is used on weaker issues to enhance the credit and make the bond more marketable.

All municipal bonds issued after 1983 are sold in book entry or registered form only, meaning the owner's name is registered with the issuer and appears on the bond. Prior to 1983, bonds were sold as bearer bonds, meaning that whoever had the bonds could clip the coupon and collect the interest.

A number of muni bonds have special features.

Municipal notes with maturities under three years have names like revenue anticipation notes (RANs), tax anticipation notes (TANs), or bond anticipation notes (BANs). As the names indicate, these notes are issued in anticipation of future revenues such as taxes, state or federal aid payments, or bond proceeds. The notes raise money now while long-term financing is being put into place.

Zero coupon municipal bonds are issued at a deep discount from par, like zero coupon Treasuries. The investor receives only one payment, at maturity, and no interest payments in between. A zero coupon municipal differs from a zero coupon Treasury in that you don't have to pay taxes on the imputed income.

A put bond is the opposite of a callable bond. The call allows the issuer to retire the bond prior to maturity. The put allows the purchaser to "put" (resell) the bonds back to the issuer at par value on a certain date before the stated maturity date. This option protects investors against interest rate increases, allowing you to redeem your bonds if rates are higher at the put date than they were at the purchase date. Put bonds tend to be less volatile in price than other bonds. Both the put and call features can be found on municipal bonds, but of course the investor or the issuer will pay for them.

Buying munis

One of the biggest drawbacks to buying munis is pricing. With so many different issues available, many of them quite small, it is inevitable that many issues can be very illiquid. Prices are available in the newspaper for some of the larger and more actively traded issues, but prices on most munis have to come from a dealer. Dealers dislike what they call odd lots, amounts less than $25,000—the very amounts some retail investors like the most. An investor can often get a reasonable offer when he or she wants to buy such a small amount, but when the investor wants to sell, the bid will build in a large enough profit margin for the dealer to resell quickly to someone else, such as another retail investor or a dealer who specializes in the issue. Dealers usually simply quote a bid or an offer that includes all transaction costs, so the customer never knows how much commission or profit he or she paid to the dealer. When buying small amounts or individual bonds, the investor should plan not to resell the bonds, because transaction costs (both on the buy and the sell) weigh heavily on the overall return.

Any broker/dealer or bank program that sells munis must have a Municipal Securities Principal (Series 53) to oversee municipal sales.

Mortgage-Backed Securities

Pass-throughs

GNMA pass-through securities were another hot investment of the 1980s. The Government National Mortgage Association (GNMA, or Ginnie Mae) is a government-owned corporation within the Department of Housing and Urban Development. A GNMA pass-through security is one kind of mortgage-backed bond. GNMAs were invented by Wall Street and require a minimum $25,000 investment. They are attractive to investors due to the unconditional backing of the U.S. government and current yield higher than that on Treasuries.

However, they are very complex instruments and, as individual securities, are probably appropriate for only the most sophisticated investors.

Although this section is based mainly on GNMAs, mortgage-backed securities are also issued by the Federal Home Loan Mortgage Corporation (FHLMC, or Freddie Mac) and the Federal National Mortgage Association (FNMA, or Fannie Mae), both of which are chartered by Congress but owned by stockholders. Due to their less direct connection to the U.S. government, both Freddie Macs and Fannie Maes trade at levels slightly higher than those of Ginnie Maes.

A GNMA pass-through is composed of a pool of FHA and VA mortgages. Ginnie Mae guarantees timely payment of principal and interest on all its pass-through securities, backed by the full faith and credit of the U.S. government. The principal and interest payments made every month by homeowners who have those mortgages are passed through every month to the holders of the securities. Investors who hold these securities receive their payments regardless of whether the mortgages are paid, and investors receive full repayment of principal even if the mortgages default.

The main problem with mortgage-backed pass-through securities is predicting cash flows. Cash flow on the instrument depends on the behavior of the consumers who have those mortgages. Because it is a mortgage, the payment the investor receives every month contains both principal and interest. An investor who wants to live on interest and reinvest principal, for example, will have to save a small amount every month until he or she has enough to reinvest in some other security. The amount of principal returned every month increases over the life of the bond, just as the amount of your mortgage payment that is principal increases over the life of the mortgage.

Furthermore, the GNMA investor cannot know with any certainty when the instrument will be repaid. GNMAs follow certain statistical models, but only when bought in quantities large enough to conform to the models. For a given investor, the behavior of a bond is completely unpredictable. All the government-issued pass-throughs are very safe investments in that investors can be assured of receiving all their money. But the fact that investors do not know the schedule for principal payments and cannot make plans for reinvesting principal can be a problem.

Most pass-throughs are collateralized by fixed-rate mortgages, although securities backed by adjustable-rate mortgages (ARMs) are also available. The mortgages comprising the pass-through securities generally have caps and floors that limit the interest-rate fluctuations.

Finally, a GNMA bond is fully taxable, a consideration when comparing the yields of GNMAs and Treasuries. Make sure you know how much of the payment is principal and how much is interest; if you report the entire amount as interest, you will overpay your taxes. Prepayments may be subject to tax as capital gain or loss.

Despite these disadvantages, GNMAs remain attractive to individual investors who need or can accommodate high cash flow and who prefer not to wait until final maturity to recover principal. Cash flow is at least as important as yield in deciding whether or not to purchase a GNMA. The typical spread of a GNMA is 50 to 200 basis points over Treasuries (and make the comparison based on duration, or expected average life, of the GNMA, not on stated final maturity). However, unless an investor can diversify appropriately by purchasing securities from more than one pool, it makes more sense to buy GNMAs through a mutual fund.

Collateralized mortgage obligations

The latest hot product among certain sectors of the brokerage community is the collateralized mortgage obligation (CMO). People are starting to receive those famous dinnertime calls offering these securities, but we are hard pressed to think of circumstances that would make these securities appropriate for the unsophisticated individual investor.

Wall Street bundled mortgages to make mortgage-backed pass-through securities and then bundled the pass-through securities to make CMOs. CMO pools are $50 million to $1 billion. The CMO slices up the mortgage cash flows into "tranches." There may be from three to 17 different tranches. Each slice, or tranche, receives scheduled interest and principal payments, but the different tranches receive unscheduled prepayments sequentially. The first tranche will receive the prepayments made for the first period of time, one or two or three years.

If we say that the first tranche is three years, at the end of that time the tranche will be retired. The next tranche will receive unscheduled prepayments for the next three years and then be retired, and so on, depending on the number of tranches that the CMO has. The early tranches are more like regular bonds than a pure GNMA, so they will have a slightly lower yield due to the lower uncertainty. Investors who buy longer tranches are looking for protection against early prepayment risk.

The final tranche is called the accrual tranche, or Z-tranche, and it receives no payments at all until all the other tranches have been retired. A Z-tranche is a strange, hybrid bond with some characteristics like a zero coupon. It is highly volatile in pricing and completely unpredictable in behavior. Certain institutional investors find the higher yields available on the Z-tranche so attractive they are willing to tolerate the risk and uncertainty, but this is in no way an appropriate instrument for an individual. One of the risks of owning a Z-tranche is that its purported high yield may never be realized.

Brokers are beginning to sell CMOs to individual investors for minimum amounts of $10,000 to $50,000. Many CMOs are available only through a certain brokerage house, so you might not be able to sell them if you change brokers. Like the mortgage-backed pass-through securities that underlie CMOs, these securities are very safe as far as ultimate payment of interest and repayment of principal. The problem, once again, is the tremendous uncertainty regarding the behavior of the bond the individual investor happens to buy. In sum, despite the enormous size of this market, if you buy a CMO you are participating in an investment experiment.

Equities

How to Pick Stocks

For individuals who are managing large amounts of money, the question for the investment advisor is what kind of research is necessary to support the recommendation of a particular stock for a particular individual. Established brokerage houses have formidable research departments equipped with analysts for every need. The overhead to pay for this research is what drives up the cost of trading stock with those companies. The trust departments of larger banks have traditionally also done the research necessary to recommend individual stocks to customers. This has been accomplished within the context of fiduciary responsibility to trust accounts. The owners of these accounts have tended to be sophisticated investors or at least individuals with significant assets. A number of the larger clearing firms have affiliations or corporate parents that can provide equity research—at a cost. An organization that is determined to recommend individual stocks should make sure it has the depth of research on which to base those recommendations.

Should Banks Recommend Stocks?

We believe the typical individual with a portfolio of less than $100,000 should not even consider investing in individual stocks. The average investor needs more diversification than he or she can get with a very small portfolio of individual stocks, and that diversification is easily available through owning two or three mutual funds.

If you have customers with larger portfolios, should your bank program recommend stocks? First you must determine whether you have access to a research source that can perform the necessary due diligence for recommending stocks. If you do, weigh the benefits against the disadvantages. Customers generally understand stock prices, and they will remember forever with absolute clarity when you recommend a stock that goes down. Somehow that memory seems to dim when your stock picks do well. If you do recommend stocks, price your services accordingly. Customers can't expect to get full-service brokerage at a discount brokerage price.

Insurance Products

What kind of insurance products are appropriate for a bank program to sell? This is an interesting philosophical question that we would like to debate in a neutral environment. For the moment, however, it seems that the better question to ask is what insurance products is a bank allowed to sell, and under what circumstances. Many banks are pushing into the gray areas of legality with the products they provide.

As we discuss in Chapter 12 on regulation, insurance sales are regulated by individual states, and we cannot detail what is legal in your state. For the sake of completeness, we discuss insurance products briefly here. We provide a complete discussion in the chapter on due diligence of some of the factors to look for in insurance companies.

There are real differences of opinion among industry professionals about the "best" kind of insurance coverage for individuals. We know agents who think it is a major disservice to a customer to sell regular traditional whole life, and we know other agents who think that whole life is really the most adequate form of insurance. In our view, agents, reps, and customers need as much education as possible to help them form their own ideas about the coverage that works best to satisfy the needs and objectives of the individual customer.

Term Life

Term life is usually referred to as the purest form of insurance. The customer pays for only mortality and expense charges, which increase with the customer's age. The insurance company's only obligation is to pay the death benefit. No cash values accumulate in a term policy.

Whole Life

Whole life is traditional life insurance. It was the only kind of insurance available to cover one's "whole" life until the advent of universal life in the 1980s.

This insurance is payable to a beneficiary at the death of the insured, whenever that occurs. Premiums can be made for a specified number of years (limited payment) or for life (straight life). Whole life can also be purchased with a single premium payment.

Universal Life

Universal life, like whole life, is permanent insurance, but it allows the policy owner flexibility in the coverage amount and frequency of premiums. The policy owner can make changes in the death benefit or payments and can vary or skip premium payments if there is adequate cash value for the insurance amount selected. This insurance first became popular with the high interest rates of the early 1980s, which allowed the policy to build up cash values faster by offering annual interest rates that fluctuate to reflect current market rates.

As it turns out, policyholders rarely use the death benefit flexibility, and premium flexibility is used more often to reduce or suspend payments than to increase them. Universal life tends to pay lower commissions on the principle that it is easier to sell than whole life and the agent should therefore be selling a much higher volume. Universal life peaked in popularity in 1985, and whole life has since regained some market share.[3] Although universal life will continue to be the right product for some customers, particularly those who need flexibility, it has less appeal now than it once did.

Universal Variable Life

With universal variable life insurance, a policyholder uses the premium payment to buy term insurance and invests the rest of the premium amount in any number of mutual funds or investment accounts, all within the context of one contract. This product is like regular universal life in that the premiums and death benefits are flexible. Once the policy owner has selected an initial death benefit (guaranteed insurance amount or GIA), the rest of the premium is applied to investments. The policy owner can choose from a variety of different investments, including mutual funds, bond accounts, and money market accounts.

The benefit of this kind of policy is that the underlying investments can grow with taxes deferred. If the investments are in equities, this can be a powerful tool for increasing wealth. The owner benefits from the same kind of professional management found in mutual funds but receives the death benefit as well.

The disadvantages are that the owner bears investment risk on the cash value of the policy, since there is no minimum guaranteed amount, and invest-

---

3   Gary W. Parker, "The Return of Whole Life," *Broker World,* July 1993, p. 30.

ment performance may not meet expectations. The risk of generating sufficient returns to pay the death benefit lies with the policy owner. However, the insurance company will offer a fixed-rate account option to provide stability.

A salesperson selling universal variable life must have both an insurance producer's license and a Series 6 or 7 securities license.

Variable Life

Variable life is to whole life what variable universal life is to universal life. A variable life insurance policy is like a whole life insurance policy except that part of the premium is allocated to various investments that the policyholder chooses. Whereas a universal variable life policy has the same flexibility as a universal life policy, a variable life policy has certain stated premiums and a stipulated death benefit. However, the policyholder does have flexibility about how to allocate the investment portion.

The salesperson must have both an insurance producer's license and a Series 6 or 7 securities license.

Selling Property and Casualty Insurance

Think for a minute about your own insurance on your car or house. Have you ever had reason to be dissatisfied with the coverage or service provided by your agent and your policy? Life insurance policies pay out only once; there is little opportunity for ongoing customer dissatisfaction with that service. But there could be numerous occasions for dissatisfaction with one's property and casualty insurance. Servicing the customer properly means providing a high level of ongoing service. Years could go by where the customer simply renews the policy and you don't hear from him or her. Then a situation might arise where you need to have extensive contact. There must be enough personnel available to take care of each customer's needs, whether it is a high contact or low contact year for the customer. Although the business demands a high level of service, it is a low-margin business.

On the other hand, an experienced property and casualty agent will be able to build up a book of business that renews faithfully and uneventfully every year, generating a constant stream of income. Any one policy brings in a small amount of revenue, so you do need the book of business to be profitable. Starting in the business will take time, but once it has been built, it will be stable. Do you have the time and/or experienced personnel necessary to build this business and service it properly?

Selling Health Insurance

Health insurance works like property and casualty in that commission profits are small, it takes some time to build a significant business, and customers demand a high level of service. It is also like property and casualty in having the capacity for a significant revenue stream. An additional disadvantage associated with health insurance, however, is that a company that doesn't manage its business expertly might be forced to raise premiums by a substantial amount in a single year: 50% is not unheard of. Then you are left with customers who are angry at you—and still demanding service.

There are many facets to health insurance. You would certainly want expert, experienced staff running this business. With the Clinton health care reform legislation on the table, now would probably not be the best time to start in this business.

Wrap Accounts

A wrap account is a fee-based asset management account. A professional asset manager manages the account, and investors pay a percentage of assets under management, something like 3% on $100,000. The individual investor stipulates his or her personal goals and objectives as guidelines for managing the account. At any time the customer can ask to realize or defer profits, depending on tax needs. At the end of the year, each wrap account provides a customized performance statement according to the specific investments in the account. The wrap account manager typically meets with the client once a quarter to review account performance and the client's investment goals and objectives.

The benefit of wrap accounts is that the percentage fee is the only fee the customer pays. There are no other transaction costs or statement charges or any of the other nickel-and-dime expenses that irritate customers. Wrap account minimums typically start at $100,000, with significant fee breakpoints at higher levels. The least satisfied customers tend to be those with account balances closer to minimums, because they pay a higher proportionate percentage of yield in fees.

According to *Financial Planning* magazine, $50 million per day is pouring into wrap accounts, and wrap account assets under management are about $50 billion (excluding commingled wrap programs). Total wrap account assets under management could reach around $1 trillion by the turn of the century.[4] Many securities professionals, whether in banks or brokerage houses, believe that ultimate success in the securities industry depends on being able to gather and manage customer assets, and wrap accounts are an extremely effective way

---

4   Thomas Kostigen, "Understanding Wrap Fees," *Financial Planning,* Sept. 1993, p. 130.

to do that. Wrap accounts are available through many clearing broker/dealers, even if a particular introducing broker does not offer them.

Some of the larger mutual fund companies have designed their own quasi-wrap programs, which allow a bank retail investment program to offer a family of no-load mutual funds. The customer fills out a form that the bank sends to the mutual fund company. The retail investment services program then charges its customers a fee for helping them allocate their funds among equity, bond, and income mutual funds. The mutual fund company processes the information according to its asset allocation model and returns the results to the bank. While this sounds simple enough on the front end, some banks have tried to do it on their own. Without the expertise of a registered rep, such programs have been less successful than anticipated.

Products for Sophisticated Investors

The most sophisticated customers will tell you about the profits they made trading options with the local securities shop, or how they bought a futures position in deutsch marks, or how they leveraged their stock position to double their money in a year. There are a certain number of customers who take an intense interest in managing their money through a variety of extremely risky investments. (You know very well that for every investor who made a killing, there were about ten times as many who lost everything, but that's another story.)

Margin Accounts

The typical agreement signed by customers of third-party provider or in-house programs is a cash account agreement. A margin account is different and must be opened separately. A customer opens a margin account to engage in securities transactions using credit extended by the brokerage firm. The amount an investor can borrow is set by regulation.

Some people might think "margin account" has a high-flyer tone (probably left over from the stock market crash of 1929), and many investors do use margin account leverage to purchase additional securities, but in fact a margin account allows customers to access the value of their investment by borrowing against it. Once a margin account has been opened and securities deposited in it, investors can borrow against the equity at any time without having to answer questions about why they want the money, since the loan is fully secured against the value of the securities. If the value of the securities falls or an investor violates any provisions of the margin account, the underlying securities can be sold and the loan repaid.

It is unlikely that many customers of community banks will borrow on margin to buy more stock (hoping the value of the stock will go up faster than the interest payments they must make to cover the cost of the margin loan). Having a margin account is not really in the same league of risky investing as trading options or owning futures, although an investor can incur plenty of risk by using the money borrowed in a margin account to attempt stock market plays. Margin accounts are an important part of the Series 7 exam, and registered reps should know how to work with them.

Should You Offer Options and Futures?

An option is a security that provides the right, but not the obligation, to purchase or sell a specified number of shares of a particular stock at a fixed price for a specified time period. An option is a wasting asset. Even if a particular option has intrinsic value due to an increase in the value of the underlying stock, if the option is not exercised or sold, it becomes worthless at expiration. A customer can either buy or sell options, and options are either calls or puts (the right to buy at a particular price or to sell at a particular price, respectively). The holder of an option can choose whether or not to exercise or sell that option.

The futures markets of the United States provide an essential service to producers, users, and buyers of various kinds of commodities and financial instruments. The futures market allows farmers to lock in the price to be paid for their crops, months in advance, or users of oil to purchase all the oil they will need for a given period of time at a given price. A futures contract is an agreement providing for the future exchange of a financial asset or commodity at an agreed-upon price in a future determined month. The seller is obligated to sell the underlying financial instrument or commodity and the buyer is obligated to purchase the underlying financial instrument or commodity at the predetermined price on settlement date. Although the contract may be sold to another investor to close out the position, the futures contract is not an option. Buyer and seller are obligated to fulfill the contract.

Customers for the essential service provided to commerce by the options and futures markets should not be confused with high-flying customers who like to speculate or investors who are so financially sophisticated and well informed that they can make money in these markets although they have no commercial interest to protect. Marketing products such as these has no place in a bank's retail investment services unit, but making them available as a service to customers who ask for them may be another story. There may be a certain number of affluent suburbs whose demographics demand a full-service investment program. All appropriate sales processes must be followed, including:

- providing qualified staff and staff supervision
- determining that the customer is truly a qualified investor
- having the customer sign risk disclosure forms
- having the customer sign forms stating that the transaction was totally unsolicited

Sales reps who sell commodity futures must have a Series 3 license (separate from the Series 7), and the financial institution must have a registered options principal on hand to supervise reps who are selling options. Qualified personnel can be available. In New York or Chicago you may find options or futures salespeople and principals who would like to get out of the fast lane of the exchanges by serving in a financial institution. Many third-party providers and/or their clearing firms can offer these services. But we caution you to be very sure of what you are doing, hire qualified personnel to run the program, determine that there is a genuine customer need to be met, and make sure that it will be economic for you to meet that need.

5

Choosing the Right Program Structure

The Banking Analysis

Once you have made the commitment to sell alternative investment products, how should you proceed? The choices are legion. You need to decide whether to develop the program yourself or go with the assistance of a third-party provider and outsource the program. If you want to do it yourself and become licensed as a broker/dealer, you have a long road of regulatory requirements and decisions ahead of you. If you decide to bring in a third-party provider, you are still left with many decisions: which third-party provider; managed program or dual-employee; Series 6 or Series 7, but the majority of the processes will be streamlined.

To make your way through these choices, you need to perform a systematic analysis of your own institution and you have to answer a number of basic structural questions. The question of "doing it yourself," whether you mean to organize your own retail investment services unit and form your own broker/dealer, boils down to asking yourself whether you have the size and the resources, including human, technological, and capital resources, and how much time you have to invest.

To help in your analysis, Figure 5.1 offers some questions. Each question gives a brief indication of what the answer might tell you about the program you should choose. Many questions refer to cultural issues. Every institution has a culture, which refers partly to the strategic stance an institution takes at any point in time, and partly to what one might call the personality of the organization. Institutions are shaped by the personalities of the people working there, but individuals are also shaped by the traditions, history, and community of the organization. Cultural issues are not "soft" issues; they are critically important to determining how the program should be structured and what kind of support the organization is going to give the new business. You should then decide how your program will present itself within your organization and its community, which means systematically defining for your organization the customer profile; the sales philosophy; and the goals and expectations for the program.

An individual institution answering these questions might not have a full understanding of its own history in regard to alternative investment products or what might be permissible activity. Please refer to Chapter 12 on regulation, which discusses some of those issues.

Figure 5.1 Questions for Your Organization

1. Given the structure and regulatory status of my organization, what avenues are open to me legally?

   Important place to begin: what is legally available?

2. Does my organization have a compelling desire or reason to own its own program?

3. Is program ownership part of my organization's strategic plan? How does program ownership tie in with my organization's mission statement?

4. Does my organization always try to vertically integrate, that is, to own every aspect of every product?

   This is truly a cultural issue. Does the institution insist on owning all business ventures? In terms of a retail investment services program, true vertical integration means not only forming a broker/dealer, but also performing every aspect of the delivery and clearance process.

5. What is my organization's level of expertise? Do we have the expertise necessary to build our own program? (Bottom line: do we know anything at all about retail investments?)

6. Do we have the human resources necessary to build from scratch?

7. If we try to build our own program, do we have the resources and/or customer base necessary to take advantage of economies of scale necessary to make a program work effectively?

   Like the legal issue, this is a "hard" constraint; develop a program consistent with the volumes you predict.

8. Do we have the time it will take to build from scratch?

9. How fast do we have to see a return?

   This is already a competitive market. Doing it yourself will take considerably longer than hiring a third-party provider.

10. Does my organization already have the sales culture necessary to make a program work?

    If the organization does not have a sales culture, what steps should you take to introduce it? How can you encourage it?

11. Does my organization already have a bond department?

Figure 5.1 Questions for Your Organization (*continued*)

---

12. Are we already selling some of the products on the list of products we would like to sell as part of a retail investment services program? If yes, how?
13. Are we already doing institutional business, and are we looking to add retail?
14. Does my organization have a trust department? If yes, what kind of business does the trust department do?

    Answers to these questions reveal what kind of expertise the financial institution already has in-house and give an indication of what kind of political conflicts might occur.
15. What kind of banking structure does my organization have: one bank, or multi-banking holding company, bank branches, etc.?
16. How will the retail investment unit fit structurally into the organization: where will it report, who will it report to, how will the revenues get split, or will the revenues get split?

    The right answer to this question is to start with a program that best facilitates business, which might not be the most obvious structure. An organization needs to make hard decisions about exactly how to structure the retail investment services unit within the organization. The flow of profits can encourage support within the organization at all levels.
17. How much capital does the organization want to invest and is it willing to invest additional capital if necessary ?

    Starting a broker dealer is not only expensive upfront, it requires ongoing commitment. Make sure your organization wants to make that commitment and is going to have the kind of volume necessary to get the required returns.
18. Are we thinking about this proactively (progressive, wave of the future), or reactively (everyone else is doing it, we better, too)?
19. Even if my organization has to use a third-party provider to do it legally, what kind of control is comfortable to me?
20. Am I willing to give up control to an outsider to make my life easier, or am I willing to commit the resources internally to retain control?
21. Will I be able to run the business efficiently enough to warrant doing it myself, or will it be more cost-effective to buy the services I need?

    Answers to these questions help determine what kind of structure will work best for your organization.
22. What is my customer/demographic profile?
23. What kind of community do I live in, and how do I position myself within that community?

Answers to the questions in Figure 5.1 will show you what kinds of services you need to provide, what program emphases are most important to you, and what particular qualities in a retail investment services program are most important to you. As you go through the process of answering these questions, keep in mind that management might change its mind as it goes through this process. Most organizations do.

Legal Structure

The very first question is to determine your legal standing, whether you are a one-bank holding company, a community bank, a savings and loan, or a credit union. We have provided a brief outline of possible regulatory options in Chapter 12 on regulations. Whatever your legal status, there is a way for you to offer alternative investment products, but you may have to find it. There are larger banks with their own broker/dealers all over the country, and there are third-party provider programs in every state. Securities laws are standard and federally-regulated, which makes the process cleaner; insurance laws are state-regulated, making each state different.

You have to conduct your own research and make decisions about the laws governing insurance sales in your own state. The law is evolving very rapidly; every day there are new interpretations of existing laws. There are many gray areas. The third-party providers have an important stake in learning how to deliver annuities or other forms of insurance in every state, and they have designed programs that work. Talk to one to get an understanding of how state laws affect your institution. However, you need to consult your own counsel for advice concerning your own institution.

Corporate Goals

The most important part of the financial institution's analysis of what kind of program to offer is that institution's strategic analysis of why it wants to offer alternative investment products. Financial institutions have many reasons for entering this business. Reasons include building customer relationships, improving fee income, increasing the service orientation of the organization as a whole, providing a more complete set of financial services, and halting the flow of funds moving out the door to the wire houses.

Set corporate goals for the program; this means ranking priorities. For example, your approach to the personnel involved will differ according to whether your first priority is developing relationships (you might want to train in-house personnel in securities products, since these people already have many customer relationships) or generating fee income (where you would definitely want to hire experienced registered reps). As we have mentioned before, the savings and loan industry became heavily involved with offering investment services—particularly annuities—in the 1980s because they were eager for fee income and recognized that insurance products could help provide additional income.

A word of advice is offered about the fee income issue: one might expect banks that are not doing well today to be the most interested in offering alternative investment products. The fee income generated might help a distressed balance sheet. In fact, it is not banks with losses that tend to be most interested in starting a retail investment services program but banks that are already doing well. An affluent, progressive bank is more likely to have the vision to understand the importance of offering the alternative investment products that will help it grow in the banking environment of the late twentieth century.

Program Ownership

This should be a business decision, not an emotional one. Some bankers' initial response to the question of program ownership is most likely to be, "I don't want outsiders in my bank's lobby!" They may feel that no one can take care of their customers the way they would; furthermore, they may have no interest in sharing their customer base in such a way as to risk losing it. As you proceed in this analysis, you should be aware of your own natural bias against sharing your customer base with anyone, internally or externally. The disinclination to share customer names with any external source is understandable, and most bankers will acknowledge this; but many traditional bankers have been reluctant to share customers internally as well. The larger the organization, the more this is the case. How well do the various parts of your organization communicate with each other in marketing campaigns, and how actively does your organization pursue cross-sales programs? How many referral programs, either formal or informal, are in place anywhere in the institution? If there are any, your organization is ahead of most. If you have an informal referral program, then you know where and with whom to start a formal program. A good referral program is one of the important factors in making an alternative investment product successful, but that will be discussed in Chapter 10.

There are some organizations that would not consider, under any circumstances, undertaking a new business venture that they did not own completely. Larger institutions especially have a tradition of making sure that any new businesses are started internally and run by institutional insiders. Such an organization will start its own check-processing unit (because it refuses to use an outside vendor or service bureau) and then find it has excess capacity or that there are economies of scale from enlarging the scope of that unit to provide service to other organizations. This is the kind of financial institution that will probably insist on owning its own program.

However, although the business of alternative investment products is not capital-intensive the way bank lending is, it is a general principle that the more of the business you build and own yourself, the higher the capital requirements will be. If you want to start your own broker/dealer, you have to look at the capital required by the NASD. Some organizations will pay any price for ownership.

In our research, we have talked to financial institutions with $250 million in assets that were eager to start a broker/dealer, and others with $1 billion in assets that couldn't imagine why they should get into that business themselves. Running your own broker/dealer inevitably diverts the focus of your business from the marketing and sales that bring in revenue. You have to spend management time and effort in dealing with administrative issues, compliance, regulation and other legal issues, accounting, and securities processing. Before embarking on that project, you need to understand very clearly why you want to be in that business. The answer could well be that you want to form your own broker/dealer in order to gain control of some very specific things. For example, one large organization decided to switch from being the customer of a third-party provider to running its own broker/dealer in order to gain control over customer statements; this organization found the statements provided by the third-party provider to be too difficult for its customers to understand. Rather than shop around for another third-party provider, this organization decided to form its own broker/dealer.

What size is required for starting your own broker/dealer? Although the answer depends on the usual confluence of factors, including customer base, market position, and all the various factors having to do with need for ownership and willingness to invest capital, many industry sources use a round number like $1 billion in total asset size as the minimum necessary to consider forming your own broker/dealer.[1] A financial institution with assets under $1 billion will generally not be able to generate the economies of scale necessary to overcome the substantial costs of developing a program on its own. A financial institution with assets greater than $1 billion will want to analyze the cost of the different ways of going into the business.

Clearing Operations

Assuming that your bank does want to offer AIPs, the next issue to consider is whether or not to provide your own clearing operations. Some very large organizations have recently chosen to eliminate their own back-office operations and use a clearing agent. The advantages are obvious in this budget-minded era: clearing costs then become completely variable with the number of transac-

---

1 Our own business has been split between potential customers of Lasalle Consultants (those customers needing consulting advice about their own programs), and potential customers of LCL Investments (smaller financial institutions that could use a third-party provider most effectively). Our cut-off point has always been $1 billion.

tions processed and can be identified with total certainty. There will be no more corporate allocation of costs for capital, space, or bank services (such as human resources); the financial institution doesn't have to continue to pay for the cost of downtime, vacations, and back-up staff when business is slow. You pay the cost of each ticket—and only that cost—for every transaction entered. (We should make it clear that we are talking here only about clearing for retail investment services units. Clearing for either dealer banks—banks that are primary government dealers—or banks that have large institutional capital markets areas is a different matter. Many of the issues are similar, relating to processing software and hardware, personnel skills, and costs, but the players and required systems are different.)

If your organization has a compelling reason to want to self-clear, there is a process involved. Most broker/dealers take it one step at a time, mastering the procedures involved in one step before moving on to the next one.

1. *Become registered with the NASD as an introducing broker, using a clearing member to process all trades.* The introducing broker does business with the clearing member on a fully-disclosed basis, which is to say, the name, positions, and complete customer activity of each individual customer is fully disclosed to the clearing firm. The clearing member might charge something like $20 to $25 per ticket; the range of charges is wider on less usual transactions. Account statements are produced by the clearing firm, and the name of the clearing firm must be disclosed to the customer.
2. *Use an omnibus account.* In this situation, the broker has one account with the clearing firm, called an omnibus account. The broker/dealer produces customer statements, is responsible for providing all the accounting and position postings for customer accounts, and sends out the customer statements. All transactions are grouped together and processed with the clearing agent through the one omnibus account. The advantage to the broker/dealer is that the cost per transaction could range from $8 to $10.
3. *Become fully self-clearing.* Like deciding to become your own broker/dealer, deciding to self-clear changes the focus of your business, which is partly why some larger financial institutions have chosen not to self-clear. You have to hire staff. A self-clearing organization has to hire seven to ten clerks: name and address clerk, transfer clerk, cashier, margin clerk, reorganization clerk, data-entry clerk, etc. However, depending on the experience of your staff, converting to self-clearing can put money in your pocket. Industry sources estimate 200 tickets per day is the minimum volume necessary to begin to make a profit by converting to self-clearing. Converting to omnibus clearing prior to converting to completely self-clearing is a way to develop

your staff and allow your employees to gain experience as you climb the learning curve. Your own geographic location will play a part in your decision as well; financial institutions located in urban centers (particularly financial centers) tend to have an easier time hiring experienced help than those located in other places.

If you have determined that you want to be in the clearing business, you might want to consider bringing in a vendor who can provide all the technological and operational resources necessary to get started. Such a vendor can provide everything but personnel. In any event, you will have to buy hardware and software, accounting systems, and sales support systems. It would be easier to purchase the package together. Otherwise, you will have to analyze each component separately and decide for each separate component what to purchase, what kind of training is necessary to make it work, and what skills are required of employees.

If you think that you will eventually have the volume necessary to self-clear, and that it is a business you want to be in, you should at the outset select a clearing member who will accommodate your business as it evolves. There are clearing firms who can operate in either fully-disclosed or omnibus mode and who can act as the vendor when you want to convert to fully self-clearing.

Some organizations are so determined to own every aspect of every business, they do everything in their power to make it almost true, even when, strictly speaking, it isn't legally true. An organization in a state where annuity sales must legally be provided through a third-party provider might use all its own employees and do everything in-house except for the "paper" part of the third-party that provides the channel legally necessary.

Ownership has its price, especially for those beginning in this business now. Make sure you are absolutely committed to this route, and understand what will be involved for you.

Capital Resource Requirements

The NASD has a scale for capital required depending on what part of the business the broker/dealer engages in, from $5,000 minimum net capital for an introducing broker/dealer, up to $250,000 for a clearing member, although there is a pending SEC proposal to increase the $5,000 requirement to $25,000. Some of the largest banks would find even $250,000 not the most expensive part of this business (compared to hiring the talent necessary to organize and manage a large institutional trading operation), but any capital investment should be included in your calculations. In addition to the significant upfront costs of becoming a broker/dealer, both in expenses and in capital, you have to keep in mind the personnel you need on an on-going basis. You have to have a compliance officer, adequate general securities principals, a financial operations principal and, if you sell municipal bonds, a municipal securities principal. You have to provide your own due diligence, marketing programs, record keeping, regulatory reporting, operations and operational control, written procedures, licensing administration, etc. There are a number of consulting companies available that have the expertise necessary to guide you through the process of forming your own broker/dealer. Considering the amount of legal and regulatory expertise they provide, the cost is reasonable, but it can be significant.

As we mentioned before, a broker/dealer is not as capital-intensive as bank lending, but not only will capital be required for regulatory purposes, large banks still allocate some amount of bank capital to each area of the bank. The capital resources necessary to hire a third-party provider are minor, compared to the above expenditures. Many third-party providers require an upfront fee, which in general pays for the upfront costs of getting a program started (marketing materials, contracts, stationery and other supplies, registering personnel, etc.). (For a complete discussion of this issue, see the section on upfront fees in Chapter 6 on choosing a third-party provider.) When the third-party provider program is dual employee rather than managed, the financial institution has more responsibility for managing the program and paying for expenses, although bottom line profits might be about the same.

Critical Mass/Economies of Scale

The answer to the question of whether your institution has the critical mass necessary to warrant starting your own program is easily quantifiable; there are no "fuzzy" issues connected to this one. Is your organization large enough to process enough tickets daily to make it profitable for you to form your own broker/dealer? (The actual number of tickets varies considerably from one clearing agent to another, and also depends on ticket size. This is something you have to evaluate for yourself in the context of your own business.) Even a wildly successful program at a community bank will never achieve the volume necessary to create economies of scale.

Required volumes go up for an organization that is looking to provide its own back-office and clearing. Both technology and book-entry securities have made a huge difference in clearing operations over the past few years, and one clerk with a computer terminal can process far more today than anyone would have dreamed of ten years ago, when operations in many back rooms were manual and dealt with physical securities. If your organization does not have the critical mass necessary to keep the minimum number of processing clerks for each part of the operation fully employed, you will be at a competitive disadvantage if you try to do so. If you decide to self-clear and do not have the economies of scale necessary to do it effectively, the already-thin profit margins from this part of the business will be eroded. And although competing for customers on price alone (in order to attract the volume necessary to create economies of scale) might not be the way to ensure longevity for your organization, compared to the importance of developing relationships and gathering assets to manage, the fact remains that bringing customers in the door with discount brokerage is one way to get accounts opened and relationships started. The number of larger players who have moved out of the clearing business recently should give pause to any organization looking to get into the business. Some of these financial institutions are large regional holding companies with a depth of management and personnel skills and fully able to afford the investment in human and technological resources, as well as the capital investment: and they choose to let a specialist do the clearing.

Prior Experience with Retail Investment Products

Many banks have been providing investment services to high net-worth individuals for many years, through the bond department or the more traditional capital markets unit. Bank bond departments have traditionally sold a variety of fixed-income products to individuals with perfect legality. High net-worth individuals who sought advice with equities were forced to work with the bank's trust department or seek a relationship with a traditional stock broker that they could trust.

An organization that already has a traditional bond department that services institutional and corporate customers should have an advantage when the bank decides to enter into retail investment services more actively, especially if some individuals are being serviced. Such a bank already has some knowledge and expertise in this kind of investing. Once the retail unit has been formed, there could be the rudiments of a customer base in place to build on. In addition, if the institution is already doing institutional or trust business, then, organizationally, there is likely to be some understanding of how markets work and how trades get cleared; there should be back-office operations already in place and operations managers eager to add retail clearing to their responsibilities. The challenge for the institution is to tap into that knowledge and expertise and utilize available resources, without starting a political fight. The organizational benefits of already having some familiarity with retail products must be made to work for you.

If a financial institution has a bond department that underwrites municipal bonds, there might be an additional synergy in starting a retail investment services unit. Many mutual fund companies offer general municipal bond funds as well as state-specific municipal bond funds. The municipal bond market is increasingly dominated by institutional buyers, and this is part of the reason. Individual investors get diversification by buying municipal bonds through the mutual fund company, so the financial institution has to compensate for the loss of those individuals by selling securities to the mutual fund company. Mutual fund companies are more likely to do business with firms that are doing business with them.

Human Resources/Expertise

It is an admirable quality for a financial institution to be so devoted to its own personnel that it doesn't want to hire new people for new programs but rather insists on using in-house staff. This may be a mistake in the case of an investment services program. Although it is possible for an investment services program to get up and running using only current bank employees, an organization climbs the learning curve much faster when it brings in outside expertise. A person with years of experience in the securities industry can be much more effective in selling securities than someone who has only just become licensed through the institution. What an individual with securities experience brings to the bank is specific knowledge about securities and the securities markets, as well as a more general knowledge of the difference in culture between a bank and a securities operation. Someone from the securities world knows how it works and how a successful operation should function, and can assist the bank in getting there.

On the other hand, as we have already mentioned, if the organization already has a bond department, or if there is a trust department that engages in certain kinds of activities, the necessary human resources might already be working for the financial institution.

In addition to needing employees with knowledge of and experience with securities, you also need to consider what kind of legal help you might need to get your unit started. No matter what route you choose, at the very least there will be contracts to sign. If you decide to form your own broker/dealer, you will have a considerable need for legal assistance. Whether or not your institution has in-house counsel, securities law requires special expertise. Legal expenses could be significant.

Technological Resources

In today's marketplace, whatever technology your organization ever dreamed of having is available—from software that offer tickler files to computers that dial the phone. However, first you need to determine what technological resources are presently available in your institution.

- If you have a bond or trust department, how are investments tracked and cleared?
- Do you manage customer data bases?
- Do you have spreadsheet programs and personal computers?
- Is there hardware in place that could be utilized, or will you have to purchase everything?

There are basically three ways to get the technology you need:

1. Use a service bureau, and have someone else do your processing for you
2. Buy your own software from a third party and run it yourself
3. Build it yourself

Which route you choose comes back to the question of human resources: do you have the personnel you need to take full and efficient advantage of the technology you own? There is so much technology available that many financial institutions would be wasting resources to try to build systems themselves or even keep the people on staff who can assist with these projects.

Structural Issues and Political Issues

As a financial organization makes plans to add a retail investment services unit, it has to decide where it will fit structurally in the organization: where will it report, who will it report to, and how will revenues get split, etc.? Although already having a bond department—which typically also serves high net-worth individuals—indicates that there is already some expertise within the institution capable of assisting in the formation of the retail investment services area, this could also foreshadow political and territorial rivalries within the organization. Is the retail investment services area to constitute part of the existing institutional investment or capital markets area? If not, will someone new be brought in to build and manage the new department?

At many of the very largest institutions, the capital markets areas and retail investment services areas are completely separate organizationally, with completely different reporting structures. At most other organizations that have bond departments or capital markets areas, it makes sense to use the structure of the institutional unit as a base when creating retail. They will be sharing information resources, back-office services, and maybe processing systems as well. If there is a current core of retail customers being serviced through the bond department, they constitute the ideal customer base for marketing the new retail investment services to, but someone is already serving those customers. Can you build a separate retail unit and then try to pull these customers into it? Do you try to force the institutional area to give up those customers, and thereby disrupt established relationships? Furthermore, the employees who are already servicing lucrative customers will fight to the death for them. Could you have a retail unit take over some of the employees who had been selling to individuals? Do you change their compensation systems? Many institutional salespeople are paid salary plus bonus, whereas salespeople serving a retail area are more likely to be paid draw plus commission.

Revenues are another question. There is a trend for larger institutions with many branches to ensure that some form of revenue sharing takes place, with referral incentive payments as well as credit for fee-income goals achieved flowing back to the branches. Whether the retail investment services area reports separate profits, or whether those profits are returned to the branches for corporate reporting, the financial institution has to work out ahead of time how the revenues will get split in order to facilitate maximum commitment to the program.

The basic structure of the financial institution has a bearing on how the retail investment services unit is itself structured. If there are many branches, then the retail unit has to work out a way to provide investment services through those branches. Keeping all registered reps at headquarters is very cost-effective—and a very ineffective way to distribute services. Talk to the larger institutions and you will find a variety of different ways to deal with the question of dividing up and assigning territories. The usual way is to assign a registered rep to any branch that is large enough to generate sales. A rep can be a circuit rider servicing two or more branches. With registered reps spread out over a large area, you have to provide customer service, information, and compliance and sales supervision.

The trust department can also form a line of potential conflict. Retail investment services managers traditionally report conflict with the trust department. A registered rep sees pure opportunity when a customer has more than $100,000 to invest. However, bank management might see a potential trust customer for that amount. Different institutions have different definitions of the minimum investment amount necessary to open a trust account. Putting aside the special services that a trust department offers and focusing only on the investment part of the relationship, based on informal surveys, the largest institutions still look for $500,000 or more to manage before a trust account is warranted. Amounts of $300,000 to $500,000 might use a money manager; $100,000 to $300,000 would use a wrap account or mutual fund. (There is great variance among institutions, depending on the focus of the institution and the technology available to it.)

The trust department is always necessary for certain types of nonstandard transactions, and there will be obvious situations: estates or certain other cases require the fiduciary guidance of a trust account. But many registered reps have the training and experience necessary to advise a customer who wants to manage his or her money actively. Such reps believe they shouldn't automatically be forced to turn the customer over to the trust area.

Furthermore, there may be other kinds of conflict among the employees of the two respective areas. Trust department officers traditionally had titles (customers love to deal with vice presidents), good salaries, and benefits, whereas the registered rep is often paid a low draw and commission, with perhaps no institutional title. This does not lead to good employee relationships. An additional conflict can arrise between a registered rep and the branch manager. The fact is that registered reps can end up making more money than branch managers if they are good salespeople and work in an busy branch.

The institution has to work out for itself what it wants the guidelines to be. The institution needs to be fully aware of the referral incentives it offers to bank personnel and needs to make sure the referral system rewards the behavior it wants to see. (Trust account referrals often pay the employee making the referral 10% of first-year trust fees, resulting in a pay-out of hundreds of dollars, versus a $2 to $40 payout for a referral to the registered rep.) There is no one right decision; just be aware that the referral system probably gives a definite bias to where the customer is referred, and make sure that that is the bias the institution means to have. The bias creates the behavior the institution desires.

It is not at all clear whether there will be interdepartmental conflict within your organization, or how much conflict there will be. (We think there must be a bank somewhere that has dealt with these issues without causing political friction—we just don't happen to know of any.) Unfortunately, we can't tell you how to resolve this conflict within your organization. The conflict has to be defused and the organization has to pull together to provide the new retail investment services area with the organizational and senior management support that is essential to make it a success. Senior management will have to analyze where the potential areas of conflict exist within your structure and decide what your institution is going to have to do to ensure the success of the program. If there is a place in this book where we would recommend that the institution use a consultant, it would be here. As consultants we have seen many situations and have the experience to work through the structural and political issues without a personal bias or agenda.

Time Available

While we don't want to induce panic in anyone, if you are only just starting to think about providing alternative investment products in your institution, you are behind the times. This business is already very competitive, and there are many other organizations with well-established customer bases (that could include customers that might have originally come from your institution). Other organizations have had years of experience in mapping out marketing strategies, ironing out the wrinkles in their operations, and developing customer relationships. As a newcomer, you will be competing with these institutions.

However, it is important for you to get into this business because offering retail investment products is going to be essential to the future of financial institutions. We do think it means that you should organize your own strategic plan in such a way as to enter this business as quickly and efficiently as possible. This could well mean hiring help to get you started, whether a third-party provider or an in-house program manager. If you choose to hire employees to run the program in-house, you have to understand that you first have to take the time to find those individuals, and then give them time to get the program going once they have been hired. It might be more efficient—depending on the needs and qualities of the institution—to hire a third-party provider to get the program up and running quickly and retain the option of bringing the program in-house after it has become established and successful.

The other time constraint is how fast you have to see a profit. At one time, banks had deep pockets for new ventures, but that time is past. Can you afford to invest a year's worth of salaries in developing this program in-house, or do you need to see returns as quickly as possible after committing the first dollar? Some third-party providers claim to be able have programs in place within two weeks of signing a contract with your institution. While we don't think that you want the two-week program, most third-party providers can have a program up and producing in 60 to 90 days.

Sales Culture and Sales Philosophy

This is a term that is often used in articles and books about banking but rarely defined clearly. As we define it, a sales culture in an institution emphasizes the importance of proactively seeking out customers through marketing, education, and systematic referral systems. A financial institution with a sales culture has a comprehensive marketing plan, an active incentive plan for soliciting employee referrals, and a formal review system for its employees that includes cross-sales efforts. A sales culture understands that you don't put up your sign for business, and then wait for customers to seek you out. You seek out the customer, provide education about the benefits of your products and services as well as the benefits of doing business with you. Everyone in the organization from the chairperson of the board to the lowest level in the organizational chart energetically promotes the establishment of as many aspects of the customer relationship as possible.

As we have explained, traditional banking never had to develop a sales or market orientation because it had a monopoly on its product, which is money. Deregulation and the creativity of competing constituencies has resulted in many different sources for money besides banks. The banker no longer has an exclusive product. Even within the bank market itself, competition is much more active.

With the advent of alternative investment products, the bank is in effect asking the consumer for his or her money, rather than vice versa. Since the consumer has dozens of alternatives for investing, the bank is forced to proactively reach out to its customers. The bank will not reach those customers if it is passive.

The bank does retain its one traditional advantage: the trust its customers have in it. The trust that customers have in the bank is why they come to the bank first, and that trust implies that the bank should do what is best for its customers, no matter what, but the institution needs to price its services fairly. Educating customers about current economic realities is the best possible way to serve that trust. If a bank chose not to offer alternative investment products in order to try to keep its core deposits and because it thought customers wouldn't notice that the world had changed, and if those customers later found out from other sources that in fact there are investment choices that are more effective in the long run than traditional bank products, how will those customers feel about the trust they placed in the bank? The bank keeps customers' trust by doing what is truly in the best long-term interests of its customers, and that means meeting their complete financial needs. Leading them through the confusion of the different investments and securities, and educating them as to what will serve them best in the long run, are services customers will pay for.

The culture of the securities markets, especially as exemplified in traditional Houston or Little Rock brokerage firms, can be sales-oriented to excess, and it is that culture that has given brokerage salespeople a bad name, although typically the bond salespeople found in banks are a toned-down group compared to those found in certain southern wire houses. An institution with a bond department probably has more organizational awareness of what a sales culture is all about and should be receptive to the idea of alternative investment products. Bond department salespeople understand the necessity of calling customers and staying in touch, searching out customers, and selling to customers to close the transaction. They understand that you have to reach out to the customer and not wait for the customer to come to you. The bond department people used to make bankers uneasy, as the bankers would sit back and talk vaguely about relationships. Times have changed, and some bankers are finding that they have to promote their products and aggressively seek customers in order to remain in business; they are finding that the bond department and its salespeople knew something after all about building a business. However, the bank broker still has a greater openness about money and compensation, and a greater awareness of what profit can be made from individual transactions, than a traditional banker would have.

On the other hand, we continue to encounter traditional bankers. In researching this book, we have had an opportunity to listen to bankers in small towns, rural areas, or smaller financial institutions talk about their customer base in ways that make one revere their special relationship with their customers. Although many bankers have been persuaded that they have to offer alternative investment products as a defensive ploy, they are not really convinced that such investments are a benefit to their customers. As a result, they are decidedly neutral about the prospect of a securities salesperson in their lobbies, and leery about introducing the sales culture that such a program represents. In our experience, this is not the best way to develop a successful program, or serve the future of banking. Bankers need to understand that educating consumers about investing does not violate their relationship of trust, nor does offering a new service threaten to disrupt every aspect of their time-honored customer relationships.

However, if the bank is firmly wedded to the idea that offering brokerage services to only the customers who ask for it is the best way to satisfy the growing interest in investment products, and if bank management feels that adding a more proactive program of any sort would violate the trust their customers have in them as a bank, then they should by all means provide only the discount brokerage service. There are many third-party providers of all sorts who will help a financial institution install a phone and provide prospectuses so that customers can place a stock or mutual fund trade of their own choice. Such a program will probably pay for itself without making much further contribution to the bank's bottom line. This is the part of the world where customers consider it risky to move from a savings account to a CD; such banks consider it a violation of customer trust to try to educate their customers.

An institution that already understands sales orientation and active marketing has an advantage. The financial services industry has become too competitive to allow any individual financial institution to believe that it is not going to have to fight actively to retain customer relationships and build new ones. As we mentioned earlier, a bank that already has an active referral system, formal or informal, department- or bank-wide, has an even greater advantage as it seeks to build its business.

Demographic Analysis/Customer Profile

An organization needs to have a customer profile that describes age and investment status (the kind we discuss in Chapter 8) and a demographic understanding of its customer base. Organizations within the same geographic area can have very different customer bases. One savings and loan might offer low-cost savings accounts and various credit products that bring in a younger, less savings-oriented customer than another one down the street that specializes in savings products. Younger customers might be more interested in alternative investment products as vehicles for building their savings, while older and/or retired customers are looking to preserve principal and maintain income.

We have already talked about institutions with customers who are unsophisticated investors seeking safety and security above all else. Bank management might think that discount brokerage is the most innovative product they could possibly offer and would see little need for a program that offered sophisticated trading instruments. Such a program might not support a full-time registered rep, especially if bank management did little to support or promote the program. Fixed annuities might be particularly attractive.

On the other hand, imagine the branch of a large metropolitan bank in an upscale neighborhood where many customers already have accounts with firms such as PaineWebber or Merrill Lynch. That bank can watch its relationships walk out the door, since such brokerage houses offer checking accounts, CDs, and jumbo mortgages. The investment program at this bank should include the broadest possible mix of securities, probably including stock recommendations. Although the upscale neighborhood seems to offer unlimited opportunity in terms of the amount of wealth that lives there, this bank is going to have to compete hard and develop a sales culture quickly (if it doesn't already have one) if it is to survive.

Perform your demographic analysis; your customer base probably lies between these two extremes. The results of this analysis will help to determine what products you should offer. This should assist you in choosing the appropriate program structure for your particular needs.

Third-Party Providers

Before talking about the advantages and disadvantages of the following types of programs, we offer some definitions. The definition of a managed program is clear: a third-party provider (also often called a third-party marketer) provides the administrative infrastructure to a financial institution, and the registered rep is an employee of the third-party provider. A dual employee reports to the financial institution, but also reports to the third-party provider. A dual employee is typically considered a "dedicated" employee, working full-time on the investment services program. However, sometimes a dual employee might have other responsibilities at the financial institution.

In a managed program, the third-party provider is essentially running its own business in your lobby, although of course in close cooperation with you. As an employee of the third-party provider, the registered rep receives all compensation from the third-party provider. The third-party provider usually supplies almost every aspect of the program except some bank mailings or advertising that is very specifically the financial institution's responsibility. The bank supplies a program coordinator. In a managed program, the third-party provider provides due diligence, sales support, compliance, marketing support, etc.—the full gamut of services necessary to run a program.

In a dual-employee program, the registered rep (or other licensed person) is an employee of the financial institution and an employee of the third-party provider. The third-party provider still provides a full range of support services, but the financial institution is itself responsible for hiring personnel and supervising them on a day-to-day basis when these employees are not involved in securities and brokerage activities. The third-party provider has full responsibility for compliance, supervision and sales management of the dual employee. In addition, the third-party provider provides due diligence, marketing services, and other services. However, the financial institution will usuall recruit and hire its own personnel with the assistance of the third-party provider. The financial institution is responsible for compensating the registered rep, who is more likely to be paid salary plus bonus rather than full commission.

In a platform program, the licensed person is an employee of the financial institution. However, the platform person is not "dedicated," and does not sell securities full-time. That person is most likely to be a customer service rep or personal banker who has a Series 6 license.[2] Generally, the term "platform" refers to an in-house program but sometimes the usage is ambiguous and simply refers to an employee who has other responsibilities besides selling only securities. A dual-employee person might be equivalent to a platform person in job responsibilities, but the "dual" part of the job title refers to the two different organizations that person reports to, both the financial institution and the third-party provider. Like the dual employee, a platform person reports to the third-party provider or in-house broker/dealer for securities and insurance activities.

There is currently a great debate going on in the industry about which kind of employees are most effective and most cost-effective. Those program managers currently in financial institutions who have backgrounds in the brokerage business express a level of grave concern about securities being sold by Series 6 personnel in whatever capacity they are employed. A Series 6 person by definition will not have the market knowledge, depth of expertise, or understanding of customer needs that a Series 7 professional will have. We have been in a bull market for more than a decade, and securities sales have been easy. When there is a correction, those customers who have received the appropriate education about risk/reward and long-term investing are less likely to complain to banks or threaten law suits. It takes a market professional with significant experience to deliver that expertise.

On the other hand, banks are starting to experiment with programs in which an employee with a Series 6 license handles routine sales of mutual funds, but is supervised closely by a registered rep with a Series 7 who can sell a broader line of securities and is comfortable with larger dollar amounts. Managers of the some of the largest programs feel that it is not necessary to pay registered reps a 30% commission to roll over a maturing CD to a fixed-income mutual fund and have started to experiment with having the Series 6 handle some of these easier transactions. We know that certain registered reps affected by this change are indignant; registered reps in some programs have reported gleefully that platform personnel often fail to pass the Series 6 exam. But a Series 7 registered rep who has been hired to work with Series 6 platform personnel can do very well, because he or she is set up for success: the Series 6 employees by definition take care of the smaller-ticket items and send over the larger and/or more complex accounts. The Series 7 person often gets an override of commissions from the

---

2   The test for a Series 6 license is two hours and 15 minutes long, has 100 questions, and allows the person holding the license to sell only mutual funds and variable annuities (as long as he or she also holds an insurance license). The Series 7 exam is six rigorous hours long, has 250 questions, and covers the full range of instruments sold in the financial markets, including mutual funds, bonds, equities, and options; additional material on the exam covers margins, regulations, retirement plans, and fundamental economic analysis.

Series 6 he or she supports. Programs in some geographic areas or community banks might have trouble finding a Series 7 registered rep to serve their institution, or might be too small to support a full-time person.

A reason to consider a program using dual-employees or platform employees is that they are likely to be a part of the financial institution already. This can help overcome the objections of the other employees and remove the sense that the program is alien to the bank and its culture. On the other hand, there is no doubt that an experienced registered rep brings professionalism and specialized knowledge that can't be acquired by passing the Series 6 exam. Even if a dual employee obtains the Series 7 license, it will take a year or two to acquire a significant level of expertise and experience.

There are some very large and flourishing programs that depend on platform employees. Other large banks, with large numbers of both registered reps and platform personnel, report that registered reps outsell platform people by large numbers, on the order of 10 to 1 or more. It is easy to imagine that the training necessary to pass the Series 6 test is not enough to help the platform employees develop a true comfort level with alternate investment products, such that they sell them as enthusiastically as they sell products they are more comfortable with. These are the same people for whom banks set up referral incentive systems, to help them overcome their discomfort and learn to refer appropriate customers to the reps who sell these products. There is one caveat about having the same platform person sell both bank liability products and alternative investment products: the financial institution must be ultra clear about disclosing that the alternative investment products are not liabilities of the bank and are not guaranteed by the FDIC. This distinction might blur when the same person sells both products.

The most important thing, as we inevitably point out, is to decide what aspects of a retail investment services program are most important to your financial institution, and to analyze how that program is going to fit into your organization's structure and culture. Only then will you be qualified to make these decisions.

Discount Versus Full-Service Brokerage

Although almost all of the retail investment services programs discussed in this book are full-service brokerage programs, it is important to understand the distinction between discount and full-service. The most important difference is the absence or presence of a salesperson to advise the customer. A discount brokerage program allows a customer to call in an order to the broker/dealer's order desk, but customers must decide for themselves what investment to purchase.

In a full-service brokerage program, there is a registered rep available to work with the customer in deciding what investments are best for that customer.

Discount brokerage programs are most typically defensive. A financial institution knows its customers are buying investment products and prefers to generate at least some fee income rather than have the funds simply go somewhere else. Discount brokerage activity tends to be heavily weighted towards stocks, because many customers are simply looking for a place to execute transactions. Discount brokerage operations usually use a toll-free line installed at the bank. The bank will often have some financial information available, such as *Money Magazine,* prospectuses, marketing literature, or research materials, but will not give advice, nor will there be a person available to answer questions. Start-up requires minimal effort on the part of the financial institution.

In a full-service program, the customer develops a personal long-term relationship with the registered rep and the financial institution. The registered rep must interview the prospective customer at length before making any recommendations and will often develop a full financial plan for the customer. Even platform personnel with Series 6 licenses are part of a full-service program because they can give advice within the strict constraints of their license and can refer the customer to the registered rep for other products. A full-service program often relies heavily on packaged products such as mutual funds and annuities.

Although bankers often see discount brokerage as a way to start offering securities without making a significant commitment to alternative investment products, in fact there is a large difference in the way these two kinds of programs operate. It is not necessarily self-evident beforehand that a retail investment services program will evolve from discount brokerage, because it is quite likely that the discount brokerage program will be only marginally profitable, and the bank could easily get discouraged about the whole idea of selling securities.

The profit potential of the two different kinds of programs varies considerably. Discount programs often just barely break even, due to the nature of the products sold and the fact that banks rarely market those services. A full-service program, with its focus on the packaged products that often generate 4% commissions, is likely to be much more profitable even after taking into account the much higher expenses of such a program. Furthermore, a bank choosing full-service will often market the program in the proactive way necessary to make it successful.

The Question of Control

To illustrate the question of control, in our research we talked to two different financial institutions in essentially the same market. Both were running successful programs. Institution A had had a dual-employee program, and Bob was the senior banker who had been put in charge of it while retaining most of his banking responsibilities. He found running the program to be a "nightmare." He didn't have the time, the expertise, or the interest to run the program. His financial institution had a number of problems to which he could not turn his complete attention because every time he did, he had to hire another rep or solve another securities problem. When Institution A finally switched from a dual-employee program to a managed program, he was greatly relieved. Furthermore, after the third-party provider brought in professional securities management, even though his percentage split of gross commissions was a smaller number, his institution's net profit more than quadrupled within a short period of time—because the right people were managing the program.

John at Institution B had a different experience. His background was in the securities industry. He came in to the institution some years ago and aggressively started a successful program, which he runs with enthusiasm. He can't imagine "giving up control to an outsider," nor does he want to have to report to another organization (the third-party provider).

The difference of course is that John has the securities background necessary to manage a program himself. Running the investment services area is his only responsibility in the financial institution, so he devotes himself to it full-time. Bob didn't know securities and didn't want to know. He saw his primary responsibility to be the problems his institution was having on the banking side, and he fully admitted his lack of specific expertise in the securities industry. Both institutions are now running successful programs which are structured very differently, and both institutions are pleased with the structure they have chosen.

Conclusion

A great many options concerning program possibilities for your financial institution have been presented. For an organization just beginning to think about structuring a retail investment services program, the choices look overwhelming. But you will find that your possibilities narrow significantly as you begin to go through the choices. Community banks don't have to think about forming their own broker/dealer, and the larger institutions will have well-established management preferences about the ways to approach a new business.

Choosing the right structure for a retail investment services and fitting it into the overall strategy is critically important to the success of your program, but so is moving expeditiously. A financial institution agonizing over strategic questions is not climbing the learning curve. Maintaining flexibility is important to allow you to make changes as you learn the business.

6

Choosing a Third-Party Provider

Before you can select a third-party provider that will be a good fit with your financial institution, you have to know for yourself what you expect from them. Why do you want to use a third-party provider—to fulfill a legal requirement or because you want to offer insurance products and need a conduit? Or do you really expect this third-party provider to set up and run the alternative investment products program? You should have answered these questions as you thought about the structure of the program your institution needs.

Now that you have decided to use a third-party provider, how do you choose the right one? The number of choices is overwhelming. Industry sources suggest there are over 100 such firms.[1] This number reaches nearly 400, if you include the firms providing service to only one or two banks.[2] The high level of economic profit involved in this industry has inspired many new entrants to this field. We had an insurance agent tell us that, "It would be like shooting fish in a barrel" if he could have an office in the local bank's lobby. We have seen this attitude many times, but we think there is considerably more involved with this issue.

---

1   Richard A. Ayotte, "Starting a Bank Investment Program," *Bank Investment Representative* Apr/May, 1992, p. 27.
2   Richard A. Ayotte, "Comparing Third-Party Marketer Services," *Bank IInvestment Representative* December 1992, p. 10-11.

Most of the larger third-party providers are owned by either insurance companies or brokerage houses. This is the first thing to look at: who owns the third-party provider? This tells you about the culture of the organization and its structure, product preference, and management style. There are firms that were also started to be just third-party providers (rather than a distribution channel for a parent company) and they have their own culture. The second question is: who else does the third-party provider do business with? Look for references of institutions like yours. Don't be impressed with a third-party provider that does business with all large banks, if you are a small bank. There are cultural differences between financial institutions of different sizes and types. As with any other product that the bank outsources, the right third-party provider is the one that meets your organization's needs, and delivers the products to you or your customers the way you would.

This is not a simple process, but we have tried to make it easier by including a checklist of factors to consider when evaluating a third-party provider (Figure 6.1). The best way to approach this decision is to perform self-analysis first. You should make your own list of essential criteria according to the priorities you have identified, which helps you understand what is important to you, before you start listening to different sales pitches. Rarely will one single factor draw you to a certain third-party provider. Rather, you should make your choice by trying to find the best possible match between what the third-party provider can offer you and what you need for an effective program in your institution. Your criteria will determine which factors are most important to you.

No third-party provider is or can be all things to all financial institutions, because different financial institutions have very different needs. Once you have interviewed a number of likely third-party providers, the organization should consider its evaluation again, reevaluate what is important to its program, and then decide on the third-party provider that best fits the financial institution's needs. It is up to you whether to put sales philosophy, fee income, service, or products first, but remember that the dominant criteria will establish the emphasis of your program. If you want a balanced program, look for the third-party provider that scores the highest in all of the categories listed in Figure 6.1.

The rest of this chapter discusses in more detail what to look for when doing your evaluation. Some of the key areas include contracts, culture, training and related services, operational support, marketing, products, and compensation.

Figure 6.1 Evaluating a Third-Party Provider

Contract or lease agreement:

1. What is the basic structure of your program: discount brokerage, managed program, dual-employee program?
2. What does the lease stipulate that the financial institution has to provide, and what does the third-party provider have to provide? The lease should spell out the arrangements for fixed physical costs, marketing, training, products, compensation.
3. Who has the rights to market what products, and are those exclusive rights?
4. What is the amount of the rent to be paid: how is it calculated, when is it due, etc.?
5. Can the third-party provider contract with a local competitor?
6. What is the length of the lease, and is it the same for both parties?
7. What are the terms and conditions for cancellation?
8. If the third-party provider and the financial institution decide to terminate their agreement, who will service the customer?
9. Do the contracts provide flexibility for a program to evolve according to the needs of the financial institution?

Customer base ownership:

1. In the event of cancellation, who has the right or obligation to continue to service the existing customer base?
2. Will the third-party provider give up the names of the financial institution's customer base to any other party (such as a mutual fund company)?

What the financial institution provides:

1. Exactly what does the financial institution provide to the program:
   - physical space and equipment?
   - technology?
   - marketing materials?
2. What kind of administrative support does the third-party provider expect the financial institution to provide?
3. What is the role of the financial institution's program manager or contact person?

Financial Strength

1. Review financial statements for the last three years. Does the third-party provider have the financial resources to deliver on its commitment to the financial institution?
2. How many financial institutions belonged to the third-party provider's program each year?
3. What percentage of gross commissions was paid out to financial institutions each year?
4. Is that percentage increasing or decreasing?
5. How does it compare with the sample calculations made by the financial institution regarding program profitability?
6. What are average gross commissions per institution?

Figure 6.1 Evaluating a Third-Party Provider (*continued*)

Management

1. Have you talked to senior management at length?
2. What is the background of the members of senior management?
3. Does senior management have the qualifications and experience to run a successful program?
4. Does management have a strategic vision? Describe.
5. Do they understand the marketplace, and their role and yours within it?
6. Did you like and can you work with senior management?

Ownership

1. Who owns the third-party provider?
2. What is the business of the owner—brokerage house, insurance company, independent?
3. How will that ownership influence the financial institution's program?

Sales process/marketing to the bank:

1. Does the organization rep have a fairly complete understanding of how his or her own company works?
2. Can the rep provide detailed information about marketing support and contract clauses?
3. Does the third-party provider organization provide information that lays out its program clearly?
4. Were you left struggling to understand how the program works?

Flexibility:

1. Does the financial institution have special circumstances that require flexibility?
2. How flexible will the third-party provider be in adapting to the needs and requirements of special situations?
3. What percentage of a third-party provider's business will your financial institution constitute?

Specialties:

1. What is the specialty of the third-party provider in terms of:
   - type of program
   - kind of financial institution served
   - size of financial institution served
   - region of the country
2. Where is the third-party provider located in relationship to the financial institution?

Sales philosophy:

1. What is the sales philosophy of the financial institution?
2. What is the sales philosophy of the third-party provider?
3. How well do those two philosophies mix?

Feedback:

1. Does the third-party provider send out surveys asking for feedback?
2. Do program representatives seek out key managers in the financial institution to find out if expectations are being met?
3. What action will the third-party provider take if it finds out there are program issues?

Figure 6.1 Evaluating a Third-Party Provider (*continued*)

References:
1. Does the third-party provider supply you with a list of references the financial institution can contact?
2. Here are some of the questions to ask:
   - How long have you been with the third-party provider?
   - How long have the reps been with the third-party provider and/or bank?
   - What is the bank size?
   - Who was the prior vendor, if any?
   - Why did you choose to make the change?
   - Who chose the third-party provider?
   - What is the quality of the personnel they use in their programs, particularly in a managed program?
   - How is service/how responsive are they?
   - Are their products competitive with those of other third-party providers?
   - Have they delivered what they promised?

Training:
1. What kind of training is offered for the following levels of employees:
   - tellers
   - customers service reps
   - personal bankers
   - other bank employees
   - senior management
   - registered reps and/or dual employees
   - customers
2. How often is training supplied?
3. Who does the training, and where?
4. How is training monitored?
5. Who pays for training?

Licensing:
1. Who pays for licensing, both initial cost and annual registration?
2. Who has responsibility for keeping records on licensing, both insurance and brokerage?
3. Does the third-party provider supply prelicensing training, or recommend how the financial institution's employees can get it?

Quality of personnel/reps:
1. How are reps recruited and compensated?
2. Who makes the decision about hiring?
3. How much input or responsibility will the financial institution have for the hiring process?
4. Does the third-party provider use a written employment agreement with a rep?
5. Has the third-party provider introduced the financial institution to some of its registered reps?

Figure 6.1 Evaluating a Third-Party Provider (*continued*)

Due diligence:

1. Have you met with the due diligence officer?
2. Review the criteria used in the due diligence process. Do the final results (products recommended) accord with the process?
3. How often are due diligence reports prepared?
4. Review the quality of proprietary products in relationship to the due diligence process. Do the proprietary products make the grade?
5. Is the due diligence officer available to talk to registered reps and answer questions?

Compliance:

1. Ask for details of how the third-party provider conducts compliance reviews of its reps and its branches.
2. How many principals does the third-party provider have relative to the number of registered reps, branch offices, or institutions served?
3. Have you discussed compliance audits and customer complaints with the third-party provider?
4. Have you reviewed the compliance manual, registered rep's manual, and procedures manual? Are procedures well-documented and thorough?
5. Does the company follow its own compliance procedures?
6. Is the compliance officer available to answer questions and provide advice?

Service:

1. What services does the third-party provider offer in terms of the following:
   - on-line financial quotes
   - problem-solving assistance
   - software to help the rep manage his or her business
   - customer inquiries concerning accounts
   - customer seminar materials
2. Who is available at the third-party provider's corporate offices to answer questions and solve problems?
3. Does the third-party provider have the capacity to handle the financial institution's business and service needs?

Sales and accounting reports:

1. How thorough are these reports?
2. Will the financial institution see full details, or is only summary information available?
3. Can you understand the reports?

Project coordinator:

1. How many financial institutions does each coordinator oversee?
2. How accessible is this person?
3. Is this person experienced, well-qualified, helpful?

Figure 6.1 Evaluating a Third-Party Provider (*continued*)

Customer confirms and statements:
1. Can you understand them?
2. Will your customers be able to understand them?
3. Who mails out confirms?
4. How fast do customers receive them?

Capacity constraints in a down market:
1. How well will your third-party provider be able to function in a "stressed" market?
2. Under normal circumstances, is there excess capacity?
3. Will someone be there to work with reps and assure customers in the advent of a down market?

Marketing materials:
1. Is the program coherent, well thought out?
2. Is the program product-specific or generic?
3. Was the program developed by the third-party provider or a product sponsor?
4. Are materials market-specific, and how do they compare with the quality of the bank's materials?
5. Does the financial institution have a choice of marketing materials?
6. Does the marketing plan attempt to reach out to new customers, or does it rely heavily on maturing-CD lists from the bank?
7. Does the marketing program reach out beyond a financial institution's current customer base to attempt to draw in new customers and funds for the investment services program?
8. Does the plan incorporate seminars, direct mail, statement stuffers, newspaper advertising, referral programs, or telemarketing?
9. Does the third-party provider offer newsletters?
10. Does the marketing plan include the design and implementation of incentive and referral programs?

Referral program:
1. Is there a referral program?
2. Is the referral program well designed and well thought out?
3. How does it work?
4. Does it seem to fit your organization?

Regional competition:
1. Ask the third-party provider for the names of all the institutions it services in your region. How many are there? Are any of them organizations you consider to be your competition?
2. Can you foresee conflicts, or competition down the street?

Figure 6.1 Evaluating a Third-Party Provider (*continued*)

Marketing research and reporting:

1. Ask the third-party provider what statistics it tracks for each institution, such as:
   - foreign/domestic funds
   - number of customers who stop by the rep's office every day
   - number of responses to a statement stuffer
   - how many customers call to thank the rep for a birthday card

2. Can the third-party provider show you examples of market research for other programs it runs?

3. Does the third-party provider have access to industry demographic information and other statistical marketing data?

4. Can the third-party provider show you how it will track results for your program?

Products offered:

1. What products are offered, and what products are not offered?

2. How does the third-party provider's product selection compare with the financial institution's strategic analysis of its market position and the products its program should offer?

3. Does the financial institution have any input into what products are offered?

4. What is the specialty of the third-party provider and how does that influence the products it offers?

Proprietary products:

1. Does the third-party provider offer proprietary products? If yes, ask to see the due diligence on them.

2. Do the proprietary products generate extra profits for the third-party provider, the financial institution or the rep?

3. Do you see any evidence of the third-party provider pushing the proprietary products over non-proprietary?

Financial planning:

1. This is an important and necessary service. Does the third-party provider offer it?

2. How quickly will a rep be able to learn the financial planning software?

Commissions and pay-outs:

1. What are the payouts and how are they calculated? Remember that high levels of payouts can mask fees and other miscellaneous deductions.

2. Upfront fees: What are the upfront fees and what do they cover?

Structure

Contracts

While the arrangement between your organization and the third-party provider is not a legal partnership, joint venture, strategic alliance, or any other legal entity, your program will be more successful if you think of it as a partnership. A spirit of cooperation and mutual enterprise between both parties to this undertaking will make a real contribution to its success.

Because a broker/dealer is not allowed to split commissions with an unlicensed entity, the kind of contract by which the broker/dealer pays the financial institution is a lease agreement. As with any contract, it is important to have the document reviewed by qualified counsel. This is a unique document; it takes special expertise to ensure that it complies with the regulatory requirements that make it legal. It is the third-party provider's responsibility to supply your organization with a properly prepared document. Review the lease carefully and make sure you understand all the provisions.

Some of the important issues include the following:

- The terms of the lease—what the financial institution as the lessor has to provide, and what the third-party provider as the lessee will provide.
- Who has the rights to market what products, and are those exclusive rights?
- What is the amount of the rent to be paid: how is it calculated, when is it due, etc?
- Can the third-party provider contract with a local competitor?
- What is the length of the lease, and is it the same for both parties?
- What are the terms and conditions for cancellation?
- If the lease is canceled, who will service the customer base?
- Who owns the customer base?

Terms of the Lease

It is critically important to understand exactly what is expected of the financial institution, and what is going to be provided by the third-party provider. Lease agreements for third-party providers are not standard in any way, although there are certain points that must be dealt with in every circumstance. There will be fixed costs, including physical space, desk, heat, electric, phone, etc. These costs are usually provided and paid for by the financial institution. Marketing, training, and products are usually provided by the third-party provider. The balance can be negotiated. The key point is to fully understand what each party brings to the table.

Rights to Products

As the lessor you will want to establish beforehand what products the third-party provider has the right to market. This means basics such as annuities, mutual funds, fixed-income securities, municipal bonds, equities, etc. It could possibly include margin accounts, options, or other, more sophisticated products. This list can be added to as the need arises, so it does not have to be all-inclusive at the beginning. Even if you would like to "ease in" to your investment services program, we recommend that you include all the basics from the beginning so you can begin your program providing a full range of products. The third-party provider will want to make sure that the list includes all the products that it plans to sell.

A financial institution contracting with a third-party provider should give its third-party provider exclusive rights to sell products within the financial institution. A community bank would not normally consider doing things any other way. However, larger organizations that are using a third-party provider only to supply products might want to have more than one product provider (meaning two different insurance companies offering two different menus of annuities and other insurance products, for example), but this gets very complicated. Competition within your organization by product providers is not healthy. We suggest, instead, contracting with one third-party provider that can provide the full range of products your financial institution needs.

Amount of Rent

The amount of rent a third-party provider pays a financial institution will vary with the level of service that the third-party provider supplies. We have seen everything from a basic program where the third-party provider provides everything and pays the equivalent of 5% of the gross revenues to the financial institution, to a program where the third-party provider provides only the structure necessary to make the program legal and receives 50 basis points on all products sold through that conduit.

Industry practice suggests a ball-park guideline. The institution should be compensated one-third of the revenues for providing the customer and the physical space; the third-party provider should be compensated one-third for providing the products, marketing expertise, and the structure; and the additional one-third should go for distribution of products (pay for registered reps or other licensed personnel). For a dual-employee program, the financial institution gets the one-third for distribution (in addition to one-third for providing the customer and physical space), but then is responsible for compensating registered reps. On the other hand, if the third-party provider compensates the rep, then it should get the additional one-third. This is only a guideline and, in most programs that we have seen, represents the most a third-party provider will pay to the financial institution or the distribution channel once the program is up and running. Be very cautious of the third-party provider that wants to buy business by paying out a high percentage rate to the financial institution (such as 80% to 90%). There are three parties involved, the financial institution, the registered rep, and the third-party provider, and each party has to be happy with its share of the compensation or the program will always have problems.

Competitors

The lease should address the issue of competition. Can the financial institution have more than one provider, and can the third-party provider set up across the street in another institution? We already mentioned the problems with having more than one product provider in the same financial institution, but what about having the same third-party provider in the bank across the street? What is acceptable to you depends on what services are being provided and what the parties involved are willing to agree on. A third-party provider who supplies only products for defensive dual-employee programs in multiple locations in the same geographic area is very different from two proactively managed programs in institutions across the street from one another. But if this is in a city, it may not matter anyway.

Length of the Lease

There is a very large range on the length of time leases are written for. If you are entering this business looking for ways to get out, you might consider not getting into it in the first place: the term should be indefinite, or as long as it is mutually beneficial. If the business is not mutually beneficial, it won't last long, and a lease cannot change that. What a lease can do is give the program the time it needs to mature. We have seen leases that allow termination in as short as 30 days' notice with notice by either party and other leases with terms as long as five years. The larger the investment each party is making, the longer the lease needs to be.

Some third-party providers have leases that allow the financial institution to terminate the lease, but they have a noncompete clause forcing the financial institution to wait a year before bringing in another third-party provider. Do not allow a third-party provider to put this clause in your lease.

Conditions for Cancellation

When a financial institution does not want to support the alternative investment products program, it's time to terminate the lease. If the financial institution wants the third-party provider out of the institution, the third-party provider should recognize the inevitable and not waste everyone's time, effort, and resources in building a program that will no longer be supported. The same is true for the third-party provider: if it wants out of a situation, it should get out. The institution will not benefit by having a third-party provider who does not support the program. The fact that two parties have a lease does not by itself make a bad situation good. If the situation has been profitable, it is unfortunate to have to unwind the agreement, but it can usually be done to the satisfaction of both parties. The reality is that most organizations don't unwind good situations, but occasionally there is a change of management that results in one party wanting to cancel the agreement. The contract should spell out who is to bear what costs of termination. It would be preferable to try to renegotiate rather than cancel, and the terms of the original contract can be changed if both parties agree.

Servicing Existing Customers

If the third-party provider and the financial institution decide to terminate their agreement, who will service the customer? If the customer's best interest is truly the objective of all parties, then the answer should be easy: if the institution is going to discontinue the service, then the third-party provider has the right and the obligation to continue to service the customer. If, however, the institution intends to replace the third-party provider with another third-party provider, the contract should stipulate that the old third-party provider will help the financial institution shift the assets of its customers to the new third-party provider. Furthermore, the former third-party provider should be prohibited from soliciting any further business from the shifted customers.

Retail investment services programs have a natural evolution. A larger financial institution might hire the third-party provider to start a program quickly with a managed program, then shift to a dual-employee program, and finally start its own broker/dealer. A contract that provides for this eventuality will allow the financial institution to grow its own program. This lease should include a method of compensating the third-party provider for having built the program.

The process of terminating or changing programs sounds straight-forward and matter-of-fact as we have described it. It is not likely to be that way in practice. The reality is likely to have anger and/or bad feelings from one or both parties. The more that is spelled out beforehand in the contract, the better. It will help if both parties remember that the program's goal is to service the customer.

Who Owns the Customer Base

Determining who owns the customer base should be of major concern to the institution. It is unquestionably the financial institution who brings the original customer base to the relationship with the third-party provider; how could anyone question that? But questions do arise. If the financial institution terminates its relationship with the third-party provider and has not made arrangements to service the customer, the third-party provider retains the relationship. If the institution has made arrangements to move the account to another third-party provider, then the first third-party provider must turn over the accounts.

Some financial institutions have tried to cancel their contract with a third-party provider only to discover that the third-party provider has retained the right to service the customer base in the event of lease termination. We can't overemphasize the need to have the appropriate clauses in the lease from the beginning. Make sure that the lease clearly stipulates who owns the customer base that the third-party provider has developed. If your organization should decide to switch third-party providers, for whatever reason, the lease should provide that the old third-party provider will assist your organization in making the change. However, the financial institution should also recognize that once they have exposed their customers to alternative investment products, someone needs to continue to service the account (or it will reflect badly on the financial institution).

The importance of customer base ownership cannot be overestimated and it is one of the most important questions to consider in choosing a third-party provider or in deciding to do alternative investment products in general. In discussing contract terms, we have already touched on the issue of customer base ownership, but we would like to elaborate.

All third-party providers will have the customer sign an account agreement in opening the account. Once it has been opened, it needs to be serviced, and the financial institution must understand this. The situation becomes more complicated as the customer does transactions with different product families. For example, a customer might purchase two different annuities from two different insurance companies. Insurance transactions are always placed directly with the insurance company (meaning there is no clearing agent or other intermediary; the insurance company knows the name of each customer who buys one of its products), so now two different insurance companies know the customer, and could possibly seek direct contact with the customer, rather than communicating through the registered rep/insurance salesperson.

Sometimes the third-party provider does its mutual fund trades directly with the mutual fund company, rather than processing the trade through the clearing agent. (See the Chapter 3 on definitions for a discussion of direct mutual fund trades.) This is a very popular way of doing mutual fund business.

Third-party providers will generally cite cost as a reason for "going direct," but your customer and financial institution are probably better served when all transactions are placed through a brokerage account. Direct trades provide the mutual fund company with the names of individual customers, and the mutual fund then sends statements directly to the customer. Some mutual fund companies do not distinguish how an account was introduced to them and will use this as an opportunity for direct marketing of other products and services to your customer—now your organization has lost control of the customer relationship. When trades are done through the clearing agent, the mutual fund company sees only the name of the broker/dealer or clearing agent. Processing all transactions through the brokerage account means all investments are collected in a single account and on a single account statement, and it is easier for both the customer and the broker/dealer to monitor customer accounts and activity. The further advantage is that the mutual fund company does not know the identity of individual customers. There is a cost for this service, but it serves the customer by providing a single statement, and it keeps the customer account proprietary.

Using the brokerage account for all transactions makes switching third-party providers much easier, should that need arise. If customers have transactions direct with the mutual fund company, each company has to be notified individually. The brokerage account makes it cleaner and easier. Your lease with any third-party provider should stipulate that it will assist with the account transfer process should it ever become necessary.

Note: Financial institutions are increasingly requiring registered reps to sign a non-compete letter or letter of agreement agreeing that if he or she leaves the financial institution or third-party provider, he or she will not solicit financial institution customers. This is especially important when the rep is the employee of the third-party provider.

What the Financial Institution Provides

The financial institution should evaluate what it is expected to supply to the program. It is standard to require office space, office furniture, phone, fax, and part-time clerical support as part of the lease agreement. Some programs require other information systems or personal computers. Although this sounds like a reasonable request at this time in the computer age, some financial institutions do not yet utilize much personal computer technology, and it might make waves in your institution if the first personal computer is dedicated to the investment rep.

As discussed below in the section about upfront fees, marketing materials, stationery, signs, etc., have to be supplied. Some institutions think their own vendors can supply such items most economically, whereas a large third-party provider could likely buy these items in large quantities and actually be the most economical supplier. The two parties need to be clear on who supplies what and who pays.

The financial institution will also be expected to supply a contact person. The third-party provider might ask for only a quasi-clerical person to fulfill this role, but the program and the institution as a whole will be much better served by having the most senior person possible fill the position of program coordinator. This person should have the authority to make decisions and should be expected to assist in the development of a business and marketing plan and support its implementation. If you are not asked to make this commitment, be suspicious. There is a direct correlation between the organizational level of this person and the organization's commitment to this program: the more senior this person, the greater the support. A senior person will build organizational support while ensuring that senior management maintains its commitment to making the program work.

Financial Strength

The next question is to review the financial strength of the third-party provider. Review financial statements for at least three years and satisfy yourself that it has the financial and capital resources to deliver on its commitment to you. This is where the deep pockets of a well-capitalized parent can be reassuring.

Published financial statements are only part of the story, although an important one. In addition, you need to know how many financial institutions belonged to the third-party provider's program each year and what the average operating expense was for each institution. Overhead per financial institution should show a decreasing trend. What percentage of gross commission was paid out to financial institutions each year? Is it increasing or decreasing? How does it compare with the sample calculations you made? Calculating average gross commissions per institution will give an indication of whether the third-party provider's marketing and training programs are effective. (Average gross commissions per institution should increase, year-over-year, showing programs that are increasingly profitable.)[3]

3   Richard A. Ayotte, "Selecting a Third-Party Brokerage Firm," *Bank Investment Representative*, Jun/Jul 1992, p. 20. (The whole paragraph is adapted from this source.)

Culture

Management

In Chapter 11 on due diligence, we recommend that a representative of a financial institution (such as the due diligence officer) visit the headquarters of any insurance company whose products the financial institution intends to sell. The due diligence officer should meet with senior management and see the insurance company's facilities and operations. If that kind of investigation is important for each separate product provider when a financial institution might have a number of product providers, then how much more important is it to visit with the senior management of the one third-party provider that a financial institution will hire? Talk to senior management, inquire into their backgrounds, satisfy yourself that they have the experience necessary to help your program become successful. If you were going to start a third-party provider organization, would you hire this person to manage the company? Does the third-party provider have the knowledge and expertise to make your company successful over the long run? You would particularly like to see significant experience in the securities industry, since knowing and understanding compliance is such an essential part of that industry. Do they have a vision of what they are creating? Do they know their business and their marketplace? If you walk away from this meeting with a positive feeling, you probably have found a good third-party provider organization.

Ownership

One of the first things you need to know about potential third-party providers is their company affiliation. It takes substantial amounts of capital to hire the people to run this business. The third-party provider's assets are its employees, and banks like to lend against equipment, not personnel. How the third-party provider capitalizes itself becomes very important. There are a number of third-party providers that are owned by large insurance companies or brokerage firms, because this kind of company has the extra capital to finance companies such as third-party providers. However, you need to ascertain if there is a hidden agenda.

If your financial institution expects its business to consist mainly of annuity sales, then a third-party provider bringing the expertise and years of experience of an insurance company can be a good fit. If company ownership raises questions about the independence of the third-party provider, you need to insure that it will not affect the product neutrality of your program. The same is true if the third-party provider is owned by a brokerage firm. What effect will this have on the product neutrality of your program? What is the culture of the third-party provider, and how is it affected by the corporate parent? You need to know this before you sign the lease.

Sales Process/Marketing to the Bank

When the third-party provider visits you to make a sales presentation, listen closely to what is presented, and then ask some of the following questions:

1. Does the organization rep have a fairly complete understanding of how his or her own company works?
2. Can the rep provide detailed information about marketing support and contract clauses?
3. Does the third-party provider organization provide information that lays out its program clearly?
4. Were you left struggling to understand how the program works?

An organization that cannot convey its message in its marketing materials to prospective institutions is likely to have the same problem conveying its message to prospective customers of the financial institution. If you have a negative impression at this point, you might want to eliminate this third-party provider from further consideration.

Flexibility

Although a large third-party provider with an impressive number of institutions might seem like the surest bet for a new program, in fact a third-party provider with fewer institutions might suit your own particular needs better. Bigger does not always mean better. The key is flexibility plus the third-party provider's willingness to meet the needs of your institution. Smaller institutions in rural areas might have constraints and unique circumstances (particularly concerning suitable staff) that require the third-party provider to adapt its program somewhat, in which case you want to hire a third-party provider who will accommodate you. Larger institutions might need less from the third-party provider, so they would want to negotiate an unbundled contract that would provide what was needed without requiring them to purchase what was not needed. Ask the third-party provider to assess what will make an alternative investment products program most successful in your organization, and see if that matches your own analysis.

Specialties

No third-party provider offers the best program of each type available. Ask each third-party provider what its niche is, and make certain that it is used to working with banks. A third-party provider with 100 managed programs and two dual-employee programs definitely has a specialty. If you need a dual-employee program, you might want to choose a different third-party provider. (However, even so, you might want to consider what that third-party provider could do for you if it was so determined to expand its dual-employee programs that it offered you some kind of special deal.) Does the third-party provider work primarily with large, metropolitan programs, or with community banks, or with holding companies with branches? Are most of its programs in $100 million institutions or $1 billion institutions? No one answer is right; the object is to find the best match between your needs and its qualifications. In what part of the country are the third-party provider's institutions, and how far away is your program coordinator and/or training programs and conferences? If the third-party provider has been regional, do you think its programs translate into success in your location?

Another place specialization plays a factor is in products offered; see separate section, below.

Sales Philosophy

Securities and insurance salespeople in financial institutions range from so low-key as to hardly exist ("I would never try to sell my customer a mutual fund"), to as fast-talking and results-oriented person as you could find in any New York brokerage house. Your task is to find the third-party provider whose sales philosophy and style matches yours and that of the community of which you are a part.

There is not just one thing that makes up a sales philosophy; a sales philosophy comprises all of the program pieces. What products you pick, your marketing plan, the referral program, and your objectives for offering this service all will be factors that help to create the sales philosophy. The registered rep is an important factor in creating the sales philosophy, because it is his or her mission to implement the program after you have designed it. It is the implementation of a philosophy that creates culture.

While in our experience the introduction of a sales culture into almost any bank can re-energize and revitalize an entire institution, we realize that many institutions have a fear of just that. If this describes you, choose a third-party provider wisely.

Feedback

This is not a critical factor for third-party provider selection, but it does illustrate something like marketing elegance: does the third-party provider send out surveys asking for feedback? Do program representatives seek out key managers in the financial institution to find out if expectations are being met? An even better question is, what action will the third-party provider take if it finds out that there are program issues? But it might be hard to get a real answer to that question.

References

Ask the third-party provider for references and check them carefully. The following are sample questions to ask the third-party provider. You can probably add a dozen more about factors that are particularly important to your financial institution, but these are a good beginning.

1. How long have you been with the third-party provider?
2. How long have the reps been with the third-party provider and/or bank?
3. What is the bank size?
4. Who was the prior vendor, if any?
5. Why did you choose to make the change?
6. Who chose the third-party provider?
7. What is the quality of the personnel they use in their programs, particularly in a managed program?
8. How is service/how responsive are they?
9. Are their products competitive with those of other third-party providers?
10. Have they delivered what they promised?

If you don't check references, you will have only yourself to blame if the program does not go well for reasons you could have uncovered beforehand.

Training and Related Services

Training

What is the third-party provider's capacity for training the different levels of employees? There should be training for all of the following:

- Tellers
- Customers service reps

- Personal bankers
- Other bank employees
- Senior management
- Registered reps and/or dual employees
- Customers

Training is one of the keys to making a program work. Do not underestimate the importance of professional sales training for registered reps. Training should include conferences for different participants in the program (registered reps and senior management both), sales meetings, and regional seminars. Some other key areas include the following:

- Individual training in product knowledge and selling skills
- Methods for helping staff understand program services and products
- Training in how to recognize a candidate for alternative investment products and how to make the referral
- Training in what nonlicensed staff can and cannot say to a prospect
- Advanced sales training in nontraditional products and/or product introductions
- Ongoing sales support to introduce and/or reinforce marketing ideas

Although the first priority is to make sure that the third-party provider offers these various training services, the third-party provider should make clear who pays for what parts of these programs. Where is training done? If it is at corporate headquarters, find out who pays for airfare, hotels, food, etc. This can be worked out in a variety of ways between the third-party provider and the financial institution, as long as the financial institution doesn't get a big surprise later on when the bill arrives.

It is very likely that the split of costs will depend on what kind of program it is. For a managed program, sometimes the registered rep will be charged for training. This is important information to know, because programs often start slowly, and the rep who needs help (sales training or specialized product information) might not be in a position to afford it. This type of system punishes slow starters or those who were not able to bring a "book" (of customers) from a former position and helps those who are in a stronger position financially. It is unlikely enough that the rep of your dreams—high producer, book in hand—is going to walk in your door, and a certain amount of development time and expense can pay off dramatically in the long run. You want to be sure the appropriate investment will be made in the rep who is to work with you.

Licensing

If you are going to have a dual-employee program, will the third-party provider provide the training necessary to lead to a Series 6 or 7 and an insurance license? If that is not provided, will the third-party provider offer advice about how best to obtain that training?

It costs $65 to have an employee register with the NASD. The Series 7 exam costs $150, the Series 63 costs $60, and then state registration costs between $20 and $235. It costs $23.50 for each person connected with the broker/dealer to be fingerprinted. Who pays this cost? There is a yearly registration fee for both the NASD and each state the rep is licensed to do business in.

Insurance registrations vary by state. They tend to range from $25 to $100, as does the annual cost of an insurance license. Many states require continuing education credit hours annually for at least a few years. These credit hours are offered through service organizations that have sprung up to satisfy this need; they exist everywhere. Any insurance agent will know where to find them. Credit hours can sometimes be acquired quite inexpensively through home-study courses shared with other insurance producers ($35), or through extensive seminar programs (up to $200). State requirements run the gamut. Check with your state insurance department.

Make sure you understand who pays the costs of initial registration plus these annual costs.

Quality of Personnel/Reps

The quality of the registered rep is vitally important to the success of your program. A well-structured program could flounder if the rep fails to fit in to the bank culture or lacks appropriate knowledge or experience. Third-party providers know how to select reps with the qualities to succeed in a bank program, but the financial institution will also want to have input. The third-party provider also wants the financial institution to have input, because the institution has a greater stake in the rep's success if it shares responsibility for who has been chosen.

The financial institution will want to know the process by which the third-party provider selects reps. Do they talk personally with references? Do they use a written employment agreement with a rep, specifying responsibilities and standards? Can you meet some of their reps?

Financial institutions establishing a dual-employee program often need guidance in selecting employees for their program, whether they are trying to work with someone already in their employ or hiring from the outside. Can the third-party provider help?

Operational Support

Due Diligence

Chapter 11 on due diligence spells out very specifically how to analyze the quality of the products offered through your financial institution. You as the financial institution should not need to perform this analysis yourself. However, you should be thoroughly familiar with how the third-party provider performs this analysis.

Before making the final selection of third-party provider, you should meet with the due diligence officer and discuss in depth how due diligence is conducted. Review the criteria the third-party provider uses, and make sure that the final result does not conflict with those criteria. (If it says it allows only funds that achieve certain benchmarks, but then appears to recommend funds that do not achieve those benchmarks, you want to know why.) Be particularly aware of any proprietary products it may offer, and make sure that those are of the same quality as nonproprietary products.

You should receive quarterly reports on the products offered. It is your responsibility to review those products and find them suitable for your customers.

Compliance

Effective compliance is an important part of any securities firm (see Chapter 13 on compliance). Appropriate compliance handles customer complaints and lawsuits by trying to avoid them in the first place, but deals with them proactively if they should arise.

Ask for the details of how the third-party provider conducts compliance reviews of its reps and its branches. How many compliance officers does the third-party provider have relative to the number of registered reps, branch offices, or institutions it serves? The NASD generally allows ten registered reps per general securities principal. Ask who the general securities principals are, and what the ratio of principals to reps is. In addition, ask to see the written documentation of the firm, including compliance manual, registered rep's manual, and procedures manual. These manuals reveal more than procedures; they also demonstrate the firm's philosophy about these important matters. Be sure to verify that what is in print is in fact what happens in reality.

Furthermore, all broker/dealers are required to keep a file of customer complaints. The broker/dealer might allow you to see its file, although there is no regulatory requirement that they do so. They should be willing to discuss customer complaints with you. They will also have a file on write-ups from NASD audits, which they should also discuss with you. The NASD itself will answer questions about the compliance record of a broker/dealer, and you should check the official record. (You can submit an NASD Information Request Form to ask for information about final disciplinary actions taken by self-regulatory organizations. The NASD will not supply information about actions pending.)

In asking for these records, you are asking for the confidential records of the firm. While many will be willing to share this information, not all will. This does not mean that it was a negative review. How would your organization respond if the third-party provider asked to see your institution's regulatory review?

It is unlikely that you will find evidence of fraud or violations of securities rules and regulations in any of the compliance checks you do. What you are looking for is the full picture of the firm's sales philosophy, because you are about to entrust that firm with your customer relationships. Is there any indication of high-pressure tactics or lack of concern for customer suitability? Are procedures sloppy and poorly implemented, which can lead to errors and customer complaints? You should also have access to the compliance department to receive guidance and counsel on securities issues as necessary. Please note that your organization must rely on its own counsel for banking regulations.

Service

Will you get the level of service you need? Service encompasses everything from product support to an 800 number for questions about accounts. While some of the larger, more-established third-party providers seem to offer outstanding levels of service, smaller institutions can also compete in this area through the classic method of "trying harder." The secret is matching the level of service to your needs.

"Client power" is the key: how much weight do you carry with the third-party provider? The reality of business is that you get what you pay for, and you can pay the third-party provider in terms of either an upfront fee or business generated for the third-party provider. Larger customers get better service. If you are a smaller community bank, you might be better off aligning yourself with a smaller third-party provider where your business has more value. Do you want to be the big fish in a little pond or the little fish in a big pond? On the other hand, large organizations should select third-party providers that are large enough to service them adequately (being too large a fish in a small pond is also deadly).

Don't be overwhelmed by expensive ads and slick marketing materials. The important thing to find out is whether you will get qualified help when you need it; having ten people available to answer the phone does not guarantee that you will get the answer you need.

The technology of the brokerage industry can be daunting. Will you need access to on-line stock quotes? Stock quotes on 15-minute delays are significantly less expensive. Will that work for you? Will you need a weekly or monthly conference call (on market trends and/or products)? Would you use it if it were available? A marketing support desk can be invaluable, especially to those institutions using dual employees or platform personnel who might have less thorough knowledge of either products or markets. A daily fax or recorded message of economic news, market trends, and product offerings can also be helpful in keeping a rep well-informed.

Does the third-party provider have software available to help the registered rep manage his or her business? Such software is being introduced enthusiastically at investment services areas in large banks and is becoming available through third-party providers. This software allows a rep to manage extensive amounts of information on each customer, including portfolio, investment goals, tickler files, and referrals. Would having this software add value to the program in your institution?

Ask about customer seminars. Does the third-party provider supply materials such as slides and slide programs? In the case of a dual-employee program, the third-party provider might need to supply the seminar speaker as well. Are those services available? Who has primary responsibility to schedule, advertise, and promote—plus send out invitations for a seminar? Who is responsible for follow-up? (If you do not make follow-up phone calls to seminar participants, you are missing one of the easiest and most profitable sales opportunities available to a retail investment services program.)

These are just some of the services available from a third-party provider, and it is up to you to insure that the third-party provider delivers what it says it will deliver. Your experiences during the initial sales process will help you gauge what level of service you will receive from the third-party provider. You can hope that the service you receive during the time the third-party provider is trying to sign you up is not the best service you ever receive; once the contract is signed, things sometimes change.

Accounting Reports

Your third-party provider has to have a complete, accurate, and understandable sales reporting and accounting mechanism. You cannot sign with a third-party provider who does not supply this. You want to see full information, not just summary information, to facilitate your ability to understand and supervise the sales process. Good reporting can come in many formats, but good reporting it must be.

Project Coordinator

The third-party provider should assign a project coordinator to each financial institution, both for the implementation phase and then on a continuing basis. How many financial institutions does each coordinator oversee? How accessible is he or she, both geographically and on the phone? This is your first real introduction to the level of service that your organization is going to receive. If you are not happy with the project coordinator or the implementation of the program, discuss it now. You deserve to get the level of service that was promised to you. There have been a number of institutions that changed third-party providers because the project coordinator did not live up to expectations and/or promises.

Customer Confirms and Statements

Asking to see copies of customer confirms and statements might seem like a small point, but we already mentioned the case where a financial institution decided to change third-party providers because its customers found statements too confusing and difficult to use. If the broker/dealer is self-clearing or uses an omnibus account, it produces its own customer statements. If the broker/dealer is an introducing broker/dealer, it is the clearing firm that produces the statement, and the broker/dealer itself may not have much input into how they look. Needless to say, make sure you understand customer confirms and statements and find out who is responsible for sending them out.

Capacity Constraints in a Down Market

Market professionals know very well that the current bull market will not last forever. The market downturn in 1987 showed the real limitations of some clearing systems. What is the capacity of the broker/dealer and/or its clearing agent to enter trades, provide service, and answer questions in a stressed market? Many broker/dealers have built clearing networks that serve well enough under ordinary circumstances, but the best broker/dealers will be able to provide good service under extraordinary circumstances.

The average community bank might have difficulty asking the questions that will get the right answers on this issue. Industry experts advise that the well-established, better-known clearers are the ones who have built the networks that will serve even through a wave of bear markets. We do not endorse a policy of bigger is better, but it probably is true that in regard to clearing services, stronger and better established is better. You might have to check with industry professionals or publications to investigate your proposed third-party provider on this issue.

Marketing

Marketing Materials

How well developed is the marketing program and marketing materials? The following are questions to ask a third-party provider during the selection process. You should have a positive feeling about the responses to these questions. (For more information, please refer to Chapter 9 on marketing.)

1. Is the program coherent, well thought out?
2. Is the program product-specific or generic?
3. Was the program developed by the third-party provider or a product sponsor?
4. Are materials market-specific, and how do they compare with the quality of the bank's materials?
5. Do you have a choice of marketing materials?
6. Does the marketing plan attempt to reach out to new customers, or does it rely heavily on maturing-CD lists from the bank?
7. Does the marketing program reach out beyond a financial institution's current customer base to attempt to draw in new customers and funds for the investment services program?
8. Does the plan incorporate seminars, direct mail, statement stuffers, newspaper advertising, referral programs, or telemarketing?
9. Does the third-party provider offer newsletters?
10. Does the marketing plan include the design and implementation of incentive and referral programs?

Referral Program

A good referral program is essential (see Chapter 10 on referral programs). You need to find out from the third-party provider if the philosophy behind its referral programs corresponds to the philosophy of the bank. Will this program offer the incentives needed to obtain the desired behavior? The referral program that was implemented in a large regional bank may not work in the small-town community bank.

Regional Competition

Does the third-party provider service other institutions within the area you consider your competition? While prior experience within your region tends to be a positive factor, locations down the street tend to be negative. Consider this scenario: Financial Institution A wanted to terminate its contract with a third-party provider. Unfortunately, it had not secured ownership of the customer base, and the third-party provider in question had branches with another financial institution within the same urban area. The third-party provider effectively prevented contract termination by threatening to transfer Financial Institution A's brokerage customers to its competitor's retail investment services program. That threat was easy to take seriously because customers would not have been inconvenienced very much to move their business down the street. It is a good question whether that ploy would have worked if the third-party provider's nearest financial institution had been 100 miles away.

Marketing Research and Reporting

We mentioned sales reporting under operational support. The kind of reporting we mean here refers to keeping track of the results obtained from marketing efforts such as mailings, letters, and advertisements. The financial institution is vitally interested in how much money going into alternative investment products comes from internal funds and how much comes from external. Reps should report how many customers stop in every day, how many appointments they have, how many phone calls result from sending out birthday cards, etc. Some of the following statistics would also be useful to track:

- What time of day is the best time to hold a seminar?
- Is attendance improved when phone calls are made the day before a seminar?
- When does lobby traffic result in the most number of customers stopping by?
- Are holiday weekends hopeless for business?
- What kind of results do cold calls generate?

The best third-party providers will have mechanisms in place to collect this information and share it with you. It should have information already available from other programs it runs, and should be able to show you how it will track results from your program. The most sophisticated third-party providers will have access to industry demographic information and other statistical marketing data that it knows how to use in relation to running your business.

Products

Products Offered

Be honest about your need for products. Do you want to hire the most sophisticated third-party provider available—who offers options, limited partnerships, or other such services—if your customers think they are taking a big risk in moving from a passbook savings account to a statement account? It probably doesn't really make a difference to you whether your third-party provider as a broker/dealer is a member of the New York Stock Exchange or whether it is the third-party provider's clearing agent that is a member. A community bank might be able to work more effectively with a third-party provider who specializes in the mutual funds and annuities that are mostly likely to appeal to 99% of its customers, whereas institutions in some suburban areas might find they have to offer the most advanced products in order to lure customers away from their current brokerage firm.

There is a debate in the industry about which products a financial institution should offer (see Chapter 4 on products), particularly once you move beyond the basic mutual funds, annuities, fixed-income securities, and equities. We suggest your institution think about this question. It may be helpful if you use the following questions to determine your approach.

- What are the demographics of your customer base?
- Define your the target market.
- Which products are most suited to your target market?
- Which third-party provider specializes in those products?

We caution you, however, not to limit your program. If your objective is to have a program that satisfies the needs of your customers, then choose a third-party provider that specializes in the products your customers want (the 90%) but can also service the occasional unusual transaction.

The program will take on the specialty of the third-party provider. If your third-party provider specializes in annuities, your program will be annuity driven; if your third-party provider specializes in equities, your program will be stock driven. Third-party providers got their specialties by doing a lot of business in the product.

Proprietary Products

Proprietary products are much in the press at the moment, unfortunately more negative than positive. Too many organizations have gotten into the proprietary product business because of the economic profits, and because they can get their organization's name on the product. The cost of doing this has been great. Many proprietary products have been unsuccessful due to poor product performance and lack of distribution, and, at the same time, have sacrificed the customer's needs. Industry sources suggest a mutual fund has to reach an asset level of $100 million in order to break even, and annuities have to reach about $50 million. (As you can see, a poor mutual fund program could be a good annuity program.)

Offering proprietary products can prove to be a benefit for a program, especially if the third-party provider has designed its products to offer some marketing twist making them particularly attractive to a certain market. This is most likely to be the case with annuities, where the proprietary product has a shorter surrender period, or higher bonus rate, etc. The size and strength of the third-party provider offering proprietary products could possibly benefit a larger financial institution which would like to sell proprietary products designed for its use. A side benefit of proprietary products—but not a reason in itself for choosing such products—is that they sometimes pay a higher commission rate.

The main caveat is to ensure that the proprietary products are as strong and as suitable for the customer as the nonproprietary products also offered. Not adhering to this practice is not only bad business sense, it could result both in customer liability suits and/or regulatory action. It is also important that use of the proprietary products does not taint the third-party provider's objectivity in making recommendations on nonproprietary products or product providers. It is extremely difficult to be product neutral if you have proprietary products that need to be sold.

Financial Planning

We mention elsewhere in this book that financial planning is an important part of a needs-based sales process, and we also note how many leaders in the industry think that asset-gathering is facilitated by financial planning. In our experience, therefore, being able to offer financial planning is critical to the long-term success of a good and comprehensive alternative investment products program.

Compensation

Commissions and Pay-Outs

A payout is the percentage amount of commissions paid to the financial institution by the third-party provider as rent. Which is a higher payout, 60% or 75%? While this sounds like a simple question, when it come to calculating payouts, it's not. We recently talked to a firm offering a 100% payout. It doesn't take an

MBA to figure that out! However, when you crank the numbers to calculate the actual dollars paid out, the real payout was something like the 70% offered by a competing firm. The firm that paid out 100% had a great cost accounting system and had totally unbundled all of their services, while the 70% firm included a number of necessary services in the base price.

All of the new entrants into the third-party-provider industry—each one wanting to outdo the other—has resulted in a myriad of payout schemes. Third-party provider firms have demonstrated great creativity in designing ways to show financial institutions that their firm has the "highest" payout—and therefore adds the greatest value. *Don't be fooled by high commission payouts:* in most cases you will get what you pay for.

In addition to this outpouring of accounting and marketing ingenuity on the part of third-party provider firms, payout schemes are so confusing due to the difference between how the securities and the insurance industries have compensated product distributors in the past. How a third-party provider approaches the compensation issue depends on the culture of the third-party provider and its owner.

As we discussed in Chapter 3, the insurance industry uses a totem pole approach. The insurance company is at the top, then a master general agent (or whichever terms the particular insurance company uses), then a general agent, and so on down the pole until you get to the guy on the bottom, the agent or even the sub-agent. Everyone takes a percentage of the spread (the difference between what it cost to produce a policy and what it was sold for) all the way down the pole. Since most insurance products are original issue and are not traded in a market place, it is possible to take a fixed spread (profit margin) off the top, making this system very profitable and easy to understand. A third-party provider might say that it pays out 100% of the gross commission on an annuity to the financial institution. It might not tell you that, because of its position in the hierarchy, it gets a 1% override on sales at the financial institution. Therefore the real gross commission is 5% and not 4%, and the financial institution is getting only 80% of that.[4] (However, because of the way insurance distribution is organized, a financial institution might get paid a larger spread by going through a third-party provider than it could get by going directly to the insurance company for product. This is due to the insurance industry's practice of paying larger spreads to the largest distributors. The more you sell of an insurance company's product, the larger the percentage profit you will make from it.)

The securities world is different. Most securities are traded in a marketplace where the spread is not fixed. (If I buy a bond at 99 and sell it at 100, it is easy to

---

4   Richard A. Ayotte, "Analyzing Third-Party Payouts," *Bank Investment Representative,* Aug/Sep 1992, p. 12.

calculate my profit. But while I own the bond, it might move either up or down in price, depending on the market. If I'm a good trader, the market moves up and I can sell it at 101, which is a fair price to the customer on the day I sell it, and I end up making two points instead of one. If the market moves against me, I might be lucky to sell at 98-1/2, thereby losing one-half point.) Making a profit on securities sales is quite different than making a profit on issuing an annuity. As a trader, I can never guarantee that I will realize a certain percentage spread or profit. A securities firm can promise to pay its distribution system a certain percentage of its profits, but it can't know in advance how many points or what the profit is going to be. The securities firm usually assumes the risk of the fluctuating spread, and in fact this is how many firms make their profits, which are trading profits.

Processing or clearing cost

Insurance companies take the point of view that since all of their transactions are original issue, the issuing company absorbs the cost of processing, which means issuing a policy. To an insurance company, this is one of the costs of doing business. Like insurance, mutual funds are all original issue, therefore the cost of processing is borne by the issuing company; there is a fixed percentage of profit on the sale of a mutual fund—the load remains constant. On the other hand, the securities industry (except for mutual funds) is organized quite differently. Because securities are traded in the open markets, not only does the profit margin fluctuate, each firm has to pay its own cost of clearing for each security it buys or sells.

In the early 1980s, financial institutions were not aware of what it cost to process a ticket, meaning one securities transaction. Each separate financial institution had its own back office, and cost accounting had not progressed to the point where a charge was assessed to each ticket. Salespeople would do transactions that generated a very small amount of profit and then would be paid a commission on that small amount. Only after that was the processing charge subtracted, leaving the financial institution with a net loss on the trade. Securities firms soon realized that processing charges had to be paid first, before profit was calculated; incentives should be paid out on any profit remaining after the ticket charge had been subtracted. Most third-party providers today use a clearing firm to process their securities transactions, which makes it possible to account for and pass these charges on to the customer.

How do you combine these two industries, brokerage and insurance, and come up with a compensation system that works well for all instruments and all parties? Most third-party providers pay incentives on a product basis, paying different commissions on separate systems of securities and insurance distribution. While this is one way to deal with the problem, we don't believe it is the best method, because the economic incentives are different on different products. This means that a third-party provider, especially one owned by an insurance company, could well pay out a full 4% in gross commissions on an annuity to a financial institution, but pay out only a percentage of the profit on a securities transaction which—if it is not a mutual fund—is almost certain to have a much thinner spread in the first place. Which product do you think a fee-income-oriented financial institution would rather sell? The profits are much larger on the insurance products. This could lead a registered rep to sell a particular product based on his (and the bank's) compensation, and not based on the client's needs. Under this system, the product paying the highest incentive will be the product sold most often.

A financial institution should carefully consider exactly what is involved in the whole compensation and clearing process and understand exactly how the third-party provider calculates payouts. The question to ask an organization that claims to have the highest payout is, payout of what?

How to Calculate Payouts [5]

Gross commissions

The first step is to start with gross commissions. You must ask the third-party provider how it defines gross commissions. There are a number of definitions in use: the amount charged the customer; the amount remaining after deducting clearing costs; and the amount remaining after deducting the third-party provider's fee. These three amounts will not be the same.

If clearing costs are deducted before the payout amount is calculated, then all parties that share in the commissions will pay a pro rata share of the clearing costs. (If the financial institution, registered rep, and third-party provider each receive a third of the payout, then each will pay a third of the clearing costs.) However, if the financial institution's percentage payout is calculated first before any clearing charges are subtracted, and then all clearing charges are subtracted from the amount calculated as the financial institution's share, then obviously it is the financial institution that pays all the clearing charges. This is not a reasonable approach.

Understanding fees

It is extremely important to understand exactly how clearing charges are defined. They can be called service fees, processing fees, or ticket charges. There

---

5   Much of the following section, "How to Calculate Payouts" was derived, with permission, from Richard A. Ayotte's "Analyzing Third-Party Payouts," *Bank Investment Representative,* Aug/Sep 1992, pps. 12, 14.

can be extra fees charged directly to the customer. Does the financial institution get a share of those? Are there safekeeping fees, handling fees, wire fees, limit-order fees, or inactive account fees? It makes sense to unbundle fees and then pay for only what you use; the critical thing is to understand beforehand exactly what you will be paying. In some circumstances, the financial institution might think it is being charged fees that make a profit for the third-party provider, whereas in fact it is the clearing agent who originates these fees and charges them to the third-party provider, so that the third-party provider doesn't make anything on them. Whatever fees are charged to you, you have to understand:

- Which party in the whole process has charged them
- Who is making a profit from them
- When they are incurred
- Who pays them
- How they affect your payout and your customers

Direct mutual fund trades

Does the third-party provider process mutual fund trades directly with the mutual fund company? We have already discussed this issue. This may be one way of lowering the processing cost. Do you think the amount saved is worth the trade-off? In addition, if your third-party provider is going direct to the mutual fund company, how is it tracking these transactions?

Other payout issues

You must ascertain whether payouts apply to every product sold through the third-party provider, or whether there are exceptions. Are there monthly production minimums that must be met before payouts kick in? Are 12b-1 fees calculated as part of the gross commissions? (Anecdotal evidence suggests that about half the third-party providers share these fees.) If the 12b-1 fee is shared, when does this occur and how is it calculated? Does your institution have to meet the minimums or are your balances counted as part of the third-party provider's totals? The 12b-1 amounts will be minuscule at first, but fee income in any amount is particularly welcome at the program's outset.

Breakpoints

If payout percentages are structured to increase as volume increases, make sure that the breakpoints are achievable for your program. Although the highest percentages are very attractive, it does not serve your purposes if your program is too small to be able to reach them within the foreseeable future. You might want to negotiate a lower top scale for the purpose of increasing the low-end payout.

Bundling versus unbundling

We cannot mention often enough how important it is to verify exactly what services are included in your payout amount. We had bankers tell us they chose to take lower payouts in order to receive some other service, such as free research. Unbundling of significant services has advantages. The amount paid out to the institution would be the maximum possible, and the third-party provider would be paid separately for each separate service. The disadvantage is that if the unbundled fees include numerous smaller service fees, the third-party provider has to pass the cost to individual customers, and both the financial institution and customers may feel "nickled and dimed" to death. On the other hand, while the payout does not sound as large in a bundled program, you can get more support and service than if you had to pay directly for each separate service (charge for the next seminar is $100, etc.), especially if you might choose not to spend the money. The traditional method of pricing for both the insurance and the securities industry has been to hide the cost to the customer with a bundled package. An informed approach is the most reasonable: sign up for the services you need, know what you're paying for and what will cost extra.

Once you have a clear understanding of how the third-party provider calculates all the various fees and how it makes payouts, it is your job to sit down with your estimates of first- and second-year volume and crank through the calculations. There is no way you can project your business with total accuracy. You have to make some assumptions, and then compare payout results across the field of third-party provider candidates you are considering. It is more important to understand the percentage breakouts of the various parts of your business than to worry about precise predictions of volume. A business that is 60% mutual funds, 30% annuities, and 10% stocks will look very different from a business that projects a large percentage of its business to be discount brokerage. Ask the third-party provider to review your calculations and tell you if your hypothetical numbers look reasonable.

There are two other approaches you might encounter. In one case, the third-party provider is paid a service fee, usually expressed in basis points. The financial institution which hires the third-party provider pays it a fee for its services, which actually makes sense in terms of the underlying business relationship. This fee can be calculated in the same way as other fees and payouts, and the results can be compared to those calculated under more conventional structures. This is a popular method used by third-party providers that are providing insurance products and the legal structure to financial institutions.

There is one more structure sometimes used by very large financial institutions that would prefer—under other circumstances—to own their own program but are prohibited by law. A new corporate entity is formed for the sole purpose of offering alternative investment products in the financial institution. This new entity is jointly owned by the bank and the third-party provider. All commissions are paid into this entity, which pays all expenses. What is left is split between the financial institution and the third-party provider. The purpose of this entity is to be able to identify very accurately the transactions done with the financial institution; the other likely purpose is probably to allow ease of ownership transferal if the laws should change.

Upfront Fees

There are a number of different ways that a third-party provider funds the initial start-up cost of a new customer, including upfront fees, which vary from zero to about $25,000. An upfront fee is a factor to be considered carefully. Sometimes a third-party provider will offer several different fees ($2,000, $5,000, or $10,000), depending on the level of support an institution wants to buy. There is a virtuous circle at work here: an institution with progressive management who is committed to the idea of alternative investment products will pay a larger upfront fee to hire the most extensive level of support offered by the third-party provider. Because they were already committed, they wanted the best support, but because they then paid the higher fee, they were more determined to make the program work and earn back the fee. Paying a larger fee definitely has an impact on the level of support an alternative investment products program receives from a financial institution. A program does not run itself, and—if the financial institution has a choice of program levels—that institution should definitely consider investing a larger amount rather than a smaller amount to obtain the highest level of support available.

Do evaluate carefully what that fee entails. A $5,000 fee might include all marketing materials needed for start-up, whereas another program, which doesn't charge an upfront fee, instead asks the financial institution to order and pay for stationery, business cards, signs, etc.—and the total could easily equal the fee charged by the other third-party provider.

Some third-party providers have structured contracts to provide for 90 days' free rent (90 days in which the third-party provider retains all gross commissions). While this would seem to be an easy answer to the question of how to compensate the third-party provider for the time and effort involved in setting up a program initially, the problem with this approach is that it provides no incentive for the institution to assist actively in getting the program running quickly; in fact, we have seen evidence of management holding back until the revenues start to flow.

The 90 days' free rent approach is even more popular for those reluctant institutions that are starting an alternative investment products program defensively. Because the institution feels it has to offer some kind of program, but it also wants to minimize use of resources, especially capital, this is an easy and inexpensive way to get started. This type of program has an air of doom from the start. Because it does not have to make the capital commitment of the upfront fee and does not receive rent for the first 90 days, the financial institution has no motivation to implement quickly. This lack of incentive causes the financial institution to deny support in the start-up stage when it is most needed.

In our experience, an upfront fee provides a financial institution with the best motivation to support the program and assist in implementing it quickly. The next best method is to agree that the third-party provider will begin to pay gross commissions to the bank after a certain level has been achieved, allowing the third-party provider to recoup some of its start-up costs, but the financial institution is interested in reaching that level quickly so it can begin receiving profits. Providing a third-party provider with 90 days' free rent is the least likely method to inspire a financial institution—especially a reluctant one.

This does not mean, however, that a financial institution should necessarily seek out a third-party provider that asks a higher fee upfront. The amount of upfront fee is a consideration in choosing a third-party provider, but not a major one. Be willing to show your organization supports the program, and make the appropriate financial commitment.

A Word of Caution

There are a number of third-party providers who, on paper, show extremely well-developed marketing materials, training programs, and promises of service and support. Will the third-party provider you select deliver on its promises and commitments? We advise you to check references carefully, visit company headquarters, and do everything in your power to determine that the program you think you are contracting for is in fact the program that will be delivered.

Think of your relationship with the third-party provider in terms of a personal relationship: do everything in your power to make it work; understand that there will be great times and some not so great times, but maintain your commitment. Give it a chance, especially in the beginning. Communication will be the key. The financial institution will be disappointed if it thinks the third-party provider already knows all its needs (because it doesn't), and the third-party provider needs to explain and educate the financial institution as it goes along. While both parties have attempted to get to know the other before signing the contract, there will certainly be surprises down the road. As with any relationship, you have to respect each other and give each other room to breathe. Give the relationship time, and don't expect results overnight. (Full implementation can take six months to a year.) After all of this, if it is still not the program you wanted, bow out gracefully, but don't be afraid to try again.

Getting Started

And now you say you are more confused than ever, because we have introduced so many factors to consider. How do you start?

Over the years, most bankers have formed a network of friends and colleagues in similar institutions who help each other with questions and problems. Turn to your network and see who has an enthusiastic recommendation. Go to a conference and talk to the experts. There are a number of trade associations, like the American Bankers Association and the Bank Securities Association that sponsor conferences that include topics for choosing a third-party provider. State banking associations also sponsor programs and conferences that either touch on these topics, or allow you to gather with your peers to discuss them. The person sitting next to you may have been where you are in the process a few years ago, so talk to him or her and build a network.

There are a number of good reference sources that can help. *The Bankers' Guide to Third-Party Securities & Annuities Programs*, by Richard A. Ayotte, is one. *Bank Investment Representative* and *Bank Securities Journal* magazines always have helpful articles, or watch the *American Banker's* section on investment products. These are just a few of the many resources available.

Interview third-party providers who seem reliable on paper, and invite them in. If you don't like the presentation, or the third-party provider representatives can't explain their business in a manner that is helpful to you, talk to another one. There are a host of excellent organizations available to you. You will find people you can communicate with and who understand your needs.

This is not a science. The right third-party provider can bring many benefits and resources to your institution. It is unlikely you will make a terrible mistake if you follow our advice and do your due diligence. If you remember to be careful about the escape clauses in your lease, at the very least you know that you can change vendors if you are not happy with the results.

7

Selling in a Bank

There are six key components to selling alternative investment products in a financial institution:

1. Choosing the right structure
2. Preserving the special relationship of trust that a financial institution has with its customers
3. Determining the appropriate sales philosophy for the program
4. Implementing a relationship (or needs-based) selling program
5. Developing an internal marketing program
6. Choosing what products are most appropriate for an AIP program.

We assume that you as the financial institution have taken the time to perform the self-analysis necessary to choose the structure for a retail investments program that is right for you. You are now ready to implement that program.

What's Special About Selling in Banks

There are two important differences between selling an investment product to a bank customer and selling that same product in a brokerage firm. First, the relationship that a bank customer has with the bank can be defined as trust. A customer does not approach a brokerage house with anything like the degree of trust reserved for a bank and any product that bank might offer. Banks take the customer relationship very seriously; one real reason many banks hesitate to go into the brokerage business is they are afraid the investment sales process will somehow force them to break that bond of trust. Banks want to deliver products that customers need but don't want to risk damaging the customer relationship.

The other main difference between bank and brokerage-firm selling is the fact that a bank customer usually has a multidimensional relationship with the bank, which includes everything from a personal checking account to possibly a corporate loan. Some banks see alternative investment products as a potential threat to the relationship that is already there. The customer of a brokerage house can become upset with his or her broker and break off the relationship, but that relationship includes only certain products within one product category (whether stocks, bonds, mutual funds, or other investments; money management products of one or another kind). A customer from the investment services unit in a bank who is not happy with the investment service he or she received represents a threat to take an entire relationship away from the bank— thereby having an impact on every department the customer did business with.

However, registered reps in banks have a wonderful opportunity because of the already existing relationship between the customer and the organization. Many brokerage firm reps see this special relationship and are trying to make the move into banks. Studies have been done demonstrating that customers trust their bankers far more than they trust their brokers; this special relationship that makes the banking franchise work. Customers have trusted their banker for years, and if the bank ever loses this trust they lose their competitive edge.

We recently met an ex-broker turned banker who had resigned from his position as a registered rep with a major bank. When asked why he had left that position, he replied, "I had burned up the deposit base," meaning he had picked off all the easy sales. He further explained that when he called a customer about a maturing CD and introduced himself, the customer would tell him that he had told the last three salespeople who called from the institution that he wanted to roll his CD over and did not want to invest it.

There are several lessons to be learned from this short story. When you hire an ex-broker for the program in your financial institution, be extremely careful to insure that the individual's sales philosophy mirrors that of the financial institution. We see this young rep's mistakes as twofold: first, he believed that he had already exhausted the potential of each customer with the transaction he had either already accomplished or failed to accomplish, as though the one- or two-time sale represented the full potential of the account. Second, he seemed to feel that when the customers from the CD list turned him down, he was not only finished with that customer but had maxed-out his sales potential in that branch.

This is not the person or the sales philosophy that I want sitting in my bank lobby, do you?

Sales Philosophy for Bank Reps

Bankers believe they must seek to protect the customer's trust above all and that the customer's best interest is of paramount importance. The best sales philosophy for selling alternative investment products in a financial institution flows from this premise. To ensure the customer's trust, you have to be product neutral, which is the central tenet of selling in a bank. When a customer walks in the door for the first time, you don't already know which product is best for him or her, which is essentially what happens when ownership of a program dictates that certain proprietary products must be sold. This can happen when the third-party provider is owned by a brokerage house or an insurance company. It can also happen when a financial institution has its own proprietary funds, which it emphasizes in some way.

A third-party provider or financial institution can offer a full range of products, including proprietary products, and still be product neutral. Being product neutral means having an entire program that focuses on the customer's needs and not the needs of the organization. This is the essence of needs-based selling. Product neutrality is violated when incentives are provided to salespeople to sell the proprietary products over the nonproprietary products. These incentives can take a variety of forms: higher commissions for proprietary products (which is essentially the same as lower or no commissions on other products); management pressure of some kind to sell the proprietary products (goals and quotas); or full marketing support for the proprietary products and very little on others. Institutions selling proprietary funds think they are limiting customers' ability to move their accounts out of the firm, but that strategy backfires if a customer ever decides that he or she didn't receive the best investment advice possible because the registered rep put the needs of his or her organization ahead of the needs of the customer.

Brokerage houses have traditionally sold on the basis of hot products. Registered reps would be told on any given day that a certain product was hot and needed to move. Special incentives would be provided to ensure that this happened. The hot product could be a new-issue security the brokerage firm was underwriting, or part of the firm's inventory position, which is essentially the firm's personal investments. "Here's the product; now find the customer." This is when the cold calling really starts. When a salesperson's need to sell a product is stronger than the customer's need to buy it, in most cases the rep has not done what is best for the customer. We have found some customers so used to getting cold calls that they enter the bank lobby asking for the hot product of the day.

While we don't want to impugn an entire industry and we recognize that the brokerage industry has many registered reps who are genuinely concerned for their customers' long-term satisfaction, there has commonly been a product orientation in the brokerage firm that is not acceptable in banks. This orientation was seen at its worst in the "bucket shops" of the 1980s, where Mr. and Mrs. Investor were easy prey for fast-talking salesmen with hot stock tips or junk bonds bearing sky-high interest rates—and risk to match. The average bank program would not be well served by such selling. The customer would not be buying a product that was a good fit and, if the customer became dissatisfied, his or her entire relationship with the financial institution could walk out the door along with the brokerage business.

Brokerage firms have traditionally compensated reps for the number and volume of transactions they produced over a short period of time, emphasizing the product-driven nature of that business. Today this is changing with the invention of such products as wrap accounts, which compensate the rep for dollars under management. Financial institutions have started to experiment with paying reps not only for completing transactions, but for assets under management, referrals made back to the bank, or other measures of performance that evaluate more than simply volume sold or transactions completed. Paying a registered rep salary plus commission rather than straight commission takes away the hungry edge that can make a salesperson desperate to close transactions.

There is a growing recognition in the securities industry that the smart money is focused on gathering assets and controlling the customer relationship, not on selling particular securities or doing one-time transactions. Bank trust departments have had this asset-gathering mentality for years. Tools like customer seminars and financial planning are strengthening these relationships. We believe transaction-oriented programs have a limited future.

Moving Beyond Maturing CDs: Needs-Based Selling

Building customer relationships has become the hot topic for any kind of selling; it is certainly one of the most important themes in the securities industry. *Bank Investment Representative* magazine sums up this topic in a note from the publisher:

There is one theme we keep hitting over and over … We made a decision at the beginning of the year to emphasize relationship building between bank customers and bank investment programs in an effort to help steer the industry away from its growing tendency to be 'single sale' oriented. In spite of all the lip service given needs-based selling, far too many reps and the programs they work for are settling for the 'easy sale.' Banking customers have money to invest, so reps are often quick to recommend a bank account look-alike product with little regard for the customer's overall financial needs. The idea of developing customer relationships is gaining momentum throughout the country. We plan to continue our efforts, so plan on reading more articles that develop the concepts of customer profiling, knowing your customer, needs-based selling, and gaining customers trust. These concepts not only help you sell more products more often, but more importantly, only when appropriate.[1]

Relationship selling, or needs-based selling, never talks about making a sale or selling a product; relationship selling talks about meeting a need or solving a problem. The sale is not your goal. You are working with the customer to help put kids through college, plan for retirement, provide adequate insurance, or otherwise meet a family's short- and long-term financial needs. Relationship selling means staying in contact with customers, offering further advice as needs change, designing a financial plan, and working with the customer to implement that plan. At its best, relationship selling educates customers, and helps them better understand their overall financial needs, both long term and short term. Few customers have that understanding at the outset.

Karl F. Gretz has been training professionals in the financial services industry for more than ten years. He points out that consultative selling means, "I'm here to solve my customers' financial problems." In the process of meeting the various financial needs they discuss with you, people happen to purchase a lot of products.[2] "The traditional salesperson 'persuades' the customer to see his or her point of view—to make the sale the overriding goal. In needs-based selling, however, the goal is to create a customer, a person who respects your opinion, trusts your recommendations and buys from you again."[3]

1 Jeffrey H. Champlin, "From the Publisher," *Bank Investment Representative*, (July/August 1993), p. 4.
2 Karl F. Gretz, "Success or Self-Destruction: Consultative Selling is the Key," talk made at the *Bank Investment Representative's* National Sales Conference, August 27, 1993.
3 Larry Chambers, "The Success of Need-Satisfaction Selling," *Bank Investment Representative*, Apr/May, 1992, p. 16

Consistent with the message that comes from the bank, you are trying to build a relationship of trust with the customer. Customer relationships are based on more than purely rational thinking. Customers come to you with their money, worried about investing it. If your customers trust you, they will invest their money with you. This is where the registered rep in a bank has a significant advantage over the registered rep in a brokerage house. The customer approaches the institution with trust. You have another advantage if the referral is made by a bank employee the customer already trusts. Now it is up to you to maintain that trust.

The First Interview

The first step to establishing a long-term relationship with a customer is to sit down and discuss his or her financial situation. Resist the urge to simply roll over the maturing CD into a CD-look-alike product. You shouldn't recommend products until you know the customer's financial objectives. The analogy is to a doctor-patient situation: you would be disappointed if your doctor prescribed medicine before he or she understood the nature of your illness. You expect your doctor to examine you and talk to you about your symptoms. Why would you expect less from any other type of professional? This defines the level of suitability as required by the regulators:

> Whether your work is with individuals, institutions, or business entities, your obligation in this profession is to properly serve your customer. The first step in properly serving your customers is to obtain a clear understanding of each customer's financial condition . . . The second step in serving customers properly is for both you and the customer to have a clear understanding of the customer's investment objectives . . . Just as your customer's financial position may change, your customer's investment objectives may change. They should, therefore, be reviewed periodically, and you should make a written record of any changes as they occur.[4]

As defined by the regulators, understanding and implementing a customer suitability program is simply the most effective way to ensure long-term, satisfied customers. However, even though customers trust their banker, they are often reluctant to give out financial information. Unlike the situation where the customer wants a loan and is willing to divulge anything to get the institution's

---

4   "Understanding Your Role and Responsibilities as a Rep," (pamphlet) National Association of Securities Dealers, Inc., ©1993, pps. 5-6. All rights reserved.

money, customers have been hounded for years by fast-talking brokers who have said that this information was being gathered in their best interest but used it to take advantage of them in the long run. Don't be surprised when your customer hesitates or refuses to give you the information needed to do a thorough job.

The organization needs to structure the first interview so that the customer learns something about the rep and the organization's services. Gradually, you as the rep can start gathering the information you need from the customer and begin to establish that all-important long-term relationship. Although you need a great deal of information about your potential customer, you simply can't start off too aggressively. Remember that most people consider financial matters to be very private; talking about their finances is like asking people to take their clothes off! Customers may be reassured if you explain that you need to know their financial objectives before making recommendations. You can also explain that the regulators require you to know certain details before making a financial recommendation. If a customer still hesitates to give you the information you need, you have to make a hard decision. Has the customer disclosed enough information so you can make a product recommendation?

A full-fledged, needs-based program, as practiced by a number of institutions, starts out with a questionnaire that may run five pages long. This obviously requires time, effort, and attention—on the part of both the rep and the customer—to complete. However, Citicorp reports that, when the needs-based process has been followed, "Customers aren't surprised at short-term changes in their portfolios—the process helps them understand short-term volatility and how to focus on the long term."[5] If your institution does not yet use such a questionnaire, you might try building one for yourself. If you are not in a position to offer financial planning services to your customers, you need to find ways to ask about other assets. You might inquire when the next CD is coming due. Servicing the customer's needs will not only ensure a long-term customer relationship but help you identify the next transaction.

In addition to asking about the customer's current financial situation, you need to probe for financial goals and objectives, concerns for the future, time horizon, tax bracket, investment experience, and risk tolerance. Ask the customer about the important issues in his or her life at the moment. The sensitive rep will try to tune in to other issues that the customer might have. Customers approach investments determined to do or not to do certain things with their money based on experiences they have had or heard about. Watch out for a customer whose mother was unhappy with a bond fund or whose neighbor lost a

---

5   Mark G. Steinbert, "Programs that Focus on Needs-Based Selling," *Bank Investment Representative,* Jun/Jul, 1992, p. 44.

lot of money with a junk bond or an Executive Life annuity. You know the stories. Those experiences form an emotional undercurrent to the customer's investment preferences, and you won't know they are there unless you listen for them.

Finally, remember that the first interview is critical to the long-term relationship. The customer is worried, insecure, afraid of making a big mistake with money he or she can't afford to lose. The customer is looking to you, the registered rep, to provide solutions, comfort, trust, and education. You need to reassure the customer, build trust and rapport, and project an image of confidence and knowledge. You can do this much more effectively if you are focusing on the customer's needs and goals instead of simply trying to sell a product. You won't need your handbook on 20 surefire closing techniques if you and your customer work together to analyze the situation and come to an agreement on how best to meet his or her needs.

A Financial Plan

Financial planning can be a powerful sales tool. New customers usually reveal only a portion of their assets to a registered rep as they begin a relationship. However, if the rep offers to produce a financial plan, the customer is likely to provide fairly complete information about finances and assets. INVEST runs one of the largest third-party provider programs in the country and does not charge a fee for financial planning services. "A recent survey disclosed that bank customers who use complimentary financial planning services disclose more than 10 times the total amount of assets as customers who did not use financial planning. Furthermore, over 80% of the assets reviewed for financial planning customers come from outside the financial institution."[6]

More to the point, using a financial plan will help you identify the customer's assets, giving you a better understanding of his or her needs. In the long run, this will create more fee income.

Designing a financial plan for a customer helps establish that the relationship is going to be long term. The customer makes a commitment to the registered rep by commiting first to giving you the information you need to complete the plan and second to attaining the financial goals outlined in it. Developing and implementing the plan gives you an excellent opportunity to enhance the client relationship. This can establish a solid foundation for needs-based selling, since the plan is built on the problems, concerns, constraints, goals, and objectives of the customer.

---

6   D. Mark Olson, "The Power of Management's Commitment," *Bank Investment Representative,* Oct/Nov, 1992, p.16.

Although some well-known brokerage houses make a business of financial planning, and many financial planners charge for financial plans, banks in general have chosen not to charge for those services. The idea is twofold. First, doing a financial plan draws in reluctant customers by giving them a valuable service rather than driving them away by charging for a product about whose value they are uncertain. Second, we believe it is a conflict of interest to get paid for the plan and at the same time recommend products on which you will earn a commission. (However, there are many people who believe—and do—otherwise.)

Presenting the Products

Only after you have learned about the customer are you ready to present products. The solutions will follow naturally from the discussion of the customer's problems and issues. At this point, exactly which product you recommend is of secondary importance to the customer as long as it meets or exceeds the customer's needs.[7] The best solutions provide an asset allocation plan and divide investments into sectors, including aggressive long-term growth, shorter-term savings, tax-deferred instruments, etc.

Education and Seminar Selling

Seminar selling is a natural part of a retail investment services program in a bank. Inviting customers to a series of seminars has two major benefits. It is a way to introduce customers to new products and investing ideas in a nonthreatening environment. And it allows them to become comfortable with the registered rep so that follow-up calls are seen as friendly, not invasive cold calls. Hearing a registered rep make a presentation about investments gives listeners a chance to test drive, so to speak, both the investment strategy being discussed and the speaker. The rep appears as a teacher or problem solver and does not generate the sales resistance that arises when seen in the role of a salesperson. The seminars should be educational, not product specific.

Cold Calling

The typical new hire in a brokerage firm will be handed either the phone book or more refined database and told to get going. As part of its basic training program, one very successful brokerage firm requires new recruits to make 1000 cold calls door to door. At the other extreme, some financial institutions prohib-

---

7   Gretz, "Success or Self-Destruction," 1993.

it telemarketing of any kind, whether the rep is calling bank customers or community residents.

In our view, the glory days of cold calling are gone for basically two reasons. The most obvious is the difficulty of getting people to answer the phone. More people than ever screen their calls, partly due to the technology that lets them do it and partly due to the proliferation of telemarketing for services of all kinds that makes it necessary. A number of laws put constraints on cold calling. The other reason cold calling can no longer serve as the basis of a marketing campaign is that one contact with a salesperson is not enough to establish a customer relationship. Competition in this industry is so tough that customers have become much more discriminating about where they establish relationships. You have to prove yourself and give customers reasons to want to do business with you.

Telemarketing to the bank's customer base does have a place in marketing securities in a bank; the call can introduce your services, invite a customer to a seminar, or let a customer know about a maturing CD. This kind of cold call is not really cold, because the customer already has a relationship with the bank, but it is a way to make sure the customer is aware of the new retail investment services program. We are not opposed to the idea of telemarketing to the surrounding community; banks are happy to have the registered rep bring in new relationships, depending on how much time the rep has. (Reps in some programs report not being able to keep up with in-house referrals, let alone make cold calls—lucky reps.)

The Long-Term Relationship

A long-term relationship with a customer cannot, by definition, develop overnight. Excellent service over time, repeated contact, and a variety of programs are necessary to nurture the customer relationship. We like to compare developing a customer relationship to planting a garden. You have to sow the seeds, add fertilizer, and water as needed over the whole season. You can't put the seeds in the ground in September, throw in some manure and water, and expect a plant to bear fruit the next day. There is no substitute for taking the actions necessary, day after day, to bring your crop to harvest. So it is with customers; to build a solid relationship, you have to nurture it over a significant period of time.

Bruce F. Wells, a sales trainer, reports that the single biggest complaint of customers is that the registered reps don't keep in touch with them.[8] Yet many reps are reluctant to pick up the phone after six months because they're afraid

---

8   Bruce F. Wells, "The Second, Third, Fourth, and Fifth ......Sale," talk made at the *Bank Investment Representative's* National Sales Conference, August 19, 1993, Chicago, IL.

they'll look too hungry! The most successful registered reps know that once a month is not too often to contact a customer. This is part of the whole customer development process. The rep should maintain the relationship of trust developed with a customer by following the customer keeper commands: Keep your promises, keep in touch, and keep the customer's best interests above all other considerations.[9]

The second sale is always easier than the first, because it's more efficient. You have already established trust and credibility; the customer is already satisfied and knows your products and services. If the customer's needs have changed, you know that because you've kept in touch. It is the second sale that bonds; it shows that you have earned the customer's respect. And you know you have succeeded with a customer when he or she calls you to talk about nonbusiness subjects.[10]

Giving a customer appreciation night or an open house is an idea we like. It will generally take the form of a seminar, but the presentation should not be heavy. The idea is to avoid any kind of direct selling, because you are thanking customers for their business. Look for other ways to get in front of customers in nonselling roles, such as advising a local club's investment committee, joining the chamber of commerce, or working with a small business club. Some reps like to buy token gifts like flowers or candy for customers; mugs, pencils, or pens also serve this purpose. Many registered reps enthusiastically recommend sending birthday cards to customers; they get a steady stream of thank-you calls for cards sent out. There are sophisticated computer programs to help you manage your customer base, including when to send birthday cards, but the standard low-tech method is to write the names and dates on a calendar.

Stay in touch with the people in the community. Sending sympathy cards is not as enjoyable as sending birthday cards, but it can make an even better impression. Mail customers reprinted articles from independent sources like *Money Magazine* recommending the mutual fund you recommended, or send them updates from the mutual fund company showing superior performance for one of their funds.

Getting Customer Referrals

There is no better advertisement for a registered rep than a happy, satisfied customer, nor is there a better source for new business. The best way to get your customers to give you referrals is to ask for them! Best of all is for your customers themselves to call a friend or colleague to recommend your services. The next

---

9 Bruce F. Wells, "The Second Sale, Repeat Business from Existing Customers," Bank Investment Representative, May 1993, p. 42.
10 Ibid. Whole paragraph, not just sentence is from source.

best thing is to have your customers give you the names and phone numbers of people you can call yourself, saying the customer recommended that you call. In a smaller community, ask customers to highlight names in the phone book.

Educating for Market Volatility

Those of us who have been in this industry for the past few years know that we have been the beneficiaries of one of the longest bull markets in history; we also know it won't last forever. The last taste anyone had of a real market dip was in 1987, and many of today's registered reps did not experience that.

A sales process based on filling customer needs will educate the customer to understand that significant market volatility is unavoidable. Asset allocation plans teach customers to put aside short-term funds for emergency needs; these amounts are safer from volatility because they are in the lower-yielding fixed-income instruments. Longer-term funds will be subject to market fluctuation, but history has shown that market fluctuation is not a danger when your time horizon is long enough. Market professionals are concerned for their reps and their customers once the bull market turns around, but we can begin to prepare for that eventuality now, by educating customers to understand asset allocation and long-term investing. This is part of the real mission of the bank registered rep. The time you spend with your customer today explaining these issues is time you won't have to spend when there's a downturn in the market.

Importance of Internal Marketing

The most important thing for a registered rep in a bank to remember is that his or her most important customers are bank employees. Every customer is valuable and represents someone who might ultimately send other customers to the rep. But each bank employee represents a steady stream of potential referrals. CSRs see many more people in the course of their everyday transactions than the registered rep. The fact that internal marketing is so important is not our unique insight, nor does it apply only to the retail investment services unit and the registered rep. However, the more a business unit and its staff are perceived to be outsiders, the more important this internal marketing becomes.

Making Your Way in the Branch

Paying incentives for referrals is the best way for the institution to encourage the front-line service employees to learn about investment services and why they are important. (See Chapter 10 on referrals.) Incentives provide an excellent way for the registered rep to begin his or her internal marketing program within the branch. However, they are only part of the marketing program the registered rep must plan and carry out. Establishing an effective internal marketing program requires maximum effort from reps themselves, in addition to the referral program offered by the financial institution.

Internal marketing is conducted much like external marketing. You create a plan designed to sell bank employees on the value and importance of your products. You have to think out how you will generate referrals, conduct training, get to know bank employees, and coordinate with branch management. You then have to do your homework and learn about the players in the branch, how the branch functions, what products are offered and how they work. Successful reps recommend a written plan.

The first task is to perform your own market research in the branch. The bank had a culture long before the investment services program arrived (whether performed by a bank unit or a third-party provider). Each bank and/or bank branch has its own culture, based on the personality of its management and employees. The registered rep has to fit in with the bank's culture. If the rep is not perceived to fit in, or if branch employees think the rep is not cooperating, there can be frustration on both sides. A retail investment services program has to form a real partnership with the bank if it is to be successful.

The registered rep's task is twofold: he or she must persuade the other bank employees that he or she is a competent person, a team player who can be entrusted with the customer relationship, can add value to that relationship, and will serve the customer in a trustworthy way. The rep must also educate the CSRs about investment products. Reps who can establish themselves personally but cannot convey information about their product will be ineffective, because the CSRs must understand the investment products' benefits well enough to see a match with customers' needs and refer them. If the CSRs understand that investments are important but don't like the registered rep, they still won't send referrals. Even worse, if the CSRs don't like the rep personally, he or she probably won't be given a chance to get the message across.

You as the registered rep have to be seen as a hard-working, dedicated employee who is devoted to the success of the financial institution. Especially in the beginning, you must arrive in the branch with the other employees and stay as late as they do. It would be a recipe for disaster to have someone come in as an outsider, get paid on a different scale, and work less than anyone else. You might think of this process as paying your dues or earning the referrals you would like to have. Another mistake is flaunting success with conspicuous consumption. This can be devastating in smaller communities. We have heard stories about bank employees sending customers to the broker down the street because those employees are so irate at seeing the rep drive up in his new BMW—when the rest of the bank can only afford a Chevy.

Getting Introduced

The first part of the registered rep's marketing campaign is to get to know the employees of the branch. Try to learn all you can about the functions and situation of each employee. (It goes without saying that you learn their names!) Ask the branch manager to make introductions your first day on the job. Ask to attend staff meetings. Although these things may seem obvious, the reality is that registered reps have their own set of priorities. Some reps are so ready to set the investment world on fire with their knowledge and experience that they may not realize the key to their long-term success lies in imparting some of that knowledge to the tellers and other bank employees who share the lobby with them.

After you have been introduced to the bank staff, the next step is asking them to introduce you to their customers. Ask the branch manager to mention investment products in as many presentations and as part of as many other kinds of calls as possible. Try to talk to the people handling rate inquiry calls. When they hear those signals from customers ("Is that your best rate?"), they should mention the investment services program.

Make sure you keep branch employees informed about your schedule. If you cover more than one branch, post your schedule for both customers and employees to see. Be very clear about how to get in touch with you and who should be making appointments for you.

Start a Training Program

What you really have to do is sell yourself to bank employees in the same way you sell your services to customers. Remember, they are your most important customers. Think out the same kind of needs-based selling strategy you use on the end customer. Start by asking what their situation is. CSRs are worried that customers will blame them if something goes wrong with the investment, because they made the original referral. CSRs have performance goals for a variety of other programs and products besides yours. Bank employees have been taught for a long time that any investments besides bank liability products are too risky for their customers. Some employees, especially if they are long-time bankers, might be hostile on principle to any product that threatens to erode the deposits that have always been so important to the survival of the financial institution.

These are some of the topics you need to address in your training program. (We describe training for CSRs at length in the Chapter 10 on referrals.) As branch employees come to better understand customer needs for alternative investment products, they will be more able to recognize that need and make referrals. In your training sessions, explain that the more ties customers have with the institution, the more likely they are to remain a customer. Tell them how the retail investment services program will benefit the bank, the customer, and the employees as well. Explain that customer funds often come from outside the institution. Customers are going to buy these products anyway, so they should buy them from the financial institution they trust. Treat your fellow employees as partners and sell the program to them. Finally, help them realize their performance goals by sending referrals back to them.

Try to make training sessions interesting. Don't simply lecture, but interact with those attending. Use role plays. Make sure you understand the way the branch or bank operates, and plan your training to harmonize with the environment. You need to remember that the alternative investment products that are so familiar to you are totally new to most bank employees. Don't overwhelm them with information. The initial training can't be a data dump; use additional training sessions to support the information you provided in the first sessions. Training is an ongoing commitment.

In addition to the certification program we describe in the chapter on referrals, we recommend that the rep devote time to bank employees one on one. Work with a particular employee, describing your products and converting him or her to your point of view. In this context, that means not only sharing knowledge and information but learning about the employee's family, job, and job aspirations. Use this as an opportunity to develop strong personal relationships with bank employees. It's easier for employees to be lukewarm about the investment program when you talk to them as a group. When you talk to an individual, you need to ask questions and learn about that person. No one can resist this. And don't forget to have fun. (One rep broke the ice with bank employees the day he dressed up as a bunny as part of a festival.) Lighten up their days, and they'll help you all they can.

Go the Extra Mile

A personal referral from the CSR, teller, or platform person will accomplish far more than elaborate, expensive, but impersonal advertising campaigns. Successful registered reps say they would rather spend a few dollars on their fellow employees paying directly for referrals or indirectly in some form of appreciation (the all-important pizza, flowers, donuts, mugs) than spending the same amount of money on advertising. The payoff is much more direct and immediate. You cannot force cooperation from other branch employees but people love to be appreciated. You need to give constant support and recognition. If you send birthday cards to customers, send them to your fellow employees.

If it is appropriate within bank guidelines, you might invite your best customers to lunch. But also take along the branch manager, particularly if he or she is not well acquainted with those particular customers.

The registered rep should make it a personal mission to work with the branch manager. The manager's support is vitally important to making your program a success. All the incentive referral programs in the world and all your personal charm cannot make the program work if you don't have active management support. To get the support of the branch manager, offer your support to him or her. Support bank programs and events; contribute ideas for seminars, promotions, and contests. And remember that the best way to get a referral is to make a referral, particularly if you have been able to develop customers from outside the financial institution.

Start an Investment Program

Alternative investment products are scary for bank employees who are being exposed to them for the first time. Try to persuade employees to open their own accounts with you. There is nothing like investing one's own money to teach an employee exactly how it works. The employee gets a statement, is confused, gets help from you—and the next thing you know, can tell a customer that it's not really very hard. Some branches have investment clubs where an individual can invest a small amount of money but still reap the reward (as far as you're concerned) of becoming familiar with your program and products.

How Larger Banks Enlist Management Support

Many of the larger banks have reorganized their budgeting process to create a structural foundation for generating commitment to the investment center's success. This process can also be applied to smaller institutions. Management has realized that one of the most important factors in getting retail investment services up and running is obtaining personal commitment from branch managers. The best method to accomplish this is to make the fee income generated by the program part of the branch budget and hold the branch manager accountable for achieving it. Management has to recognize that some short-term disintermediation is inevitable and remove penalties for branch managers when deposits are down (because investment amounts are up).

Most larger banks have developed some system for making branches accountable for fee income. Sometimes it's shadow accounting or double counting. In several significant cases, the financial services unit has stopped reporting separate profits; it returns gross margins (revenue minus expenses) to the banks or the branches where they originated. Although this view is not popular everywhere, it's increasingly accepted that growing the bottom line is what's important, not how it gets there.

An investment rep cannot force management to include goals in the branch's budget for fee income generated by the investment services program. But this factor should be understood by both third-party provider and bank management. Those from the investment services side should ask for such accounting whenever possible.

Appropriate Products for Banks

It is interesting that banks have come to define trust, as far as investments are concerned, so narrowly as to mean safety of principal. In community banks in particular, bankers often avoid trying to educate their customers about investment products that do have principal risk but are probably in the best interests of their customers in the long run. Educating customers about their long-term investment needs might satisfy the requirements of trust more broadly.

We suggest that it does not necessarily serve customers' best interests to fail to educate them about changing economic realities. One banker told us he has been selling bank certificates of deposits for years, but he believes that a bank CD is no longer a suitable investment for IRA money. Look at the marketing materials from equity mutual funds and you will see charts and graphs making the point that as soon as you have a time horizon beyond 15 years, the investor's money should be in equities. "Ibbotson & Associates reports that for any 15-year holding period between 1940 and 1990, stocks have beaten inflation 92% of the time compared with 62% for Treasuries and 31% for bonds."[11] When the time horizon is long enough, equities always outperform bonds or other fixed-income products.

What most customers fear most is losing their money, but times have changed since the Depression. What customers should fear most is loss of purchasing power.[12] When a customer retires at age 62 or age 65, what is his or her time horizon? Probably more than 20 years, which means that the traditional

---

11 Thomas G. Drobka, "Selling Stock Funds Through Bank Investment Programs," *Bank Investment Representative*, Fall 1991, p. 4.

12 Nick Murray, "Off the Path of Least Resistance: Equity Mutual Funds in Banks," talk given to the *Bank Investment Representative's* 1993 National Sales Conference, August 19, 1993, Chicago, IL.

wisdom of shifting most assets out of equities and into fixed-income instruments as one approaches retirement is an outdated strategy.

Registered reps selling in banks have traditionally focused on selling annuities and fixed-income mutual funds, the products that look the most like the
CDs bank customers are used to investing in. While we do not have the space
here for a long discussion of personal investing, we suggest that bank management keep an open mind about the products sold through retail investment
programs and not necessarily push for a fixed-income orientation. Customers
are best served when they are well informed about the economic reality of a
changing marketplace.

8

Who Is the Customer?

It is safe to say that it is the goal of every citizen to live a long and healthy life; most people would like to have a prosperous life as well. This goal seems straightforward enough. In the normal course of events, children receive formal education (some more than others). They grow up and get jobs or start careers. Then the objective is to enjoy life (some also do this better than others) while trying to achieve some measure of financial security. With any luck, one retires while still youthful and healthy enough to enjoy the remaining years.

Individuals have many goals. Many of those goals require additional financial resources, increase the needs of the individual, and make the goal of financial security more challenging. The individual may choose to become a family and take on the responsibility of dependents. Currently the median price for a home in America is $100,900.[1] This is the largest single expenditure that most individuals will make. Another major financial commitment is education. A child's college education (or a degree for a parent) also requires financial planning. A four-year college education at an elite private institution currently costs $92,000; by the year 2000, one year could cost $40,000.[2] A four-year education at even a public college now costs almost $25,000 for a state resident.[3]

There was a time when individuals relied on their employer to provide for them when they retired, including medical care. The employer relied on the

1   *The World Almanac and Book of Facts*, 1993, pub Newspaper Enterprise Association, NY, NY. p.714.
2   John Elson, "Campus of the Future," *Time*, April 13, 1992, p.54.
3   *The World Almanac*, p. 195.

employee to work for the same company for thirty years. Today the employer/employee relationship has changed radically. Employees have become more mobile and less loyal to one company, with good reason, since employers are now quick to institute layoffs when company fortunes falter. Employers no longer provide the employee with the security of a pension plan or even profit-sharing programs. Retirement is now provided through the means of a 401(k) program which shifts the responsibility of funding retirement back to the individual. The major advantage of a 401(k) is that it moves with the employee when he or she changes jobs; it was designed for the mobile society we have become.

Social Security exists now, but many question its long-term viability. Even if it doesn't collapse completely, how much of a living will its benefits supply? The social security system was set up to supplement employers' programs but now it is the main source of retirement income for many retirees. The burden of providing for retirement is being shifted from employers and the government to individuals. Financial planners say that something like 90% of the individuals retiring cannot afford to retire. We believe this trend will continue.

The largest investment that an individual will make is his or her own retirement. If you don't take care of yourself, no one else will. This is why we believe everyone is a potential customer of alternative investment products. Taking into account day-to-day needs and long-term goals, individuals need to be more aggressive in managing their money. Most individuals work hard to get money, but they are afraid to let their money work hard for them. They have little experience as investors. At best, they have been savers for most of their lives.

Savers are those individuals whose main financial concern has been principal risk rather than risk of losing purchasing power. Most savers have been profoundly affected by their own experiences or the stories they've heard about family experiences during the Depression. They think that losing one's money is the worst thing than can happen to a person financially. By contrast, investors are willing to risk principal to gain additional purchasing power. A person can be both a saver and an investor. In fact, a well-balanced investment portfolio would include both savings and investment instruments.

Investor Profiles

Individuals tend to follow what might be called a financial life cycle. There are certain economic and financial stages that most people go through. These stages can be characterized in terms of how individuals live, work, spend, invest, and save at each period. The investment needs of individuals change with the different life stages. The life stages themselves might seem obvious enough, but understanding how investment needs change is harder. In Figure 8.1, we have sketched out the characteristics of each stage, along with the likely components of an investment portfolio. In every case the particular investments made will be adjusted to the needs and circumstances of the individual, but this gives an overview of the process.

About Retirement

The average age of Americans is going up, from 33.0 years in 1990 to 38.9 in 2010.[4] Life expectancy is climbing; it was 69.7 years in 1960 and 75.4 years in 1990, and it's expected to reach 77 years in 2000 and 77.9 in 2010.[5] A Merrill Lynch publication quotes the U.S. Bureau of the Census: "By the year 2030, the number of Americans age 65 and over will more than double to 65 million, and 10% of the population will be over the age of 75. The fastest growing age group is the 85+ population. Their numbers will almost quadruple over the next 50 years, to more than 12 million."[6] According to *Financial Planning* magazine, U.S. Census figures predict that most Americans will spend one-third of their adult lives in retirement. Furthermore, 5% annual inflation would result in the purchasing power of retirement income being cut in half in 15 years.[7]

What's new about retirement now is that a 60-year-old has a time horizon of 15 years or more. Until recently, most people lived only a few years beyond retirement. A woman who was born in 1950 and reaches the age of 65 is projected to live to age 87, and a man to age 81.[8] Furthermore, "the mature market (defined as those households headed by an individual over 50 years old) holds 77% of the wealth in the United States, controls 42% of all disposable income, [and] owns half of all corporate stocks, two-thirds of all investment portfolios, and 65% of all bank deposits."[9] This suggests that the elderly continue to control a large proportion of the wealth in this country, but they need help in directing those investments so that they will have the wealth they need for the longer lives they will lead.

The greatest financial danger for individuals is outliving their financial resources. Individuals need to be educated about their need to save and invest

4   "Baby Boomers: Comparing Fund and Nonfund Owners," *FUND, Mutual Fund Research in Brief*, ICI Research Department, July 1992, p. 1.
5   "Demographic Trends and their Implications for the Mutual Fund Industry," *FUND, Mutual fund Research in Brief*, July 1993, p.1.
6   "Retirement Savings in America," *The Fifth Annual Merrill Lynch Retirement Planning Survey*, June 1993, p. 2; quoting U.S. Bureau of the Census. "Projections of the Population of the United States, by Age, Sex, and Race: 1988 to 2080," by Gregory Spencer. *Current Population Reports* Series P-25, No. 1018 (January 1989).
7   Amey Stone, "Baby-Boomers Head toward Their Retirement Years," *Financial Planning*, February 1993, p. 29.
8   "Retirement Savings," 1993, p. 6; quoting Source: NCHS, Middle Morality Projections, 1990..
9   Michael P. Sullivan, "Aging Population Provides Planners Wealth of Opportunity," *Financial Planning*, February 1993, p. 75.

Table 8.1 The Typical Investor Profiles

Age 20-35: The early investor

Investor profile:

- Early stages of career
- Beginning to establish family
- Improving lifestyle

Financial goals:

- Establish and maintain good credit
- Begin to pay off college loans
- Save for down payment on a house
- Save for own further college education
- Provide for family in case of death (life insurance)

Investment portfolio:

- 10% protection
- 15% growth and income
- 25% long-term growth
- 50% aggressive long-term growth
- Tax-deferred investing for long-term growth: IRAs, 401(k)s, variable annuities

Age 35-50: The seasoned investor

Investor profile:

- Well established in career
- Children growing up
- Have purchased home
- Starting to think seriously about investing
- Consuming as well as starting to accumulate wealth

Financial goals:

- Save for children's college expenses or paying for children in college
- Start to get serious about retirement
- Save for shorter-term goals like vacations, consumer goods
- Upgrade house

Investment portfolio:

- 10% protection
- 20% growth and income
- 40% long-term growth
- 30% aggressive long-term growth
- 25-40% of investments are done through tax-deferred vehicles: IRAs, 401(k)s, variable annuities, municipal bonds, variable universal life insurance

Age 50-60: Pre-retirement

Investor profile:

- Earnings at their peak

Table 8.1 The Typical Investor Profiles (*continued*)

- Children out of college
- Caring for elderly parents
- Worried about own long-term care
- House fully paid for
- Increasing time for leisure and travel
- Tax bracket at peak
- Starting to think about estate planning and the transfer of wealth

Financial goals:
- Maximize investing for retirement
- Reduce tax liability
- Enhance living standards
- Save for vacations or a second home
- Accumulate wealth in estate

Investment portfolio:
- 10% protection
- 15% income
- 20% growth and income
- 35% growth
- 20% aggressive long-term growth
- 25-40% of investments done through tax-deferred vehicles: IRAs, 401(k)s, variable annuities, fixed-rate annuities, municipal bonds

Age 60+: Retirement

Investor profile:
- Ready to retire or just retired
- Want to enjoy the fruits of a working life
- Mortgage paid off
- Very concerned about preserving independence

Financial goals:
- Preserve capital
- Protect savings from inflation
- Maintain standard of living in retirement
- Estate planning: living trusts, education trusts for grandchildren, etc.
- Continue to build value in estate
- Emphasize current income

Investment portfolio:
- 15% protection
- 25% income
- 25% growth and income
- 35% growth

for their retirement. "According to published research, the typical 50-year-old has only $2,300 in financial assets, excluding the primary residence. And 15% of 45- to 65-year-olds are saving nothing at all. On average, people plan to retire at age 61, which indicates that many individuals in this middle-age segment need to increase retirement savings significantly."[10]

A number of studies about baby boomers indicate that they are not yet serious about retirement. An Investment Company Institute (ICI) study shows that 34% of boomers who already own mutual funds have retirement as their primary financial goal, compared to 13% of those who do not yet own mutual funds. Looked at another way, 66% of those who know about investing and 87% of those who do not own mutual funds are not saving for retirement. For baby boomers as a whole, 83% are not saving for retirement.[11]

These facts, although somewhat contradictory, reveal the extent of the problem. While many of the younger people who should be starting on a retirement program are not now your customers, they should be, because there is a genuine customer need for financial planning and investment services. Your marketing should reach out to give these people the education they need to make decisions about investments. If you help them find solutions to their retirement problems, in the process you will also sell a lot of product.

When a 60-year-old prospect comes to your desk and wants to put all his or her money into fixed-income investments to be "safe" for retirement, how should you respond? As soon as an investor has a 15-year time horizon, he or she should be investing, at least to some extent, in equities. And a 60-year-old most definitely has a 15-year time horizon. A retiree would probably rather have the growth component of the portfolio invested in growth funds and stocks rather than aggressive growth funds or high-yield funds, and there might be an income component to that mutual fund as well, but it would be a disservice to the customer to move him or her completely out of equities.

Marketing to the mature market has always been vital to the success of a retail investment services program, but it is taking on a new importance. A number of consultants have made it a specialty. The mature market and the elderly have special concerns as well as different physical realities, such as not being able to read fine print or glossy paper. It is well worth your while to take note of the special needs and concerns of this part of the marketplace, because these customers, above all others, have assets to invest.

---

10 "Demographic Trends," p. 1.
11 "Baby Boomers," p. 1.

Portfolio Components

Asset allocation has become a buzzword in the financial industry, for good reasons. It refers to the process by which individuals divide up their investment portfolio among different sectors of the market, and is another term for talking about how to structure an investment portfolio. We have suggested portfolios appropriate to individuals in different age groups, but portfolios for individuals of every age should include certain kinds of investments. We call this the investment pyramid.

- Speculative
- Aggressive growth
- Growth
- Growth and income
- Income
- Protection or foundation

At the base, for everyone, should be a certain component of very safe and liquid investments that can be tapped for emergencies or short-term needs. This protection category includes savings accounts and very short CDs, money market accounts, and other money market instruments. It also includes basic insurance needs such as disability and life insurance. At the top of the pyramid are speculative investments such as futures and options. Speculative investing has no place in the average investor's portfolio; it's for the sophisticated investor who has money to lose. On the other hand, growth investments have a place in every portfolio, even for the person about to retire. Aggressive growth investments should be heaviest in the early years, when there is a long time before retirement. They should be transferred to growth as retirement gets closer. The income sector of the portfolio is the opposite. In the later years, when earned income starts to taper off, the growth portion of the portfolio should be shifted to income.

This is a very simple asset allocation model. You can best serve the needs of the individual by doing a personal financial plan which is reviewed regularly.

Defining Portfolio Segments

It's easy enough to say that one's portfolio should contain 25% growth investments, but how do you know which products constitute growth? Here are some general indications of which products go into each market segment.

Protection:
- Money-market mutual funds
- Tax-exempt money-market mutual funds
- Money-market investments, including CDs, Treasury bills, and BAs
- Savings accounts
- Life insurance
- Disability insurance

Income:
- Intermediate Treasury and agency notes
- High-quality corporate bonds
- Mortgage-backed mutual funds
- Mutual funds with the stated goal of income
- Strategic income or global income mutual funds

Growth and income:
- Utility stocks and utility mutual funds
- Stocks that pay stable dividends
- Mutual funds with this stated goal
- Asset allocation mutual funds

Growth:
- Stocks
- Zero coupon bonds
- Mutual funds with a growth objective
- Global equity funds
- Small-cap equity funds

Aggressive long-term growth:
- Equity investments of all kinds, including both stocks and stock mutual funds
- Mutual funds and variable-rate annuities invested in mutual funds (for professional management)
- High-yield mutual bonds (which manage high-yield bonds)

Speculative:
- Futures
- Options
- Gold bullion

Tax deferred: Tax deferred means the taxes have to be paid once the investment profits are used after age 59-1/2. Classic tax-deferred investments include:
- Fixed-rate annuities
- Variable annuities
- Variable and universal life insurance policies
- IRA and SEP contributions

Tax free: This includes only municipal bonds. On all other investments, the tax must be paid at some time.
- Municipal bonds and notes
- Zero coupon municipal bonds

Who is Investing in Mutual Funds

Mutual funds offer investors a number of advantages including diversification, professional management, market liquidity, and low cost of acquisition. (See Chapter 4 for more details.)

The Investment Company Institute has done a number of studies about mutual fund investing. Its 1992 statistics estimate that 27% of U.S. households own mutual funds. Demographic and financial characteristics of new and seasoned investors can be seen in Tables 8.2 and 8.3.

From the group of investors surveyed, one in ten bought their first mutual fund after January 1991. It is those new investors who are profiled in the column "New." They are younger, have lower incomes and have fewer assets to invest than seasoned mutual fund owners. It stands to reason that 85% of those who fall into this category are employed; younger investors would not have the resources to invest if they weren't employed. Fewer of the new investors are married, although in other characteristics they resemble seasoned investors.

Baby Boomers

Any study of potential investors should include a separate study of the baby boomers, who comprise 76 million people age 29-47. In the year 2000, baby boomers will be age 36-55 (the baby boom lasted from 1945 to 1964). The first boomers will start to retire at age 60 in 2005.

The boomers are starting to worry about retirement, according to the ICI, and they should get more worried as retirement approaches. The ICI suggests that "targeting communications to meet the retirement needs of boomers will

Table 8.2 New and Seasoned Shareholders, Demographic and Financial Characteristics

Demographic Characteristics		
	New	Seasoned
Median age	37	46
Median income	$40,000	$45,000
Male decision-maker	58%	57%
4-year college degree		
or more	51%	50%
Completed graduate school	14%	16%
Married	62%	73%
Employed	85%	71%
Retired	9%	25%

Financial Characteristics		
	New	Seasoned
Average per household		
Financial assets*	$60,000	$121,000
Financial assets in funds	$21,000	$ 45,900
Number of funds owned	6.9	6.0
Percentage of financial assets in		
Mutual funds	35%	38%
Individual stocks	14%	15%
Individual bonds	5%	6%

* Excluding real estate and assets in employer-sponsored retirement plans.
Source: "Profiles in Fund Ownership," ICI.

help ensure that mutual funds are an investment option that boomers under-stand and consider using to meet this long-term goal."[12]

Boomers who already own mutual funds have demographic and financial characteristics very different from those of nonfund-owning boomers (Table 8.3). According to the ICI, 27% of them (about 21 million individuals) own mutual funds. "Boomer fund owners have greater wealth, better education, a higher incidence of home ownership, and are more likely to own IRAs or Keoghs than the nonfund-owning members of their generation."[13] In short, they

12 "Demographic Trends," p.1.
13 "Baby Boomers," p.1.

Table 8.3 Baby Boomers Who Own Mutual Funds Versus Those Who Don't

	Fund Owners	Nonfund Owners
Median income	$52,000	$33,000
Average savings/investments*	$62,000	28,000
Male decision-maker	59%	54%
Employed full or part-time	89%	84%
Married	76%	67%
Dual-income household	54%	45%
Completed college	51%	24%
Own home	78%	62%
Own personal computer at home	44%	22%
Have children under 18	67%	70%
Respondent or spouse has:		
Pension plan at work	76%	64%
IRA or Keogh account	62%	28%

* Data excludes primary residence and may include 401(k) and IRA investments.
Source: "The Baby Boom Generation: A Financial Portrait," ICI, 1991.

exhibit characteristics that make them the kind of customers every bank would like to attract and form long-term relationships with.

The study further shows that boomers who own mutual funds keep 36% of their assets in mutual funds and 21% savings accounts; nonfund-owning boomers keep 69% of their financial assets in bank products, mostly savings accounts.

These numbers lead to a double conclusion for designing a marketing strategy for retail investment services programs. First, as we suggested, boomers who already own mutual funds are prime candidates for a wide variety of bank services. They are already buying mutual funds from someone; if the financial institution can attract them with retail investment services, it has a good chance of establishing a multifaceted relationship with these desirable customers.

Second, nonfund-owning customers are already heavy users of bank savings products. The financial institution has a wide-open field to educate these customers about different investment vehicles, since they are already coming to buy savings products. Their current reliance on savings products makes it less likely that they would take their money out of the bank to buy mutual funds or other alternative investments.

Who is the Sandwich Generation?

There has been a great deal of discussion in the press recently about the sandwich generation, people who are being squeezed financially by both the need to pay the soaring costs of college education for their children and medical and long-term care for their aging parents. Add to that paying for their own retirement, and you have a triple squeeze.

But Cynthia Taeuber, an expert from the Census Bureau, says that women and men who are now age 55 to 70 and still working are likely to feel the greatest crunch. For one thing, only about 6% of all Americans have kids age 18 to 24. Furthermore, the parents of many baby boomers are no older than 75 now, since their mothers tended to have babies earlier than women today. It's at age 80 and over that elderly people really start needing substantial assistance. [14]

On the other hand, the financial press is buzzing with talk about the "greatest transfer of wealth from one generation to the next that the world has ever seen . . . as $8 trillion in assets is transferred from aging or deceased parents to their baby boomer offspring."[15] We had bankers telling us about this before we ever read it in a magazine. Assets of $8 trillion represent a lot of investing power. Now is the time to start marketing to the people who will be holding that wealth in a few years.

There will certainly be a tremendous squeeze on those who have to support elderly parents, plan for their own retirement and possible long-term care, and provide for children and their college education. There is some debate about exactly which segment of the population will be most adversely affected. However, in light of the Clinton tax increases and the continuing sluggish economy, most adults will probably feel the pinch. This means financial planning and investment advice will become even more important for all sectors of society.

Potential Customers

Community bankers continue to ask us where they will find customers for their retail investment services programs. Demographically speaking, we think *everyone* is a potential customer, but we would like to offer a few suggestions.

Doctors and lawyers are some of the most overtargeted people we can think of—especially young doctors, who are far more likely to have six-figure debts, not incomes. However, it does still make sense to target these people in community banks, where the registered rep or the financial institution is approach-

---

14 "Baby Boomers May Not Face Tight Squeeze," *Wall Street Journal,* June 29, 1993.
15 Stone, "Boomers Head Toward," p. 30.

ing them as a current customer and a warm lead, not as a cold call from a brokerage house. The people in these professions are attractive potential customers for more reasons than just their incomes. They come into contact with a wide range of the public, and lawyers especially are in a position to know about the situation and finances of their clients. If you can convert a doctor or a lawyer to a client, you have also won a potential stream of referrals. The same goes for accountants, who are in an excellent position to know which clients need financial counseling.

The presidents and owners of businesses are another interesting group, because they can be customers for both their own investment needs and the needs of their employees. While registered reps are very happy to assist individual customers with pension planning, assisting a company with its pension plan for all employees offers even more potential.

Above all else, the first target market for your retail investment services program is your institution's top 200 to 300 depositors, who may or may not already be investing in alternative investment products. The best place to look for customers is in your lobby. The next place to look is in the competition's lobby. Draw their customers in with your marketing expertise and referral programs (see Chapters 9 and 10).

Rule of 72

Somewhere in this book we have to talk about the rule of 72, a simple arithmetic rule that allows you to calculate compound interest quickly in your head. It is a powerful tool for selling to younger customers, who can use the rule of 72 to see why they should put compound interest on their side as soon as possible.

If you divide 72 by the interest rate on the investment in question, you find how many years it will take for the funds in that investment to double. For example, at 10%, it will take 7.2 years for an investment to double. At 2%, it will take 36 years for an investment to double; at 3%, 24 years. A higher-risk investment at 15% will take only 4.8 years to double.

If a young couple starts out with $10,000 at age 25, at 15% that money will be able to double eight times before they retire, to yield $2,560,000 at retirement. At 2%, that money will double only once in 36 years, to yield $20,000. (Although past performance in no way guarantees future performance, a number of mutual funds have yielded an average of 15% or more, year after year for 15 years.)

9

Marketing

We have mentioned elsewhere in this book why banks historically have not had to develop the kind of marketing skills that characterize other industries. At one time, banks were not only the low-cost providers of their product—money—they were the only providers. Anyone who wanted to borrow money had to get it from a bank. Businesses and consumers borrowed money on the bank's terms and at the bank's convenience. Furthermore, bank savings and checking accounts were the only way customers could save. Of course, the capital and stock markets have been available to individual investors for this entire century, but many people would not consider investing their savings in these markets, especially after the stock market crash of 1929 and the Great Depression. Even those individuals who did invest in the stock market needed a way to accumulate savings and keep a certain amount of liquidity on hand, in addition to long-term investing.

Every aspect of this scenario has changed. On the bank lending side, most consumers receive an offer for them to borrow money at least weekly. Those offers come from banks, near-banks, credit card companies, finance companies for mortgages and car manufacturers, etc. They arrive in the form of direct mail or dinnertime phone calls. The recent slowdown in economic activity means lending activities of all kinds are less in demand. (It wasn't that long ago that there was a certain amount of credit rationing.) At the commercial level, the disintermediation of bank lending means that larger companies that can raise their own capital and satisfy their own funding needs go directly to the market themselves.

On the investing side, consumers have a wide array of products from which to choose. Money market mutual funds are as liquid as bank accounts, for all practical purposes. Our chapter describing alternative investment products is so long because there are so many different choices, an investment choice for every possible permutation of consumer need. Banks have to compete not only with all the products that are offered directly to consumers, but with a variety of distribution choices, including brokerage houses, discount brokers, and other banks.

For the first time, banks have to reach out to the individual consumer; they can't wait for consumers to come in and ask to do business. Consumers still need to borrow money, and they still like to borrow from banks, but banks are competing against each other as never before. How does a bank lure a potential customer onto its premises? Traditional banking cultures don't know how, because they have never developed marketing orientation or expertise. Banks are slowly learning how to survive and thrive in a new environment; many banks are only starting to realize the need for better marketing, let alone develop the expertise to carry it out.

Then comes the culture shock of alternative investment products. We have used the term third-party provider throughout this book to refer to the securities organization that comes into a financial institution to provide AIPs to that institution's customers. In the industry, however, "third-party marketer" means the same thing, and it might be a more relevant term in the context of this chapter. Third-party providers provide not just products but an entire distribution system. They know you can't just put up a sign and expect customers to flock in, even though there is a real consumer need for these products. Customers must be made aware that the products are available and educated as to features and benefits. They also have to receive service before, during, and after the sale. These are the skills and the orientation that third-party providers bring to banks.

And this is where friction begins, because the third-party provider (third-party marketer) knows more about marketing than the bank knows. Bankers like to retain control of their own customer base and everything that goes to it, and it is only human that they think they know their own customer base better than anyone else could know it. They think they have a better understanding than anyone else could possibly have of what their customers need and how they should be approached. They think that their customer base is unique and that they alone have insight into how it operates. We understand why banks feel this way, but we think many of them could use some help.

There is tremendous confusion about the role of "marketing" in banks. Many banks have marketing departments or an employee who is in charge of marketing. What that means in the context of an individual bank varies widely. A bank marketing department might really be the public relations department, or the product development department, or the communications department. That is, the marketing department might handle the bank's relationship with the media; or design new products, carry out advertising campaigns or develop brochures for products; or foster internal communications in some way. Many people define marketing by just one of its aspects and some bank marketing departments perform just one part of the marketing process. We would like to diminish the confusion by laying out systematically what we mean by marketing and what role marketing should play in a bank.

Developing a Marketing Plan

Every bank should have a master marketing plan. "Marketing is a social and managerial process by which individuals and groups obtain what they need and want through creating, offering and exchanging products of value with others."[1]

This is one definition of marketing. We like it because it encompasses the process we understand as marketing. Marketing is not simply advertising or brochures or signs in the window. In terms of a retail investment services program, marketing is the entire process by which alternative investment products are delivered by your institution to your customers. The marketing process includes

- defining the target market
- positioning the program within the institution
- positioning products within the program
- attracting customers to the program
- identifying customer needs and objectives
- obtaining the products that satisfy customer needs
- servicing the customer after the sale

These are the broad categories of a marketing program. We believe all other materials and activities are subsets of these categories that support the program within the context of these definitions.

You can't have a successful retail investment services program without a clearly defined, written marketing plan. This plan should encompass every aspect of your program. The securities area, whether it is a bank department (in an in-house program) or the third-party provider, must develop a plan in con-

---

1   Philip Kotler, *Marketing Management, Analysis, Planning, Implementation and Control,* (New Jersey: Prentice Hall, Inc., 1991), p.4.

junction with bank management. The TPP will be the marketing specialist or consultant and should be able to propose an overall plan, which can then be adapted to the specific needs of your institution. One word of caution: do not allow a traditional bank marketing program to limit the effectiveness of the TPP's marketing program.

Defining the Target Market

It is essential to define the target market in terms of both target segments within the bank customer base and potential customers who are not already part of the bank customer base. You have to reach out beyond the bank's current customer base to build new relationships. Different financial institutions have different target markets overall. For example, there are upscale banks, savings and loans that offer attractive credit products to a younger clientele, banks in retirement communities that appeal mostly to the elderly, and banks in urban settings that have ATMs in foreign languages. The target market for the retail investment services program should be a subset of the target market for the bank as a whole. It should include those potential customers who are not currently customers of the financial institution but would mesh well with it. The marketing plan should include a way to bring in those new customer relationships that are essential to the long-term success of both the retail investment services program and the institution itself.

Positioning the Program Within the Institution

How will you set up your program so that it generates maximum cross-sales opportunities within the financial institution? As we have discussed in other chapters, there are numerous ways to structure and deliver a retail investment services program. Who the retail investment services program reports to organizationally can make a substantial difference in how it functions. For example, a program reporting to or aligned with the trust department produces one type of sales philosophy and product orientation. If the program reports to the retail department of the bank, you get an entirely different product emphasis and sales philosophy.

There can be organizational synergies when a bank has both retail investment services and a capital markets area. For example, the capital markets area might underwrite municipal bonds that can be sold to tax-exempt mutual funds. The bank can potentially profit from underwriting bonds, selling the bonds to the mutual fund, and then selling the mutual fund to individual investors.

Positioning Products Within the Program

Many retail investment services programs are quite similar in the product categories they offer, but they differ as far as the exact product. That is, bank retail investment services programs tend to focus on packaged products, but which mutual funds and annuities a particular program sells depends on whether that program has proprietary products, how many different mutual fund families it wants to have a relationship with, or even on how the due diligence is done. The presence of proprietary products, whether of the third-party provider or of the financial institution itself, can make a great deal of difference to a program, as does cooperation between a mutual fund company and a capital markets area.

Proprietary mutual funds in an in-house program can provide a real focus for a financial institution's support of alternative investment products. Managers of retail investment services programs in money center banks report that proprietary products help senior management focus on the importance of alternative investment products. Since the program does not come from outside the bank, it is seen as one more way for the institution as a whole to grow and prosper. The bank accepts ownership of proprietary funds, which are often the trust department's general trust funds converted to retail mutual funds. This creates another synergy and profit potential; because the trust department receives additional fee income for services performed, it encourages the growth and continuing success of these funds.

Programs that depend heavily on Series 6 individuals to sell alternative investment products will have to deemphasize individual stocks, bonds, or other products and rely totally on packaged products. Affluent neighborhoods might want programs that offer sophisticated products to meet the needs of their customers and remain competitive. Less affluent neighborhoods or a customer base with a predominance of older people might dictate other product choices.

In general, most programs are well advised to offer all the various categories of funds (from fixed-income and money market funds to aggressive growth and high-yield funds). What a program comprises beyond that should be a strategic decision. If you are offering alternative investment products through an in-house program, we assume that you have the expertise to make that decision. If you are using a third-party provider, listen to it, because it has the expertise.

Attracting Customers to the Program

This is the slice of a marketing plan that many people think of as marketing, because it encompasses advertising, slogans, and media presentations. One does attract customers through the various media and printed materials, and those activities and materials have to be designed and coordinated. But to us, this is only one small part of the whole marketing plan. In fact, it's only one part of attracting customers to the program. Ways to attract customers include:

- educational seminars
- telemarketing
- target-market mailings
- a grand opening party
- a referral program
- lobby signage
- advertising
- statement stuffers
- free financial planning
- newsletters
- brochures and product information

These are all essential parts of the marketing program. As a whole, they go far beyond designing a brochure or a newspaper ad. They are all ways to make customers aware that the institution has a retail investment services program, staffed by professionals. If customers know of the program, when they need its services they know that the registered rep can help them reach their investment objectives. This awareness is the prerequisite for the educational process the rep will employ to help customers explore their needs and focus their attention on how alternative investment products can help them. The key to developing a long-term relationship with a customer is education—which is why educational seminars and financial planning are such good ways to help cement a relationship.

Identifying Customer Needs and Objectives

This part of the marketing plan should be similar for most bank programs. Bank programs should specialize in the kind of needs-based, consultative selling we discuss in this book. The sales process for a bank should emphasize those elements of commitment and overall customer benefit that will ensure long-term customer loyalty and an enhanced customer relationship.

Obtaining the Products that Satisfy Customer Needs

There is usually more than one product that will suit a particular situation, but satisfying the *customer's* need is what is important here. If the broker/dealer carries significant inventories or sells proprietary products, you might wind up with products looking for homes. This comes back to product neutrality. The sales process that focuses on customers' needs and objectives must have the flexibility to obtain products from a wide variety of sources.

Servicing the Customer After the Sale

Customer rapport must be established before the first sale can take place, but the customer relationship truly begins after the sale. You might even say the customer relationship isn't established until after the second sale. The first sale can be mostly a matter of luck, of being in the right place when the customer has a maturing CD. But the long-term investment in the customer, the repeated contacts and seminars and mailings, begins to pay off when the registered rep makes the second sale. As we have stated before, the second sale is far more efficient, because the customer already knows the rep and the routine as far as doing a trade. The rep will have to find out what financial facts have changed but won't have to start from scratch, and there may be a financial plan already in place.

Before a customer does business with you, make sure that your service is so excellent that that customer never wants to do business with anyone else. This level of service must continue after the sale has been made. Many registered reps miss out on easy business because they don't stay in touch with customers who are favorably disposed to do more business. This is the essence of a successful program, one that could live off repeat business. The brokerage world, for the most part, manages this aspect of the business very well, as does the lending world, because lenders have to stay in touch with borrowers (for good business reasons, since they are watching their money). Banks have not successfully stayed in touch with depositors, and this is one area where they will have to improve.

This part of the marketing plan includes follow-up calls from the registered rep at least monthly. The rep can also use mailings to stay in touch with customers. Providing information about different topics of interest can keep the rep's name in front of customers and supplement his or her telephone calls. Offering seminars is another way to stay in touch and keep customers focusing on financial needs and objectives.

The Marketing Manager

The financial institution has to have someone who looks at the entire marketing picture and understands the complete master marketing plan. It is important to have a person perform this function for the whole institution and, in some cases, for each individual department. We will call this person the marketing manager, but the role and function vary according to the size and environment of the institution. In a community bank, this role could be performed by the president; in a large regional bank, the retail investment services program will probably have its own marketing manager; in a mid-size bank, the institution as a whole will have a marketing manager. This role is analogous to that performed by a product manager or brand manager in a manufacturing environment. The marketing manager is responsible for designing and delivering the product, as well as servicing all the needs of the customer base.

Without one person to oversee the entire marketing plan, various parts of the process will be designed by each participant, resulting in, at best, an unfocused program or, at worst, hostility among competing segments. Suppose the registered rep decides which target market he or she would like to serve. The rep asks the "marketing person" to design a brochure, which may or may not be aimed at the target market the rep has designated, which may or may not be the target market bank management has in mind. Then the bank president decides that there is a need for a particular product.

There needs to be one person who understands both the objectives of the retail investment services program and the long-term strategic plan of the organization as a whole. It is essential that this person understand how the retail investment services program fits into the whole strategic plan of the bank. He or she must also have the power to ensure that all parts of the program be made to fit together.

Fitting Retail Investment Services Into the Bank

When financial institutions start their own in-house retail investment services programs, they tend to make the culture of that program fit only too well within the banking culture—bankers are often tempted to structure the program too defensively. One way to counteract this tendency is to hire people with securities and marketing backgrounds who can help design a program that will reach out to pull in customers, including both current bank customers and outside customers.

There is likely to be a greater culture clash when a third-party provider comes into a traditional banking culture and introduces its marketing program. The TPP is an experienced, well-oiled marketing organization. The marketer looks at the bank's customer base and makes plans for a marketing campaign. And then we often see bankers resist, as though the third-party provider were the enemy. (The real enemies are the brokerage house and the bank down the street, as well as the various other competitors that are forcing the traditional bank to change its marketing approach.) Although bankers think they know their own customer base much better than any outside organization can, the third-party provider will usually know much more than the bank about the profile of an average bank customer and how that customer behaves.

Elsewhere in this book we stress the importance of choosing a third-party provider whose sales philosophy meshes with the sales philosophy of the financial institution. That is an important factor, but most TPPs have a stronger marketing program and orientation than the bank has. Be open-minded and use their expertise. Allow the third-party provider to provide information about your own customer base and use this information to design more effective marketing programs bankwide. Bank management can maximize the success of the retail investment services program by working with the marketing organization. The bank can gain additional benefits by applying some of these marketing methods to more traditional bank products.

In our experience, a retail investment services program needs to be initiated and managed by a company with marketing expertise and experience. This is one of the main reasons why having a local broker or insurance agent set up a desk or an office in your lobby may not result in a successful program. The person may have product knowledge and sales skills, but he or she probably cannot supply the kind of proactive marketing information and support that a professional organization can give you. Reaching out to customers is the essence of the marketing that will make your program flourish.

Marketing Information is the Future

Information is the key to marketing in the 1990s. The large mutual fund companies today have incredible amounts of information to drive their marketing process. In fact, they are virtually marketing machines. Look at the materials supplied by mutual fund companies. In addition to lavish, multimedia campaigns, they produce gorgeous, full-color ads, brochures, and sales literature that position their product to a well-defined target market. Their marketing plans could be used to teach state-of-the-art marketing at any university. However, beyond the visuals lie research capabilities far beyond the dreams of the banking industry, much less a community bank.

Many banks store a certain amount of customer information but they tend not to use it or know what to do with it. How do you take that information and use it to design a marketing system?

One of the most advanced marketing methods we know of for selling mutual funds involves comparing the customer's name and address on the bank's system to a publicly available database (for example, the Polk directory) and looking for matches. The Polk directory has public information about individuals you can cross-reference with the bank's customers. The marketing company will end up with a significant amount of information about each customer that matches. This information is then compared to the statistical profile of a mutual fund buyer. The end result is a list of the financial institution's customers ranked according to their potential for buying mutual funds. This is real target marketing.

It seems obvious beyond stating that the whole point of advertising is to produce results. We have talked to community bankers who place advertising in newspapers. When you ask what the results have been, some reply offhandedly that advertisements usually bring in some business, but they can't quantify it; maybe four or five new customers. Why invest the money in a marketing campaign if you aren't going to track and follow up on the results?

Bankers need to develop and implement the systems necessary to run more effective marketing programs, but they have to develop an orientation to marketing information first before they can build systems to acquire and process effective customer information. The bankers can start by tracking the results of each kind of marketing campaign the organization does. If your marketing campaign can't be tracked, you may need to devise another kind of marketing program. Campaigns must have objectives, and you must compare them to results achieved to obtain efficiency ratings. This is not high-tech marketing; it is a reasonable and frugal use of marketing resources.

A midwestern grocery chain has just designed one of the most brilliant marketing research campaigns we have ever seen. This store's new customer preferred card is also its check-cashing card. If you sign up for this card, there will always be certain items you can buy at a sale price. Furthermore, the card takes advantage of the zebra bar codes that identify products and their cost. Everything you buy on every trip to the store is recorded on its master database under your name, which is also cross-referenced to the financial information you supplied when you applied for the check-cashing facility. The grocery store can now compile a thorough, 100% correct profile of you, Mr. or Ms. Consumer. It knows what sales you respond to, how your financial situation cross-references to your taste in potato chips, and what kinds of advertising affect you. Imagine the kind of target marketing it can do with all of this data. (The real question is, what will the store do with all this data? Is it going to use it only for its own purposes, or sell it to vendors, or otherwise repackage it for use by others?)

This is the kind of information banks need to be competitive in the 1990s. Many community banks can't provide a list of their top depositors for a simple mailing or don't have the systems capacity to manage the customer information they already have. Some don't even have enough word-processing capability to do a customer mailing. Compare this marketing approach with that of the grocery store or a major mutual fund provider and decide for yourself which organizations have the competitive advantage.

Proactive Marketing and Customer Education

Customers do have immediate needs. A customer has a maturing CD. When the customer has cashed in the CD, he or she needs to do something with the money at that moment. When the person has a cashier's check in hand, it is probably too late to get that customer to invest in your retail investment services program, because he or she has already decided to do something else with the funds. Interestingly enough, there are entire bank alternative investment products programs structured around not approaching customers about their investment needs until they are walking out the door, check in hand. It will not be easy to make a success of a program with that kind of defensive sales philosophy! Defensive marketing focuses on trying to save lost relationships—and by that point, it's usually too late.

Current marketing research says it is not possible to persuade a customer to do business with you (whatever your business) until you have contacted that person eight or nine times. In our view, what is important in proactive marketing is reaching customers before they identify a need for investments or investment advice. You can't know ahead of time exactly when an individual customer will reach this point, so you have to stay in constant contact until the need arises. Customer education reaches out to satisfy the long-term needs of customers. We believe that this is how you build and truly strengthen customer relationships.

10

Referral Systems

A good referral system is critical to the success of an investment services area in a financial institution. Investments tend to be a subject that not only customer service reps and tellers but, in some cases, bank management are not comfortable with. These are products that most bank employees have never owned or had to deal with except to tell customers not to buy them. Banks traditionally have emphasized the risk and uncertainty of alternative investment products and have stressed the advantages of investing with FDIC-insured bank liabilities instead. Alternative investment products were products only for the wealthy or for risk-takers who were willing to accept the fact that principal could fluctuate and there was no FDIC insurance.

Now these same bankers are being asked to identify customers who may be potential investors in these products. It is no wonder that they are unsure of how to approach the customer and are insecure in their knowledge and understanding of how investments actually work. Yet they are asked to put their personal credibility as bankers on the line and send their customers to the bank investment rep, who may or may not be part of the organization.

The fastest way to motivate individuals to learn about a new program and become comfortable with the products is to offer them an incentive to do so. The referral incentive provides a stimulus in an environment where approaching customers with a suggestion or recommendation, particularly about a new product or service, is new. A referral program serves to signal employees that management has a sincere desire to educate employees and better serve the

needs of its customers. A good referral program allows all employees to participate. An incentive for the employee's extra effort and for a job well done makes
that employee feel he or she is being recognized for performance. It also helps
reinforce the idea that the new retail investment services program is not hurting
the bank, but in fact is an important part of the bank's future profitability.

A strong referral program is even more important when a third-party
provider enters an institution. The third-party provider has all of the negatives
mentioned earlier associated with retail investment services, plus the added
burden of coming into the institution as an outsider. Employees of the third-
party provider will be viewed as alien to the entire banking culture as well as to
the financial institution itself. Employees of the investment services areas are
sometimes treated as outsiders even when they are part of the same organization, as in the case of programs run by larger banks, but this is usually due to
the internal politics of the organization.

Bank employees at all levels have access to individuals who represent bona
fide prospects for investment products. All branch/bank employees should be
part of the referral system, from the branch manager and lending officer
through the teller line. These employees represent the customer contact group
that is the most important part of the organization's marketing efforts.
Customers are likely to listen to the suggestions of the bank employees they
know, respect and trust, and interact with daily. Suggestions from bank
employees can accomplish more than expensive advertising campaigns.
However, a formal marketing program will help to reinforce and support the
employee's efforts.

The Referral Program

There are three essential parts to a making a referral system work. They are:

1. management support
2. tracking system
3. program design

Management Support

We cannot over-emphasize the need for management support for the referral
program. Without management support, you will fail. (See Chapter 2 on management support.) Management at all levels throughout the organization
should participate, and actions speak much louder than words.

There are any number of ways to design a referral program, but, in the final
analysis, there is an optimal approach for your institution. The program that

works for you should both motivate the employee to behave as management desires and have the institution's commitment to make it work. Some examples of referral programs that appear to be strong and well-designed on paper actually make essentially no difference at all to program success because management commitment is lacking. This might be the same management that will tell you it supports the program whole-heartedly, but when you ask the direct question, "Do you personally have an account with the bank's program?" or "Who was the last person you referred to the bank's program?" the response will be an excuse. (But management wants you to know how strongly it supports the program!)

Tracking System

The second key to a successful program is the tracking system. Do not start a program that cannot be tracked and monitored. If you have told employees that they are going to receive an incentive, they must get what is due or the program will fail. Management should communicate clearly what the incentives are and how they are earned, and ensure that the incentive pay-outs (or prizes) are delivered to employees as promised. This communication will help generate awareness of the program, and that awareness will provide the constant positive feedback necessary to keep it going.

The tracking system can run on software that the financial institution already uses, or it can be a simple program that combines a spread sheet and some database management. It is essential to be able to sort information and create reports that will monitor the results of the program. Larger banks have started to create technologically sophisticated networking programs to send referrals electronically to branches, but that is not necessary for a successful tracking mechanism. It is necessary for the institution to be able to monitor the program and reward the results. Monitoring is the only way to tell if the desired behavior is being obtained, and the rewards will keep it happening.

Program Design

A poorly-designed program can survive if the first two keys—management support and an accurate tracking system—are in place, but the better your program is designed, the better the results will be. A program that motivates the behavior that management desires will not only bring greater results, but quicker results. In addition, if the program achieves management goals, management is more likely to support it. What the institution will quickly realize is that the referral system is adding value to the organization, not increasing cost.

In the beginning the referral program might be a stand-alone program, but it is far preferable to integrate the program into a much larger, bank-wide marketing or cross-sales program. There should be bank and branch awareness of the program's goals and procedures, and a genuine understanding of what role the retail investment program plays in the organization.

A well-structured referral program will be easily understood and predictable. To make sure it works, the reporting system should take the mystery out: it should show every referral made every month, every transaction, and all income. Incentives should be distributed in a timely fashion since enthusiasm can be dampened if there is no immediate gratification. "Timely" is defined as follows: as soon as possible to make it meaningful.

The time-honored principle used in structuring a program is to provide an incentive for the behavior you are trying to motivate. For this reason, it is preferable not to make the reward, or an increased reward, contingent on whether the sale is made. If you are teaching your employees to make referrals based on appropriate signals from customers, then the employee has done everything in his or her power to facilitate the transaction. The precise circumstances of the customer's situation or the skill of the registered rep are what determine whether or not the sale is made, not behavior attributable to the referring employee. Since the referring employee, therefore, has no further control over the situation, an incentive cannot be provided for behavior out of that employee's control.

Incentive programs work as follows: If you make a referral, you get X for the referral, and the behavior of the customer doesn't influence your incentive. Some programs take the referral to the next step and are structured so that a bona fide referral has been made when the appointment is *made* or *kept* (which is one step more than simply sending the customer over to the rep). Depending on how mature your program is and how many referrals your employees are sending your registered rep, you might consider this approach. This will make the person making the referral start to prequalify the prospective customer. A customer who has been prequalified is more likely to be interested in talking to the registered rep and listening to the presentation because the customer has either indicated interest and/or has a financial situation the information applies to.

To summarize, if you want to increase the number of referrals, provide incentives to employees who supply the customer name. If you want to decrease the number of referrals but get better referrals, provide the incentive when the appointment is made or kept. And if you want to target your referrals even further, you can provide incentives for a personal introduction from the employee to the rep. Still another possibility is paying a differential amount depending on whether invested funds are internal or external.

Keep in mind that the program structure you choose depends on what behavior you want and what fits your institution and its goals the best. For example, incentives need to be on a scale that fits in with overall bank compensation. In a large urban bank with a relatively high pay scale, $2 incentives might not provide much motivation for anyone, but introducing $50 incentives in a community bank might upset other areas of the bank. It is likely that the right program is a combination of all three types (pay incentive when teller supplies customer name, pay incentive when appointment is made, pay incentive for a personal introduction), with different incentives paid for different types of referrals.

Choosing the Appropriate Incentive Program

There is no right or wrong incentive. Here are some of the more commonly-used programs:

- merchandise
- vacation trips
- dinners
- cash
- contests
- "attaboys" (recognition)
- points towards a variety of prizes

However, as we stated earlier, simple is better, which means to most people paying out in cash. Many people believe that money is the best motivator; in doing our research about the best incentives to offer, money was the big winner. "Give people cash and pay out monthly," is what we heard. "Employees need to know that if they make a referral, they're going to get money." All of this is true, in our opinion, but not for the obvious reason.

As most people have learned in organizational behavior classes, money does not in itself motivate. However, money is something of value that is simple and basic, easy to understand, and easy to track. In fact, if you owe me money, I will track it for you. A referral program that uses cash as the incentive is probably the easiest to implement, but that does not mean it is the best program for your organization. Some of the most common incentives are listed below.

Merchandise

With a merchandise program, the employee gets points, and these points can be saved or used to purchase a consumer item such as a watch, microwave, or television. The rationale for this program's effectiveness is that a $30 after-tax monthly incentive does not really seem like a significant amount, whereas by accumulating points the employee can set a larger, more desirable goal. The merchandise program will work best if the employee sets a goal for a large item that needs a significant number of referral points to acquire. In this way, not only is the prize more meaningful, but the employee must make a larger number of referrals to obtain it. Another side benefit is that employees always remember how they got such items, which reminds them to continue to make referrals. Cash has a tendency to get used like other compensation the employee receives; it gets lost in day-to-day expenses and does not remain separate and special. However, remember to keep the program manageable; it is possible to set up programs with elaborate gifts and rewards that can become very difficult to track and monitor and could end up requiring a full-time plan administrator.

Recognition

"Attaboys" or recognition can have a strong influence. A program of systematic recognition can be effective. Systematic means reporting the number of referrals made and who made them. This can then be followed up with a simple note from the bank president, thanking the employee for his or her efforts in making this program a success. In some circumstances the note would be more effective coming from an employee's senior or executive vice president, because the employee might see it in a career-advancing light. This can be as powerful as paying cash for referrals, or more so, depending on how many notes get written. While this type of an incentive seems to be the least costly because there is no cash outlay, it is the most costly to implement in terms of time—which is what makes it so effective. Registered reps should also go out of their way to praise and thank the employees who make referrals.

Finally, do not overlook one of the oldest, simplest motivators there can be: a thank you to the referring employee and a commendation to his or her boss. This works best when all employees (registered reps and tellers) work for the same organization, rather than in the case of a third-party provider. However, the theory is the same. If the head of the investment services area is known to praise customer service reps or loan officers to the "big boss," word spreads like wildfire through the organization. A little thank you and some recognition never lose their power to motivate.

A Little Something Extra

Pizza, donuts, and flowers provided by the registered rep, branch management, or the bank also have their place. Personal attention and recognition for goals achieved or a large number of quality referrals—whatever the reason—can make a significant contribution to enthusiasm and morale among the troops in the branch. However, it is an unusual organization where this type of incentive is sufficient. These things should be adjuncts to a systematic referral program.

Contests

There are other ways to structure effective referral programs. A large financial institution can organize a referral program like a sweepstakes. The referring employee gets a sweepstakes ticket for every referral made. The ticket has a scratch-off section, which might include only a sweepstakes entry, but might be an instant winner for some significant prize. Such a sweepstakes program would typically have a theme which relates to the grand prize and instant prizes.

On the other hand, one organization rewards its CSRs for the most number of referrals that *don't* lead to sales. The rationale is that the person who refers the most number who don't buy is also referring the most number who do buy.

Contests can be effective within the context of a larger program, but they generally cannot constitute the main source of support to the program. The main drawback to making contests central to the referral program is that people then participate only when contests are running. In a typical contest, there will be a 25% spike in referrals, with 10% of those eligible giving the most referrals and 50% giving none. Contest prizes can include dinners, barbecue grills, lobsters, and other prizes.

Prizes

Referral programs can be set up awarding a weekly prize for the most referrals in the preceding week. The prize can be a gift certificate for merchandise or lunch at a local fast-food restaurant. Each facility can award this prize. All referrals from the preceding week are put in a hat, and the name of one employee is drawn. This prize can be the same as the award for most referrals. Then add a monthly drawing. It can be structured to enter an employee as many times as he or she made referrals or to enter each employee's name only once. The prize for this monthly drawing should be significant in comparison to the other prize, such as lunch at a local restaurant that would be thought of as something special. Better yet, maybe the rep takes the winner to lunch, talks about how the employee got the referrals, and works with him or her to get the next one. A great kick-off method, at the inception of the program or every Monday, is to offer $10 cash to the first person who makes a referral. This gets them started.

All of the incentives discussed are short-term methods to get referral programs up and running. The point of these programs, as stated in the beginning, is to bring about desired behavior. Unless a referral program can become totally systematic and ingrained in the behavior of the institution, it will eventually run out of steam.

Once you have created the behavior you desire and have had employees do it long enough so that it becomes part of their daily habits, the next step is to incorporate that behavior into job descriptions and the formal review process. Employees know that, instead of getting something extra for making a referral, making referrals is an expected part of their job function; their reviews will reflect it if they fail to make them. This is the step that moves the program from being above and beyond into being part of an employee's daily routine. When it has become second nature to employees to refer business to the registered rep, then you are on your way to great success with your investment services program. This is the point at which you could say that a sales orientation has been introduced to your organization.

Who Makes Referrals

Referral programs, for the most part, have been described in terms of the tellers, customer service reps, and other first-level customer contact personnel who constitute the front line of the bank's customer relationships. These individuals are the most likely to have day-to-day interaction with the customer; these are the people who populate community, rural, and branch banks.

However, banks have to face the issue of paying other employees—lending, trust, and mortgage officers, for example—who are also in a position to identify prospects for retail investments and make them aware that their institution offers such services. If an institution encourages and pays for referrals, there should be a pay-out no matter what the level of employee. The program will grow and gain momentum faster if employees throughout all levels of the institution make referrals, are aware of and use investment services, and recommend these services to their friends, family, and customers. A number of institutions recommend that branch managers be paid a small fee for every referral made by a branch employee, with payouts to be made on a schedule that allows the amount to be significant, such as quarterly. However, the pay-out amounts become less significant as you work your way up through the personnel ranks (and pay-scale).

The next question is, should registered reps be required to make referrals to other areas of the bank? One institution we encountered required each investment rep to refer enough customers to open 200 new quality checking accounts annually. This institution does the marketing necessary to draw in foreign customers to the investment services unit and expand the bank's base of customers. The program manager believes that increasing checking account deposits is a way to lower the overall cost of funds for the organization and, therefore, lower the rates on loans and still maintain the spread. Using the retail investment services program to achieve this strategic goal makes perfect business sense. This is one example, but there are many more.

It is very important for the registered rep to cross-sell bank products. The rep may have excuses as to why he or she can't, but those excuses resemble those from customer service reps as to why they can't cross-sell investment products. A little incentive and a lot of education go a long way towards improving cross-selling skills and getting both sides involved. In fact, the best way to motivate more senior people in the organization to give referrals to the rep is to have the rep give one first.

Investment reps in some organizations complain that their referrals to lending and mortgage areas are not paid (or recognized), whereas, when the referral goes the other way, the lending vice president can get paid as much as $50. In a more relationship-oriented institution, the registered rep may be required to make two referrals a month to other areas of the institution. Another bank circulates a monthly list that shows all referrals made in all directions, although without dollar amounts. This promotes a feeling of teamwork and shows others in the bank which individuals and areas are trying hardest to win new relationships for the institution.

The real answer to the question of whether reps should be paid to make referrals, and the solution to the fact that higher-level employees find pay-out amounts to be less significant, is to encourage a spirit of cooperation and sales-orientation bank-wide. What the rep can do for the lending officer or mortgage officer that's more valuable than any pay-out is to demonstrate that doing business with the investment services unit can result in increased business for other areas of the bank. The rep needs to show the lending officer that he or she adds value to the customer and the customer relationship overall. There are really three aspects to this increased value. First, when the registered rep sends a customer to another area of the bank, the employee receiving the referral is happy for the increased business. Second, the registered rep provides investment services which the customer finds valuable. Finally, the customer relationship overall is strengthened as a customer does business with more parts of a financial institution.

In the long run, there is no substitute for the kind of personal relationships that smart registered reps build with the employees of the bank. In fact, the smart rep thinks of bank employees as his or her customers, and makes a point of socializing with the customer service reps, understanding the loan officer's function, and coordinating in general with all the functions of personal banking. (See Chapter 7 on selling in a bank.)

Informal Referral Systems

A financial institution that does not institute a referral system to promote the investment services area is missing an opportunity to support the program. However, there are many institutions in this category. Employees should still be encouraged to make referrals, and the registered rep should do what he or she can to promote the program. When an employee makes the first referral to the registered rep, he or she is testing the rep and the program. If the customer contact goes well and if the employee is given feedback about the customer, that employee will probably be willing to make more referrals. On the other hand, if the rep doesn't keep the lines of communication open, his or her business is doomed to fail. The bank employee doesn't begin by providing every referral he or she has. If the first couple of referrals don't go well, the rep will never get the rest of them.

Successful investment reps know that the only way to make a success of the program is to make yourself such an important part of the team that referrals go easily in both directions. Even when the referrals to the bank are not paid or required, it is essential to the success of the program that the investment rep make them whenever possible.

The Regulator's View

The NASD is very clear on the subject of splitting commissions with unlicensed persons: it is not allowed under any circumstances. That means that a referral program may not be structured so that an unlicensed person (such as a teller) making a referral receives a referral fee proportionate with the size of the investment made (such as receiving 5% of the gross commission generated by a sale). To the NASD, that would be splitting a commission.

The OCC guidelines take this one step further for national banks. The guidelines state, "Bank management should ensure that compensation programs do not operate as an incentive for salespeople to sell retail nondeposit investment products over a more suitable option. If tellers participate in referral programs that include compensation features, banks should not base such compensation on the success of the sale."[1] This is generally interpreted to mean that not only may salespeople not receive a percentage of the commission, they may not receive an incentive payment based on whether or not a sale was made.

---

1 "Retail Nondeposit Investment Sales," Washington, D.C.: U.S. Comptroller of the Currency, Administrator of National Banks, 1992, p. 6.

Who Pays for the Referrals

It is obvious that referrals are paid out of the income generated by sales of alternative investment products. At what point the referral expense is subtracted determines essentially who pays. If the referral fee is subtracted before the profits are divided, then every party who participates in the profits pays a percentage share of the referral fee. In the case of a third-party provider, if the referral fee is subtracted first, the result is to split the fee among the third-party provider organization, the bank, and the registered rep. Sometimes the registered rep is required to pay the fee out of his or her commissions.

Determining What to Pay

How does an institution decide what to pay? This is a subject that financial institutions have been debating for years. Typical amounts paid out for making a referral range from $2 to $10, with an additional amount, maybe $5 to $10, paid out if an appointment is made or if a brokerage account is opened. To a $7 per hour employee, three good referrals in a given month can be equal to an extra hour's pay. But be aware of the tax consequences of incentive pay-outs (amounts inevitably look more meager after taxes).

A number of large banks who own their own programs pay $40 to $50 per referral and have a flourishing investment area as a result. Is that too much? Obviously these banks don't think so, but we assume they have done their own analysis of how much they make from each investment and feel comfortable paying this larger amount. The bank that pays amounts of this kind is definitely the bank that is committed to its investment program and wants it to be successful. This is not a bank running a defensive program.

Individual bank programs must do their own analysis and decide on amounts. What if the investment amount is too small to justify such a large referral fee? When the referral fee is as large as $50, there have to be investment minimums large enough to generate the income necessary to cover the referral fee, such as $5,000 for a mutual fund trade.

Some of the banks that still pay $50 are considering reducing the amount. Receiving a $50 referral fee must be a sweet experience for a teller or customer service rep, but it seems the days of such programs are now numbered in most cases. This reduction is being driven by the fact that investment products in these days of low interest rates are not nearly as hard a sell or as alien a product as they might have seemed some years ago, when this industry was in its infancy. Referral programs have worked, and both employees and customers are becoming more educated.

What is it worth to a bank to receive a referral from a customer service rep that results in a $100,000 mutual fund or annuity investment with money that comes from outside the institution? That investment could well result in a gross commission of approximately $4,000. How much would you pay in marketing costs, seminars, advertisements, or customer entertainment to earn that kind of fee? Would you pay 3% of the amount earned, or $120? What if the entire $100,000 came from foreign funds?

Bankers will generally agree with the trend of this argument until they realize that an employee who makes two referrals per month for $120 each over the course of a year will receive an additional $2,880 in income annually—which could equate to something like a 15% to 25% increase in income to the low-paid employee. People from the brokerage business, where cash bonuses are the norm and registered reps openly discuss compensation and pay-outs, find this kind of pay-out normal, but there's something about those amounts being paid out to a teller that makes bankers profoundly uneasy.

The problem is not that the banker necessarily resents the lower-level people getting paid something extra. The problem is that amounts like this paid out in incentive compensation can distort a bank-wide compensation system which has been carefully worked out over the years. The traditional culture of banking believes in pay hierarchy, and bankers are unhappy to see a new product produce "bulges" in pay for certain employees who are traditionally at the bottom of the pay scale. A teller who sees a steady stream of customers all day and is therefore in a position to make numerous referrals might receive more total compensation than a bank officer who does not make referrals. Even when higher-level employees receive incentive payments, their compensation will not be affected as much on a percentage basis. Furthermore, CSRs might find themselves being paid significant percentages of their compensation to support one part of a bank's business. Although we laid out the reasons in this chapter why we think it makes good business sense to pay incentives for a business which is unfamiliar to so many bank employees, the fact remains that it is only one part of a bank's business. The branch would not be well served if branch employees neglected other parts of their job functions to focus exclusively on sending referrals to the retail investment services program.

Cross-selling

What if one then introduced referral and incentive systems for other bank products? To some of us, this seems like the best solution of all. Incentive-based pay has become a hot topic lately, and not only in banks, as one way to help introduce a more sales- and service-oriented culture into an organization. The referral system introduced for the investment services area can provide the bridge to introducing a bankwide referral system. A truly incentive-based system would see base pay cut and a significant proportion of compensation for all bank employees resulting from incentive pay. Pay-per-referral would diminish in importance and other forms of incentive-based pay would be used. Making referrals from and to all parts of the financial institution would become increasingly important and an important part of each employee's formal review process, from CEO to teller.

This is not a new topic; it has been talked about for years. Some banks have implemented cross-sales programs, shrunk base salaries, and begun to reward employees based on performance. The problem many banks have with paying incentives for opening checking accounts, referring mortgage customers, or introducing customers to other parts of the bank, is that most banks can't quantify the value of many of their products. They don't have good cost accounting systems in place, and, because most of these products are well established, it is very difficult to create such a system. Determining profitability is easier for investment services because of the nature of the business and the fact that most organizations are adding it today. On a new product or service, it is much easier to determine marginal cost and profitability, which makes compensation and incentive decisions much easier.

One of the tasks that banks must complete if they are to reinvent the retail bank is to determine precisely how profitable each product is. How profitable are checking accounts? If asking those questions produces information that leads to startling conclusions about the businesses banks should be in, no amount of rhetoric about traditional banking can change the hard decisions that banks must make if they are to remain profitable—either make that product profitable, or stop offering it. Once banks have determined the profitability of a product, they can determine how much they are willing to pay to sell one more unit of that product. Banks can use retail investment services as their model, whether or not traditional bankers realize it.

Let us conclude by offering a final word of caution. When you introduce your new program, tell the employees that the referral program has a deadline; tell them that if it works it might be continued, and if it doesn't it will either be changed or terminated. This should increase the rate at which you start to receive referrals. If you do not receive the behavior you anticipated, you have the opportunity to change or finetune the program. People in general hate change. If you tell them at the outset that change is possible, they will at least expect it. Your brighter employees will view this as a game and will look for the loopholes. This is fine if the program is well-designed and you create the behavior you want, but if you have holes in the program, these employees will find them. An example of this is the employee who was offered an incentive for each referral name provided. This employee ran a bank customer list and filled out a referral card for each customer. Needless to say, if that had been what you wanted, you didn't need to pay a referral fee for the name, since the bank already had the name. Make sure that you clearly define the behavior you are trying to motivate, and then let your best employees try to win the game.

Monitoring the Referral Program

How will you know if the referral program is successful? This is an important question for programs as they move beyond initial implementation. There should be an initial spurt of referrals because employees will think of the easiest ones first and will be enthusiastic and motivated as a result of the initial training. In the long run, the financial institution and/or third-party provider have to track, report on, and monitor referrals and referral results in the same way that every other aspect of the program should be tracked and monitored. If the program is very successful but referrals are down, there is probably room for the program to be even more successful. If referrals are down, what are the reasons? It could be due to new employees who have not yet attained a comfort level with these products, or because there are competing referral programs, or a variety of other reasons. It is important to isolate the reasons for changes in results, and then take corrective action.

Training for Referrals

Tellers often make referrals enthusiastically for new checking account programs or other bank products that they understand and believe in. That same level of enthusiasm for alternative investment products is often lacking, especially at the outset of a program. The whole referral program should be designed to help employees overcome the uncertainty of dealing with these new and unfamiliar products. However, the referral program does not run itself. The training that is essential for every component of retail investment services is also important in teaching employees to make referrals.

Generate Awareness

At the outset of the investment services program, you have to generate awareness. Some of the key concepts employees need to know include the following:

- Demonstrate the benefits of alternative investment products
- Identify who is a likely prospect

- Outline what signals to listen or watch for from a customer or in processing a customer transaction
- Explain how to make the referral

Employees need to feel comfortable that the services they are recommending are appropriate for their customers and need to have confidence that the registered rep will offer good service. Bank employees are happy to promote alternative investment products when they understand the features and benefits of those products as well as they understand the features and benefits of checking accounts. It is the responsibility of those running the program to provide them with that understanding. The faster you can get "buy-in" from bank employees, the faster you will get your program up and running. Finally, employees need to know the process by which the referral program works.

It would be a mistake to assume that any level of bank employee automatically knows how to recognize a potential customer for investment services. Although general awareness of the investment world is probably higher now than it has ever been, we strongly encourage every institution to institute training at all levels. Our focus here, however, will be on training the "front-line" employees: customer service reps, tellers, and those who open new accounts.

Performing Ongoing Training

Once a referral program has been put in place, ongoing commitment and monitoring are important. You have to continue to reinforce its goals and objectives and perform ongoing training, both to keep employees focused and the momentum going and to contend with the normal turnover among employees on the front line. Spending an occasional 15 minutes with each of these employees will go a long way to help that employee understand what the rep really does. It will also add the personal connection that will make the employee want to help the rep.

A regular method of communication such as a newsletter or meeting can help promote continued involvement. Update topics can include the status of current participants (winners and big winners), techniques that have worked, ideas for cross-selling other products, and current and future marketing campaigns. Using a newsletter to announce winners, or announcing winners in meetings, serves to provide more recognition and appreciation. It can also serve to build a spirit of team rivalry and peer pressure. Different branches can have contests to see who generates the most referrals, offering those old favorites of pizza and donuts as prizes.

The Training Program

A "certification" program for CSRs and tellers is another way to provide training. The employees need to attend a training program given on multiple days, with a final exam designed to verify that they have absorbed the materials. The course and exam are not designed to present intellectual challenge but to ensure that everyone has uniform awareness of the program. Oftentimes, saying there is going to be an exam is like asking them to pay attention. Requiring certification is a way of ensuring that all affected employees have learned about the products and that new employees are provided with proper education before being asked to make referrals. Successful completion of the course is what allows the individual to be registered to participate in the referral program. It also ensures that any new employees learn about the program and receive the same information as employees who have been at the institution for a longer time.

The training program should cover the following areas:

- why the bank is offering alternative investment products
- how the alternative investment products program works
- what products are offered
- how the referral program works:
  - objectives of the referral program
  - referral program incentives and pay-outs
  - how to fill out and process a referral card
  - how to spot a referral candidate
  - what to say to a referral candidate
- if the bank is using a third-party provider, it should also include:
  - how this relationship works
  - why the particular third-party provider was chosen

"Do's" and "don'ts" must be clearly presented without making employees feel intimidated or reluctant to talk about alternative investment products. They need to know that restrictions are due to regulatory requirements and that it is important to understand the rules.

Employees need to hear that the objectives of the referral program are to identify customers who buy investment products, stop deposit loss to other institutions, generate fee income, bring in new money from outside institutions, and cross-sell all bank products. These objectives are not inherently obvious to employees. The usual initial reaction is fear that the program will hurt the bank.

Recognizing a Potential Customer

Employees need to recognize that certain signals could indicate a receptive candidate for alternative investment products. Your customers will tell you when they are ready to be responsive to suggestions about alternative investment products by expressing themselves in some of the ways described in Figure 10.1.

Mentioning Alternative Investment Products

There are other times to mention alternative investment products. For instance:

- When a customer service rep is completing a loan application with a client who lists savings bonds, IRAs, and CDs as assets
- When cashing in a savings bond, CD, money market account, or savings account for a customer
- When closing an account for a customer
- When a customer asks about savings bonds
- When a customer states that he or she is no longer eligible to make IRA contributions
- When a customer mentions a need for investment income or guaranteed lifetime income
- When a customer makes an inquiry or statement about interest rates on investment products
- If a customer has a larger-than-average balance in a NOW account, checking account, money market account, savings account
- If a customer deposits checks from stock brokerage or investment firms, or deposits dividend checks from stocks
- If you see a customer studying the rate board

While providing service to the customer, the CSR should mention the investment department, and look for customer interest. If the employee becomes aware of one of the situations described in Figure 10.1, he or she should take that customer over to the registered rep and make the introduction. The CSR should fill out a referral card and give it to the rep. If a registered rep is not available, the CSR should give the referral card to one of them at the first opportunity. The CSR must let the customer know that the registered rep will call. In return, the CSR receives a referral payment, recognition in the branch, and the customer's respect for being knowledgeable and having his or her best interest in mind. The CSR should ask commercial customers these same questions and look for the opportunity to make commercial referrals.

Figure 10.1 Listening for Customer Clues

- Unhappiness or frustration with low rates on passbook accounts or CDs
  - "Is that your best rate?"
  - "Could I get a better rate if I added more money?"
  - "Did you know that XYZ Bank down the street is paying a higher rate?"
  - "Rates are really low!"
  - "Do you know of any other products that would give me a higher rate?"
- Dislike of taxes
  - "I'm taking a beating on my taxes."
  - "I can't believe what I have to pay on my income taxes!"
- Lump sums from retirement or severance payouts
  - "I just got laid off and will have to take my 401(k) money."
  - "I lost my job and don't know how to figure out whether to take my pension money now or leave it with the company."
- Sale of an asset (such as a home, business, or stamp collection)
  - "I just got a sales contract on my house."
  - "I got a really low price for my condo, but at least I won't have to worry about it any more."
- Receiving a large settlement, whether a law suit or an inheritance
  - Parent or uncle dies
  - New widow or widower
- Response to advertising or marketing
  - "I noticed your card in with my checking account statement."
  - "I saw the ad in the newspaper."
- Income needs
  - "I need a higher rate than this to pay the rent!"
  - "I can't live on these rates."
- Future needs
  - "How will I ever be able to retire?"
  - "I need to save money to send my children to college."
- Interested in investments and the stock market
  - "What's the market doing today?"
  - "XYZ stock is up."
  - "Do you sell mutual funds?"
  - "Do you have discount brokerage services?"
  - "I was reading in *Money Magazine* . . ."

The same signals and situations might come up outside the bank environment with family members or at social situations. Employees can use the same responses: "My bank offers tax-deferred annuities that might apply to this situation and help solve the problem. Could I have John Doe, our registered rep, call you?"

A note on training other levels of bank employees

The investment services area should arrange to give seminars to all levels of bank employees covering the same basic topics covered in the training program given to CSRs, making adjustments as necessary for the level of education and financial sophistication. However, it is wise not to make assumptions about any employee's level of expertise concerning alternative investment products.

Any lending officer who covers small businesses is a candidate for making referrals about 401(k) plans and other pension investments, key person insurance, or financial planning. There are business account customers who frequently move or shift short-term, jumbo CD money; these should be referred to the investment area.

11

Due Diligence

What Is Due Diligence?

ue diligence is not an easy topic for the average person to understand, nor does the industry seem to have agreed on a definition. We searched through industry literature and reference manuals but were unable to come up with a definition for due diligence. Everyone knows you need to do it, but no one has defined it. Due diligence is an evaluation process, which is why it is so hard to define; it is often confused with other forms of evaluation. This evaluation is performed to gain an understanding of the investment (its soundness and creditworthiness) and the risk of the investment (how the risk affects the soundness and creditworthiness of the investment). The due diligence process is very important when discussing alternative investment products, because those products have certain characteristics and certain risks. However, do not be misled into thinking that because we can study risk, we can eliminate it.

Due diligence can be described as the process, performed in a reasonable fashion, of seeking to understand risk and how risk affects any or all of the concerned parties. Due diligence must be done on all of these parties if the financial institution wants to provide optimal service to its customer and, at the same time, minimize its liability. To understand risk, you must analyze and evaluate the soundness or creditworthiness of the following parties:

- the investment itself
- the company issuing a security or other investment product
- the firm marketing the product, including a third-party marketing company
- the investor

You must be thoroughly familiar with each of these parties, both for investing in general, and specifically for the investment you are considering. Notice that we used the word "reasonable" to define how much is enough; this is similar to the "prudent man" rule of fiduciary responsibility. What do we mean by soundness or creditworthiness?

Determining Soundness or Creditworthiness

If we were talking about the process of underwriting a new issue security for a particular company, the underwriter would be responsible for performing the due diligence on the issue before the company brought it to market. The underwriter would verify that the information being reported to the public was in fact correct, the facts were presented fairly, no material facts were being withheld, the assumptions used to create the projection were in fact reasonable, and that the all statements and claims made in the report were true. Furthermore, the underwriter would also attest that, if the plan were carried out as proposed, the projected returns were likely to be realized. This does not mean the underwriter warrants the sales projections as stated in the plan. What it does mean is that the factual information underlying those projections can and should be verified. The underwriter has an obligation to examine the books, records, and business plan of a corporation before it brings a security issue to market, so that an investor can know the full facts and risk of the investment before he or she commits any money.

Most companies have no desire to publicize their entire business plan, since competitors are always watching. Information meant for public release will certainly leave out proprietary details. There is a conflict between the potential investor's need to know and the need to restrict some information. But how can an investor make an informed decision without all the facts? The markets have adopted a compromise method of dealing with these issues. The company shares proprietary information with the issue's underwriter, and it is the responsibility of the underwriter to assure the investor in all of the four ways listed below.

1. The due diligence process has been conducted in a reasonable manner.
2. To the best of their ability, what is stated is correct.

3. The investment is as it has been presented.
4. The risks are as stated.

When the underwriter can make these claims, the due diligence process is complete.

For example, if this had been a privately-held company going public, the underwriter would verify that the reported sales numbers were in fact the actual sales numbers from the period in question. If the company stated that an escrow account had been set up with a stated amount of money or securities in it, the underwriters would have to verify that the account had actually been set up. If one were talking about alternative investment products, part of the due diligence process would be verifying an insurance company's assertion that it had no junk bonds in its portfolio. For mutual funds, there must be verification of a mutual fund company's earnings and method of calculation; certain independent third-parties (such as Morningstar) usually provide this service.

For a financial institution starting a retail investment services program, one of the most important parts of the due diligence function is performed on any third-party provider it is proposing to hire, because, later on, the financial institution will rely on the third-party provider to provide due diligence on the products it provides to the financial institution's customers. If the third-party provider tells you it never handles customer funds, then the financial institution should verify the process of how a customer pays for a transaction, how the funds really flow, and compare this to what is stated. This is not to say that companies lie or even intentionally mislead an investor; however, misunderstanding either an investment or its risk can easily lead to loss.

Suitability

The question of whether or not a particular investment is appropriate for a particular investor is called suitability, and it is generally not considered to be a due diligence issue. However, in order to determine what is in fact a suitable investment for a specific investor, the registered rep must perform a process like that of due diligence on the investor to determine the credit standing and financial situation of the investor as well as his or her tolerance for risk.

The suitability of a particular investment for an individual investor is one of the greatest concerns of all the regulators. It is discussed again in Chapter 13 on compliance. A regulator will not ask a registered rep if he or she performed the necessary due diligence on that customer before the investment was recommended or made. The regulator is more likely to ask if this was a *suitable* investment—did the rep follow a process of getting to know the customer before making the recommendation? Determining the suitability of a particular invest-ment for a particular customer is really the heart of the investment business, and it is something the regulators always ask about.

Due diligence is more than just evaluating a mutual fund or insurance com-pany; it is actually a much larger process. The due diligence process looks for a high degree of probability that the companies or products recommended can deliver the features claimed for them, and make good on implicit promises about benefits. Due diligence also requires that the investor has had the implicit risk explained to him or her and understands it. This kind of rational approach evaluates a number of factors, but of course *the due diligence process supplies no guarantee.*

The Due Diligence Process

The due diligence process actually started the minute your organization started talking about offering alternative investment products. Your retail investment services program depends on the quality of the products offered, and any dis-cussion of the program should include discussions on how products are chosen and evaluated. The way your financial institution decides to structure its pro-gram—whether you form your own broker/dealer or hire a third-party provider—will determine how you approach due diligence. Each decision about structure has a bearing on due diligence. What varies is who performs the due diligence initially and who reviews it later. If you are running your own program in-house, you will have to provide your own due diligence; if you are using a third-party provider, the third-party provider will provide the due dili-gence, and you will review it. However the program is structured, it is the financial institution's responsibility to ensure that the due diligence process has been performed adequately.

Doing the Due Diligence on the Third-Party Provider

If your financial institution decides to institute a program run by a third-party provider, selecting that company is critically important to the success of your program. This information has been covered at length in Chapter 6. Figure 6.1 constitutes a due diligence worksheet on the most important factors to consider.

The Role of Third-Party Providers

If you are running a managed program, it means that your financial institution monitors and approves the work done by the third-party provider, rather than performs original research. If your organization is using a dual-employee program, you might want to take a more active role in the actual decision-making process. Although the third-party provider is still in a position to provide you with all of the necessary information for either type of program, when your program is dual-employee, the registered rep is actually an employee of the financial institution, rather than of the third-party provider, and that implies an even greater level of responsibility on the part of the financial institution. Even when you are relying on a third-party to provide you with due diligence, it is part of your organization's responsibility to your customer to oversee that process and to ensure that it has been performed to your satisfaction.

The duties of the third-party provider to the financial institution, and the financial institution's responsibilities to the customer, include providing the following services:

Mutual Funds and Annuities:
- Approve all product groups sold through the third-party provider.
- Approve all product-provider organizations that sponsor or issue products.
- Approve the suitability (due diligence process) for investors.
- Assure that the third-party provider is in compliance with all securities and insurance regulations

Fixed-Income Products:
- Approve all product groups sold through the third-party provider.
- Establish minimum credit criteria by product type.
- Approve the suitability (due diligence process) for investors.

Equities, Precious Metals, Futures, and Options Products:
- Approve the suitability (due diligence process) for investors. This is critically important for these products, which are for more sophisticated investors.
- Provide service by one of three methods: 1) perform the due diligence yourself in-house, if you have the capability; 2) subscribe to a service that provides due diligence for this kind of investment; or 3) if you have determined that this product is in general suitable for your customer, ask the customer to sign a form stating that this is an unsolicited investment and that he or she understands that it might be considered a risky investment.

If the third-party provider provides you with the information, you should understand how it is done and review updates. The reports should come on an as-needed basis, which means quarterly at a minimum. There is nothing magic about quarterly updates, but a three-month period is long enough for new information to emerge, whereas little changes month to month. Monthly updates would involve a constant analytic process to little end. Annual updates don't provide quite enough information; companies can change dramatically within a year.

If your financial institution has done appropriate due diligence in selecting a third-party provider, then you should have confidence in the products chosen by third-party provider. If you don't have that confidence, we suggest redoing the due diligence process on the third-party provider to determine why.

As a final note, the bank has to accept the responsibility for ensuring that the bank has met all of the regulatory requirements established by its regulators. Do not leave this up to the third-party provider.

In-house Programs

For an in-house program, or when the organization is using a third-party provider only for legal reasons, we recommend that a financial institution form a due diligence committee. The point of this is not to be bureaucratic but to assemble the expertise needed to make informed decisions. Similar in importance and responsibility to the loan committee, this group will establish the policies and procedures necessary for the alternative investment products program. However, just as the loan committee doesn't make loans, this group doesn't make the investments. Rather, it establishes the guidelines to operate by. Even a community bank would be well-served by a due diligence committee.

The committee members would include the compliance officer, investment principals from the bank, representatives from sales or distribution and in-house trading, a senior credit or loan officer, and an analyst. The most senior people possible should serve on the committee. The mission of the committee should include all of the following:

- manage the due diligence process
- review the research on products (whoever actually performs the research)
- choose the product providers (which might include a third-party provider)
- advise on product distribution
- establish investor suitability requirements
- insure regulatory compliance
- insure proper licensing

The due diligence committee allows the bank to manage the investment program proactively, reduce the probability of liability, and confront any problems in a professional and timely fashion. The committee should meet regularly. As the program begins, it should meet as often as needed to make the appropriate decisions; in an ongoing program, monthly meetings will probably be sufficient. The committee should meet at least quarterly to evaluate all products offered.

Products

Mutual Funds

Every institution needs to develop a preferred list of mutual funds based on a rational assessment of several significant factors. These factors are derived from an analysis of quantifiable historical data, on both absolute and relative bases.

Organizations approach the task of developing a preferred list of mutual funds in a variety of ways. The customer's best interest is not best served by approving mutual funds on the basis of bigger is better, or by choosing the best-known fund families and recommending the entire fund family. For a mutual fund company, there is minimal marginal cost to adding a new fund to an already existing product line; therefore, the majority of the largest fund companies have gone to great pains over the years to offer every kind of fund imaginable, from short-term municipal bond funds to equity growth funds specific to certain regions of the world. It is unlikely that any given fund family can be excellent with every type of fund, although some of them have done very well with a broad variety of funds.

The best way to derive a preferred list is to evaluate as many of the different funds as possible, on their own merits, and to select the two or three best funds in each category. The broader the range of customers you are servicing, the broader the range of different categories. This list is the preferred list and might have up to 70 different funds (these are individual funds, not fund families). The funds that are most often represented on this list will then tell you which fund families to choose if that becomes important to your investor. You should also have a "select preferred" list, which consists of what you consider to be the single best fund in each category, without giving any consideration to what fund family it is a part of or whether there are other funds in the same family that are also on your preferred list.

Customers vary in how much interest they have in selecting the mutual fund they will invest in; this is a factor in deciding how many different funds you will recommend. Some customers like to look at more than one fund, and make the final selection. (Show them the two or three choices in the preferred list, and allow them to pick out the one they like the best.) Some customers prefer to stick with large fund families, because they anticipate wanting to move their funds from one fund to another within the family. Some customers might be putting away IRA money for retirement and simply want the best growth or aggressive growth fund you can recommend. In that case, recommend the fund from the "select preferred" list, which will be the best fund for that category.

The significant factors for mutual funds are listed below and include a brief description. These factors are discussed at greater length in Chapter 4 on products.

Return history. The total return of a fund over the short and long term.

Volatility risk. A measure of the variability of a fund's returns over time; that is, how stable have the fund's returns been from year to year.

Market risk. The sensitivity of a fund to factors independent of the securities in the fund. Such factors include changes in the business cycle, inflation, unemployment, war, and political events.

Each risk measure is evaluated both on an absolute basis and relative to the risk characteristics of other funds in a given category. All else being equal, only those funds with relatively low risk profiles should be given further consideration.

Expenses and fees. The annual expense ratio of a fund indicates what percentage of fund assets are withdrawn each year to pay the costs of operation.

Consistency of purpose. Has the objective of the fund been stable over the life of the fund?

Consistency of holdings. Occasionally a fund may hold securities that are not consistent with the objective of the fund. Only funds that consistently hold securities appropriate to the objective should be given further consideration.

Consistency of portfolio statistics. Portfolio financial ratios such as price to earnings, price to book value, earnings growth, and dividend yield must be consistent with the objectives of the fund. This requires a thorough understanding of the fund's investment style.

Fund management. The investment community has a bias in favor of investing with a fund manager who has a longer track record. If one is of the opinion that an individual can add value to the analysis of stocks, then one would note who the fund manager is and how long he or she has been managing a particular fund.

Commissions. Although this should not be the first consideration, it is certainly a factor. Is the commission in line with what other products pay?

Fixed Annuities

Beyond the due diligence performed on the insurance company, the banker needs to be aware of the different annuity products. There is a wide variation in how annuities are structured. The annuity characteristics to be analyzed include the following:

Initial interest rate. This is the rate at which an annuity earns from inception.

Interest-rate guarantee. It is guaranteed that the renewal rate will never fall below this level.

Bailout rate. This feature is offered on some annuities and allows the customer to surrender the annuity with no penalty if the interest rate falls below a certain floor.

Surrender charges. How long does a customer have to hold an annuity before there is no penalty imposed by the insurance company for withdrawing funds?

Portfolio rate. The rate on the underlying portfolio of bonds that is allocated to funding the outstanding annuities.

It is helpful to prepare a grid with all of the features listed for each product. This makes it easier to compare each product.

Variable Annuities

A variable annuity is a hybrid product; it is a tax-deferred insurance product that uses the investment amounts to invest in mutual funds or an insurance company account that acts like a mutual fund. Selling variable annuities requires both an insurance and a securities license (Series 6 or 7).

The first step is performing the due diligence on the insurance company offering the fund, using the techniques outlined below for analyzing insurance companies. Next, look at the mutual funds or insurance company accounts used for the investment. The mutual funds offered by various insurance companies often have the same fund names as some of the most well-known mutual funds. There might be a catch, however. In some cases, even though the fund has the same name and is run according to the same stated objectives as the well-known fund, it is not the same fund. It is a mirror fund, and could have differences.

It is important to take a close look at the expenses involved in the variable annuity. (We discuss this in Chapter 4 on products.) Variable annuities carry both insurance charges and the same kind of management fees and transaction expenses found in mutual funds. This can add up to a significant ongoing load in such policies. The investor needs to compare the expense ratios in the variable annuities with the performance of the mutual funds or insurance company accounts to determine total performance. Some variable annuity policies have other features, especially concerning the way death benefits are calculated; the investor should of course select the features that serve his or her needs.

Fixed-Income Products: Corporate and Municipal Bonds

For years the market has relied on the bond rating systems of Standard & Poor's, Moody's, and Duff & Phelps to determine whether a particular bond is a sound investment. Asking about a particular bond will inevitably get you an answer in terms of ratings. A smaller factor, but one that counts with retail investors, is name recognition. Many retail investors will prefer a name they know—Merrill Lynch, IBM, DuPont—to a name they don't know. Ratings have served the market well for years, and the rating agencies are very fast to downgrade bonds.

An additional guarantee for municipal bonds is bond insurance, which is offered by several different organizations. The insurance guarantees the payment on new bond issues, and offers a higher level of safety than might otherwise be available.

Company

Insurance Companies

At one time, due diligence on insurance companies was mostly a matter of finding out what ratings the company had. However, the oft-repeated story about how Executive Life maintained an A+ rating until shortly before bankruptcy has changed the infallible image of the rating agencies in the eyes of consumers. Rating agencies have responded with expanded rankings and have gotten tougher.

Ratings

As a first step in evaluating an insurance company, look at the ratings. The four major agencies that rate insurance companies are A.M. Best, Standard & Poor's, Moody's, and Duff & Phelps. A.M. Best has historically been the agency most relied on to rate insurance companies, but that is changing. Not every agency will rate every company. The insurance company has to pay for the rating, which can get to be expensive. It is not common for an insurance company to have more than two.

Many financial institutions feel that, since there are so many different insurance companies available, why take a chance with a rating below A? However, there are many sound insurance companies offering excellent products that have ratings below AAA, and there could well be sound business reasons to offer the insurance company's products anyway. We look for an insurance company's ratings to be above an A. M. Best A-. In fact, we know of insurance companies with B+ ratings that we might consider recommending, except that it is so difficult to persuade a financial institution that such an insurance company is sound. As you proceed in your due diligence, note the ratings and proceed with the analysis.

History of Company

The next part of the process is what an analyst we know calls "kicking the tires." Look at the company's history. Has the company been stable or volatile? Bankers tend to find an undistinguished but rock-solid stable performance preferable to high but volatile returns. How stable has senior management been? How long has the company been in business? In business 60 years or more indicates a company that has survived the Depression, World War II, and numerous business cycles. Has the company had the same ownership for ten years? Is the company owned by an insurance/financial services company, not by a company from an unaffiliated industry?

Look at the income statement and historical financial statements. Analyze the company's annual reports, financial statements and structure, and overall condition of the company, its parent company and/or any subsidiaries that may exist.

If at all possible, visit the company and senior management. Get comfortable with their abilities and their vision for the company. Evaluate their focus and sense of direction, and the focus and direction they give the company. A tour of their operational facilities is even better. Try to determine how well their back office functions and how much administrative support there is for the product. Can you do some basic networking among current customers of the company to find out if the administrative staff are easy to work with, competent, and accessible? How quickly do they return phone calls? What is the company's reputation for fairness?

Current Portfolio

Look at the current portfolio holdings of the company. You want to know what is in the portfolio and evaluate whether it is conservative enough for your own comfort, but you also want to evaluate how consistent it is with the interest rates on their products as well as on guaranteed rates of interest. Extraordinarily high rates of interest with a conservative portfolio don't make sense and should constitute a red flag for the analyst. How are they doing this? Usually there will be offsets, such as longer surrender periods, larger early withdrawal penalties, or lower commissions. Look for those offsets.

How consistent has the portfolio been? Has it been stable, year-over-year, or has the company invested heavily in one sector of the market in one year and next year heavily in something else? Are investments risks appropriate for the kind of insurance the company sells (in terms of type, term, and diversity)?

What is the quality of the portfolio? Is it conservative enough to offer in banks to the customer looking for a CD alternative? The analyst should perform some ratio tests: the percentage of assets made up of high quality investments; surplus-to-assets ratio. Does the company match asset and liability duration?

Are commissions consistent with portfolio and credited rates of interest? Are commissions paid frequently and accurately?

How well does the company's performance overall mesh with the products it offers? A well-run company with strong internal controls might offer products that underperform the market. Similarly, excellent products—or products that seem too good to be true—offered by a poorly-run company might not survive long enough to deliver on their promises. A customer would be better off with a lesser product offered by a more stable company.

If this is a life insurance company, has it done an AIDS study? Does their surplus cover their worst case scenario?

In terms of product support, does the company provide software for producing customer illustrations, both basic and advanced? What kind of marketing support does the company provide? Can you find out anything about how long it takes to underwrite and issue policies?

Investor

The entire process of determining what investment is appropriate for which individual is usually referred to as suitability; the regulators use this term in this way as well. We prefer to divide this process into two different categories: due diligence and suitability. Due diligence for the individual investor involves determining his or her economic status and risk tolerance. The registered rep has to know this before making any product recommendations. Only then can one determine if a particular security is suitable for that investor in terms of soundness, creditworthiness, and risk tolerance.

When doing the due diligence on an individual, the registered rep must first determine if the individual is defined as sophisticated or unsophisticated as defined by the NASD. The registered rep needs to know the following:

- legal age
- annual income
- net worth (excluding home)
- investment objectives
- tolerance for risk
- years of investment experience
- other investments
- employer

The regulations are designed to protect unsophisticated investors (widows and orphans) much more than sophisticated or professional investors. This is discussed at greater length in Chapter 13 on compliance.

Rating Agencies

The rating agencies can be of major assistance in performing due diligence. They are an excellent place to start; but you can't rely on them completely. Fixed-income securities are rated by Moody's, Standard and Poor's, and Duff and Phelps. Mutual funds are rated by Morningstar. The insurance companies are rated by A. M. Best, Moody's, Standard and Poor's, and Duff and Phelps. Companies generally apply for only two ratings. Needless to say, they choose the two companies that will give them the highest ratings.

Morningstar

In this great age of mutual fund investing, it's hard to imagine anyone involved with mutual funds, whether from a personal or professional point of view, who hasn't heard of Morningstar. Morningstar publishes a comprehensive guide to mutual funds that is used as a reference point for much of the industry. Morningstar publishes extensive statistics on every aspect of mutual fund performance, including comparisons to a relative index and against other funds with the same objective, lists current holdings, and gives a short verbal analysis of fund characteristics and outlook. Our own analysis points out that Morningstar's ratings system isn't perfect, but it provides so much comparative information that any disagreement one might have with any particular aspect of the analysis is insignificant.

Morningstar provides analyses of 1,240 mutual funds in its written format. Subscribing to the CD ROM version adds 1,800 more. Morningstar will generally not include a fund until it has a three-year performance, although this is not a hard-and-fast rule; there seems to be some flexibility in how quickly funds are added, especially if the manager of a new fund is well known. Morningstar has started to add some of the bank proprietary funds, but many are too young to be included.

The Morningstar rating system employs a risk-adjusted performance measure to rank funds from one star (lowest) to five stars (highest). The star rating, though useful, has two limitations. First, each fund is evaluated assuming it constitutes an investor's entire portfolio. This is a very unrealistic way of looking at a portfolio, because very few investors have only one investment in their portfolio. It also means that, in Morningstar's terms, a low return/low risk fund is equivalent to a high return/high risk fund. In Morningstar's analysis, the investor should receive a return in accord with the risk he or she takes, and whether that return is low because the risk is low, or the return is high because the risk is high, the fund is awarded the same four- or five-star rating. This is misleading for the individual investor, who might think that a five-star fund is going to give a great return; furthermore, an individual is more likely thinking in terms of high rate rather than rate relative to risk. Second, the risk-adjusted measure is a moving average of historical performance using quarterly data. Extraordinary quarters either subtracted-out or added-in can result in variability in the star rating quarter to quarter.

Morningstar also publishes analyses on variable annuities, and this allows the analyst to spot the differences between the stand-alone mutual funds and the similar funds sometimes used for the variable annuities. If a variable annuity uses funds that exist only for the annuity, these call for the same kind of rigorous analysis used in the mutual fund due diligence.

Other Rating Agencies

The four major rating agencies are Standard & Poor's (referred to as S&P), Moody's, Duff and Phelps, and A.M. Best. Each of these ratings services has supplied us with information about how they determine ratings and has given us permission to quote their materials. We supply that information below.

Standard & Poor's[1]

What the Debt Ratings Mean

AAA   Debt rated 'AAA' has the highest rating assigned by Standard & Poor's. Capacity to pay interest and repay principal is extremely strong.

AA   Debt rated 'AA' has a very strong capacity to pay interest and repay principal and differs from the highest-rated issues only in small degree.

A   Debt rated 'A' has a strong capacity to pay interest and repay principal although it is somewhat more susceptible to the adverse effects of changes in circumstances and economic conditions than debt in higher-rated categories.

BBB   Debt rated 'BBB' is regarded as having an adequate capacity to pay

---

1   Used by permission of Standard & Poor's Corp.

interest and repay principal. Whereas it normally exhibits adequate protection parameters, adverse economic conditions or changing circumstances are more likely to lead to a weakened capacity to pay interest and repay principal for debt in this category than in higher-rated categories.

BB   Debt rated 'BB' has less near-term vulnerability to default than other speculative issues. However, it faces major ongoing uncertainties or exposure to adverse business, financial, or economic conditions which could lead to inadequate capacity to meet timely interest and principal payments. The 'BB' rating category is also used for debt subordinated to senior debt that is assigned an actual or implied 'BBB' rating.

B   Debt rated 'B' has a greater vulnerability to default but currently has the capacity to meet interest payments and principal repayments. Adverse business, financial, or economic conditions will likely impair capacity or willingness to pay interest and repay principal. The 'B' rating category is also used for debt subordinated to senior debt that is assigned an actual or implied 'BB' or 'BB' rating.

CCC   Debt rated 'CCC' has a currently identifiable vulnerability to default, and is dependent upon favorable business, financial, and economic conditions to meet timely payment of interest and repayment of principal. In the event of adverse business, financial, or economic conditions, it is not likely to have the capacity to pay interest and repay principal. The 'CCC' rating category is also used for debt subordinated to senior debt that is assigned an actual or implied 'B' or 'B' rating.

CC   The rating 'CC' typically is applied to debt subordinated to senior debt that is assigned an actual or implied 'CCC' rating.

C   The rating 'C' typically is applied to debt subordinated to senior debt which is assigned an actual or implied 'CCC' debt rating. The 'C' rating may be used to cover a situation where a bankruptcy petition has been filed, but debt service payments are continued.

C1   The rating 'C1' is reserved for income bonds on which no interest is being paid.

D   Debt rated 'D' is in payment default. The 'D' rating category is used when interest payments or principal payments are not made on the date due even if the applicable grace period has not expired, unless

S&P believes that such payments will be made during such grace period. The 'D' rating also will be used upon the filing of a bankruptcy
petition if debt service payments are jeopardized.

Speculative grade: Debt rated 'BB,' 'B,' 'CCC,' 'CC,'and 'C' is regarded as
having predominantly speculative characteristics with respect to capacity to
pay interest and repay principal. 'BB' indicates the least degree of speculation
and 'C' the highest. While such debt will likely have some quality and protective characteristics, these are outweighed by large uncertainties or major expo-
sures to adverse conditions.

What Is S&P; What Is Its Role

S&P is a credit rating agency that operates under these basic principles:

- independence
- objectivity
- credibility
- full disclosure of criteria and rationales

In 1923, S&P began rating the debt of corporate and municiple issuers and
now monitors the credit quality of more than $1.5 trillion worth of bonds and
other financial instruments worldwide. Much of this growth has taken place
over the last ten years. Rating criteria and methodology—the foundation of
S&P's business—have not only kept pace with market developments, but have,
in some cases, been ahead of the curve. For example, S&P was the first major
rating agency to rate the claims-paying ability of insurance companies (1971),
financial guarantees (1971), mortgage-backed bonds (1975), mutual funds
(1983), and asset-backed securities (1985).

It must be emphasized that an S&P credit rating is S&P's opinion of the creditworthiness of debt based on relevant risk factors. This opinion is stated by a
recognizable letter-grade rating symbol (see list). Over the years, S&P's credit
ratings have achieved wide investor acceptance as easily usable tools for differ-
entiating credit quality because an S&P rating is judged by the market to be reliable and credible. Credibility arises from S&P's objectivity and independence as
well as the validity of its analyses and criteria.

S&P operates with no government mandate and is independent of any
investment banking firm, bank, or similar organization. Recognition as a rating
agency ultimately depends on investors' willingness to accept its judgement. In
addition, S&P believes it is vitally important that investors understand how it

Figure 11.1 S&P's Rating Process

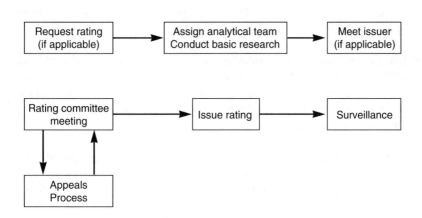

arrives at the ratings so it provides detailed reports on the rating criteria and methodology.

It is critical to remember that an S&P rating performs the isolated function of credit risk evaluation, which is only one element of the investment decision-making process. A rating does not constitute a recommendation to purchase, sell, or hold a particular secutity as it does not take into consideration factors other than credit. In addition, a rating is not a general purpose evaluation of an issuer.

Moody's Rating Definitions[2]

Long-Term

Aaa   Bonds which are rated Aaa are judged to be of the best quality. They carry the smallest degree of investment risk and are generally referred to as "gilt edged." Interest payments are protected by a large or exceptionally stable margin and principal is secure. While the various protective elements are likely to change, such changes as can be visualized are most unlikely to impair the fundamentally strong position of such issues.

Aa   Bonds which are rated Aa are judged to be of high quality by all standards. Together with the Aaa group they comprise what are generally known as high-grade bonds. They are rated lower than the best bonds because margins of protection may not be as large as in Aaa secutities,

---

2   Used by permission of Moody's Investors Service.

or fluctuation of protective elements may be of greater amplitude, or there may be other elements present which make the long-term risk appear somewhat larger than the Aaa securities.

A   Bonds which are rated A possess many favorable investment attributes and are to be considered as upper-medium-grade obligations. Factors giving security to principal and interest are considered adequate, but elements may be present which suggest a susceptibility to impairment some time in the future.

Baa   Bonds which are rated Baa are considered as medium-grade obligations (i.e., they are neither highly protected nor poorly secured). Interest payments and principal security appear adequate for the present but certain protective elements may be lacking or may be characteristically unreliable over any great length of time. Such bonds lack outstanding investment characteristics and in fact have speculative characteristics as well.

Ba   Bonds which are rated Ba are judged to have speculative elements; their future cannot be considered as well-assured. Often the protection of interest and principal payments may be very moderate and thereby not well safeguarded during both good and bad times over the future. Uncertainty of position characterizes bonds in this class.

B   Bonds which are rated B generally lack characteristics of the desirable investment. Assurance of interest and principal payments or of maintenance of other terms of the contract over any long period of time may be small.

Caa   Bonds which are rated Caa are of poor standing. Such issues may be in default or there may be present elements of danger with respect to principal or interest.

Ca   Bonds which are rated Ca represent obligations which are speculative in a high degree. Such issues are often in default or have other marked short-comings.

C   Bonds which are rated C are the lowest rated class of bonds, and issues so rated can be regarded as having extremely poor prospects of ever attaining any real investment standing.

Moody's bond ratings, where specified, are applied to senior bank obligations and insurance company senior policyholder and claims obligations with an original maturity in excess of one year. Obligations relying upon support mechanisms such as letters-of-credit and bonds of indemnity are excluded unless explicitly rated.

Obligations of a branch of a bank are considered to be domiciled in the country in which the branch is located. Unless noted as an exception, Moody's rating on a bank's ability to repay senior obligations extends only to branches located in countries which carry a Moody's sovereign rating. Such branch obligations are rated at the lower of the bank's rating or Moody's sovereign rating for the bank deposits for the country in which the branch is located.

When the currency in which an obligation is denominated is not the same as the currency of the country in which the obligation is domiciled, Moody's ratings do not incorporate an opinion as to whether payment of the obligation will be affected by the actions of the government controlling the currency of denomination. In addition, risk associated with bilateral conflicts between an investor's home country and either the issuer's home country or the country where an issuer branch is located, is not incorporated into Moody's ratings.

Moody's makes no representation that rated bank obligations or insurance company obligations are exempt from registration under the U.S. Securities Act of 1933 or issued in conformity with any other applicable law or regulation. Moody's also does not represent that any specific bank or insurance company obligation is legally enforceable or is a valid senior obligation of a rated issuer.

Moody's ratings are opinions, not recommendations to buy or sell, and their accuracy is not guaranteed. A rating should be weighed solely as one factor in an investment decision and you should make your own study and evaluation of any issuer whose securities or debt obligations you consider buying or selling.

Moody's Rating Philosophy

What is a rating? A rating is an opinion on the ability and legal obligation of an issuer to make timely payments of principal and interest on a security over the life of the instrument. A rating is also designed to rank, within a consistent framework, the relative risk of each debt issue and issuer. Because it pertains to the future, a credit rating (like all other long-term financial analysis) is necessarily subjective. Its reliability stems less from precise methodology than from the balanced opinion of experienced, well-informed, and impartial analysts.

In arriving at our conclusion on an issue's rating, Moody's stresses the examination of the specific circumstances of each issuer and each debt issue. Moody's adopts a long-term view that extends beyond a brief earnings period.

The foundation of Moody's rating methodology rests with one basic question: What is the level of risk associated with receiving timely payment of principal and interest on this specific debt security and how does the level of risk compare with that of all other debt securities?

Duff & Phelps Credit Rating Company[3]

Duff & Phelps began issuing public ratings of the Claims Paying Ability (CPA) of insurance companies in late 1986. A Claims Paying Ability rating is an objective evaluation, based on an established scale, of an insurance company's ability to meet future obligations under the contracts it issues. Currently, they have issued 195 public Claims Paying Ability ratings, and expect that this rapid growth will continue.

There are four major reasons for this interest in public Claims Paying Ability ratings:

- Marketing considerations
- Pricing advantage
- Management review
- Rating agency relationship

Summary

Claims Paying Ability Ratings

These ratings are playing a larger role in the marketing and operations pictures for insurance companies because of their importance in marketing insurance products. Ratings can facilitate a company's entrance into certain markets; they can enable a company to price more effectively and profitably; the rating process itself acts as an important management review tool and is the basis for establishing an ongoing rating agency relationship that can help with the development of additional ratings that may be required in the changing marketplace.

What is a Claims Paying Ability Rating?

A Claims Paying Ability rating is an independent evaluation of an insurance company's ability to meet its future obligations under the contracts and products it sells.

---

3   Used by permission of Duff & Phelps Credit Rating Company

Why does an insurance company need a Claims Paying Ability rating?

As insurance products and insurance company structures have become more complex, purchasers of insurance and investment products are demanding more sophisticated, in-depth, independent analysis of the ability of insurance companies to meet their future contractual commitments.

Brokers and distributors of insurance products in the performance of their due diligence requirements want, and in many cases require, independent evaluations of the claims paying ability of the insurance companies with which they deal.

A Claims Paying Ability rating from Duff & Phelps will enable a company to compete more effectively and profitably in the marketplace without using "top dollar" or "low ball" rates.

A Duff & Phelps Claims Paying Ability analysis provides an excellent review for management of an insurance company's ability to compete effectively in today's market.

A.M. Best's Rating System[4]

The objective of A.M. Best's rating system is to evaluate the factors affecting the overall performance of an insurance company in order to provide an opinion of the company's financial strength, operating performance, and ability to meet its obligations to policyholders. The procedure includes quantitative and qualitative evaluations of the company's financial condition and operating performance.

Evaluating the financial condition of a company is not an exact science. This is particularly true of insurance companies, whose assets are largely interest and economic sensitive investment, such as bonds, stocks, and real estate, and whose liabilities, such as loss and policy reserves, are based primarily on actuarial projections of future claim payments.

Determining the adequacy of loss reserves for property/casualty companies has become increasingly more difficult due to the liberalization of insurance contract interpretation and the expansion of theories of tort liability, particularly in the area of environmental pollution liability. These developments have seriously challenged the ability of insurers to predict with confidence the loss reserves they must establish today to meet future obligations.

Likewise, determining the adequacy of a life insurer's investments, cash flow and liquidity to meet policyholder obligations also has become increasingly more difficult due to the complexity of investment-oriented life and annuity

---

4   Used by permission of A.M. Best Company.

products, interest-rate volatility, the reduced certainty of future cash demands and growing policyholder and public perception concerns regarding the stability of the industry.

These issues have contributed to a waning level of consumer confidence which has increased the potential for "runs on the bank" which life insurance companies, in particular, do not have the liquidity structure to satisfy. Ultimately, these factors have led to the placement of several once highly regarded and prominent life insurance companies under state insurance departments' "protective" supervision.

12

Regulation[1]

Understanding bank and financial institution regulators and regulation is one of the most confusing and difficult aspects of the financial markets, for a variety of reasons. First of all, there are a number of different regulators, depending on the kind of financial institution, and regulation takes place on both a national and a state level. We are going to try to shed some light on the subject in a way that people who aren't lawyers can understand. Our goal is to lay out some of the basics, but please understand that we are not lawyers and there is no substitute for the advice of your own counsel. You should also be aware that the laws are undergoing a process of tremendous change at the moment, and the courts and the regulators are coming out with new rulings and guidelines every day.

The Regulators

Banks, other financial institutions, securities firms, insurance companies, and investment products are regulated by a number of different entities. The following is a brief definition of who the regulators are and what they regulate. (It is *not* a comprehensive discussion of bank regulation.)

---

1 We are deeply grateful to Ronald R. Glancz, Esq., a partner in the Washington, D.C. law firm of Venable, Baetjer, Howard & Civiletti for this chapter. He allowed us to start with material he had already written for publication elsewhere and assisted us with writing the historical and explanatory material we added.

A bank is either a state bank or a national bank, depending on who issued the charter. The main regulator of a state bank is the commissioner for the state in which it is located. A national bank is regulated by the Office of the Comptroller of the Currency (OCC). A national bank is required by law to be a member of the Federal Reserve System. All holding companies are regulated by the Fed, even if their only subsidiaries are state banks. If a state bank is not a member bank (of the Fed), its federal regulator is the Federal Deposit Insurance Corp. (FDIC).

Savings and loans are regulated by the Federal Office of Thrift Supervision (OTS). National credit unions are regulated by the National Credit Union Administration. State-chartered credit unions are regulated at the state level.

Insurance activities are regulated at a state level, by each state's department of insurance. Securities activities are regulated by the Securities and Exchange Commission (SEC), the NASD, and the MSRB. There is also a certain amount of state regulation of securities firms by state departments of securities.

The Federal Reserve System

The main function of the Federal Reserve System is to act as the central bank for the United States banking system. The Fed has the power to regulate commercial banks and bank holding companies. Fed regulation has played an important part in the expansion of banks into securities and insurance activities.

Comptroller of the Currency

This is the primary regulator of national banks. The OCC exercises general supervision over the operations of national banks. The OCC and its regulations concerning the securities and insurance activities primarily determine what is and is not allowable for banks.

Federal Deposit Insurance Corporation

The FDIC is an independent executive agency that was established by the Banking Act of 1933. It administers the system of nationwide deposit insurance for U.S. banks and has important supervisory and examination powers, making it the third federal banking supervisory agency (along with the Comptroller of the Currency and the Board of Governors of the Federal Reserve System).

As fiscally conservative Americans of all ages know, FDIC insurance covers bank deposits of every kind up to a maximum of $100,000 per institution. A number of rules concerning account ownership determine exactly which accounts of an individual are covered in one institution. If a bank goes into receivership, the amount of each depositor's insured deposit will be paid according to those rules and up to $100,000.

To pay for this insurance, insured banks are assessed a premium using a risk-based formula that is a percentage of total assessable deposits.

Office of Thrift Supervision

The OTS is a relatively new regulator. It was established in 1989 as part of a major reorganization of the thrift regulatory structure mandated by the Financial Institutions Reform, Recovery and Enforcement Act (FIRREA). The OTS is the primary regulator of thrifts belonging to the Savings Association Insurance Fund (SAIF).

The OTS supersedes the old Federal Home Loan Bank Board (FHLBB). The federal deposit insurance that used to be provided by the Federal Savings and Loan Insurance Corporation (FSLIC) has been rolled into the FDIC, which insures deposits in savings and loans as well as banks.

National Credit Union Administration

National credit unions are regulated by the National Credit Union Administration, which was established by Congress in 1934. This regulator is funded entirely by credit unions and receives no taxpayer dollars. NCUA supervises and insures over 8,000 federal credit unions and insures almost 4,500 state-chartered credit unions. The National Credit Union Share Insurance Fund is managed by the NCUA Board. It insures member accounts (shares) up to $100,000, and is backed by the full faith and credit of the U.S. government.

The Securities and Exchange Commission

The SEC has three major responsibilities:

1. to ensure the provision of full and fair disclosure of all material facts concerning securities offered for public investment;
2. to litigate for fraud when it is detected; and
3. to provide for the registration of securities offered for public investment.

Later legislation has given the SEC a mandate to facilitate the establishment of a national market system for securities as well as a nationwide system for the clearance and settlement of securities transactions. Clearing agencies are registered with and report to the SEC. All NASD members must also be members of the SEC, and the SEC assigns enforcement powers to the NASD.

National Association of Securities Dealers

All brokers and dealers, as well as all registered reps, must be members of the NASD. The NASD fulfills its regulatory responsibilities through an integrated program that includes nationwide field inspections of member firms; centralized computerized surveillance of the trading of 4,300 securities in the Nasdaq market; enforcement of rules governing special product areas such as municipal securities and government securities; review of underwriting arrangements for the public distribution of securities; testing of personnel; and cooperative action with the exchanges, the states, and the SEC.

If an organization wants to share commissions on the sale of securities, it must be NASD licensed. (See Chapter 13 on compliance for further discussion of the NASD.)

The Municipal Securities Rulemaking Board

The MSRB was created in a 1975 amendment to the 1934 Securities Act to oversee practices within the municipal securities industry. It is an independent, self-regulatory organization and is the primary rule-making authority for the industry. The MSRB is concerned with standards of professional practice, including qualifications of broker/dealers, rules of fair practice, and recordkeeping. The MSRB does not have inspection or enforcement authority; that role is fulfilled by the NASD.

Applicable Statutory Provisions

Glass-Steagall Act

Glass-Steagall is the popular name for four provisions of the Banking Act of 1933 (12 U.S.C. §§ 24, 78, 377 and 378(a)). It was enacted to separate commercial and investment banking activities. Four sections of the act prohibited banks from certain investment banking activities: sections 16, 20, 21, and 32.

As discussed more fully below, the federal banking regulators and the courts have determined that financial institutions may engage in securities brokerage activities without violating Glass-Steagall, provided they properly structure the activity. *See, e.g., Securities Industry Assn. v. Clarke*, 885 F.2d 1034 (2d Cir. 1989) *cert. denied*, 110 S. Ct. 113 (1990); *Securities Industry Assn. v. Bd. of Governors*, 458 U.S. 207 (1984).

Bank Holding Company Act

Section 4 of the Bank Holding Company Act of 1956 (BHCA) prohibits a bank holding company or its nonbank subsidiary from engaging in nonbanking activities, except as otherwise provided in the BHCA. Under section 4(c) of the BHCA [12 U.S.C. §1843(c) (8)] and Regulation Y (12 C.F.R. §225.25), a bank holding company or its nonbank subsidiary may engage in a nonbanking activity, including a securities activity, only if the Federal Reserve Board determines that the activity is "closely related to banking" and if the provision of such activity would likely result in public benefits that outweigh the possible adverse effects.

State Banking and Securities

State-chartered institutions, of course, must also consider applicable state banking and securities laws. After FIRREA and FDICIA, state-chartered institutions generally are limited to the activities that are permissible for federally chartered institutions.

Laws Pertaining to Savings and Loan Associations

Savings and loan associations are permitted to engage in securities brokerage activities through a service corporation. Federally chartered associations, including savings banks insured by the FDIC, must comply with applicable federal regulations. State-chartered institutions must comply with applicable state regulations.

A Brief History of Banking and Brokerage

Bond Departments

Banks have traditionally had a number of different ways to offer either capital market departments or retail investment services. Traditional bank bond departments are also known as "section 16s," after the relevant section of the Glass-Steagall Act. Section 16 (12 U.S.C. ¶24) authorizes a national bank to purchase and sell securities without recourse for the account of its customers—i.e., brokerage activities. This section prohibits national banks from underwriting securities except those designated as "eligible" securities. Section 5(c) (12 U.S.C. ¶335) applies the same restrictions to state member banks. Bank bond departments could not underwrite, sell, or trade corporate obligations or securities of any kind (commercial paper, corporate bonds, or equities). Eligible securities include U.S. government obligations and municipal obligations, which are also called exempt securities (because they are exempt from all requirements of this act). Securities issued by the U.S. government or any of its political subdivisions, issued or guaranteed by an agency or corporation created and controlled by the U.S. government, or issued or guaranteed by a national bank, are all exempt. Exempt securities, therefore, included bills, notes, and bonds of the U.S. government and all its various agencies, certain types of municipal securities, and various bank liabilities such as certificates of deposit (CDs) and bankers' acceptances (BAs), issued by either the bank itself or other banks.

Many traditional bond departments almost drifted into serving individuals. Banks would have a few customers who were interested in managing their own money beyond just buying jumbo CDs in the lobby. These customers would talk directly to employees of the institutional bond department, buying bankers' acceptances directly or commercial paper that the bank could sell as agent; municipal bonds; U.S. government bills, bonds, and notes; CDs of all types, including large institutional CDs and those issued by other banks; and Eurodollar time deposits if they were qualified. This took care of investment needs for many individuals. With interest rates as high as they were in the early 1980s, this was all the money management many individuals needed. Some banks formed personal investment areas adjunct to the institutional capital markets areas. A bank could further serve these individuals by acting as agent for the customer and charging only a fee for execution. The bank could thus offer equities, mutual funds, and other nonexempt products to such individuals.

The OCC originally interpreted the legislation of the 1930s as prohibiting banks from engaging in brokerage activities. The OCC began to change its views in the late 1970s, and Security Pacific was allowed to establish a discount broker subsidiary. The Fed then allowed a bank holding company to acquire Charles Schwab & Co., a discount broker. By now there had been a dramatic change in the regulatory climate for such activities in banks and bank holding companies.

Holding Companies and Section 20s

Section 20 (U.S.C. ¶377) prohibits member banks from being affiliated with any organization engaged principally in underwriting, distributing, or selling securities. In the mid-1980s, the courts sustained the Federal Reserve Board's interpretation of "engaged principally" to permit a BHC subsidiary to underwrite certain bank-ineligible securities constituting 5% to 10% of its gross revenues. (The Fed allowed this activity because the holding company was not engaged principally in this business; it was a small side business.) This meant the Fed granted approval to certain of the largest bank holding companies to form separately capitalized subsidiaries to sell commercial paper, certain municipal revenue bonds that banks had not been able to sell before, mortgage-backed securities, and asset-backed securities. Such organizations were called "section 20" subsidiaries. To do this, the section 20 had to become a member of the NASD, and its employees had to be licensed as registered reps under the NASD.

Section 21 (U.S.C. ¶378 (a)) prohibits any company receiving deposits from engaging in underwriting, distributing, or selling securities—except for certain "investment securities." The courts have held that section 21 is coextensive with section 16 and that nonbank subsidiaries of bank holding companies are authorized to engage in brokerage activities to the same extent as national banks under section 16. The courts have also held that section 21 does not prohibit state non-member banks, otherwise authorized by state law, from engaging in securities underwriting.

Thrift Institutions

The Office of Thrift Supervision permits a service corporation of a thrift to provide brokerage services. The Federal Home Loan Bank Board was the first banking regulator to determine that providing discount brokerage services was a permissible activity of federal associations. The brokerage services, however, had to be provided by a service corporation of the thrift. The FHLBB granted approval to four savings and loan associations to create a jointly-owned service corporation subsidiary known as INVEST that would offer stock brokerage and investment advisory services to customers of participating savings and loans on a nationwide basis. INVEST would execute shares of mutual funds on behalf of and for the account of customers but would not offer discretionary accounts. INVEST would also provide standardized investment advisory services. The INVEST decision was upheld by a federal district court. *See Securities Industry Assn. v. Federal Home Loan Bank Board*, 588 F. Supp. 749 (D.D.C. 1984).

The FDIC, the OCC, and the FRB subsequently approved INVEST-type programs. Dual employees of the brokerage firm and the financial institution may receive commission-based compensation. Dual employees must be licensed members of the NASD.

Sometimes particular regulations applying to certain types of institutions require that the brokerage services be offered by a service corporation. This service corporation is a subsidiary. Thrift service corporations must meet the OTS' separate organization requirements. That is, the thrift and the service corporation should operate such that (1) their respective business transactions, accounts, and records are not intermingled, (2) each observes the formalities of their separate corporate procedures, (3) each is adequately financed as a separate unit in light of normal operations reasonably foreseeable in a business of its size and character, (4) each is held out to the public as a separate enterprise, and (5) the thrift does not dominate the service corporation to the extent that the latter is treated as a mere department of the former.

According to 12 C.F.R. §545.74(c)(4), service corporations can engage in certain types of securities brokerage and investment advisory activities on a pre-approved basis. The service corporation must file a written notice with the appropriate regional director at least 30 days prior to commencement of the operations. The regional director may request additional information if he or she has supervisory concerns or questions concerning whether the activity as described is in fact pre-approved. Within 30 days after filing, the regional director may (1) give written approval or "approve" by letting time elapse, (2) determine that additional information is required, (3) determine that the service corporation may not engage in brokerage activities due to "safety and soundness" concerns, or (4) forward the notification to the OTS Corporate Activities Section because the notice raises a significant issue of law or policy. The notice is institution specific. However, the OTS will accept applications for a delegation of authority that could allow a third-party broker/dealer to begin operations with different federal associations, at least theoretically, with less difficulty than through an institution-by-institution notice.

In order for brokerage activities to be considered pre-approved, they must comply with the requirements set forth in the regulation. The regulation, among other things, requires that the separate corporate identities of the service corporation and the federal association be maintained; advertising indicates that the federal association is not providing the brokerage service; the third-party broker/dealer indemnifies the service corporation and the association; transactions are on an agency basis except for "riskless principal" transactions; and association employees may receive referral fees only if the association has received a no-action letter from the SEC stating that the association is not required to register as a broker/dealer under the Securities Exchange Act of 1934.

The Regulations Today

National Banks

The authority for national banks to engage in bank brokerage and related activities has developed incrementally, as the practice expanded, by order or interpretive letter issued by the OCC. It is by now well established that national banks and their subsidiaries may perform brokerage services under section 16 of Glass-Steagall. The OCC has also determined that national banks may provide investment advice and that the combination of these otherwise permissible activities does not violate Glass-Steagall. Thus, a national bank may provide full-service brokerage, combining brokerage and advisory services to customers. If this service is operated directly out of the bank, the brokerage operation is not required to become a member of the NASD. Bank subsidiaries conducting brokerage activities are required to register as broker/dealers with the SEC and to become members of the NASD. There may be requirements such as disclosure and recordkeeping, as well as federal securities law requirements in connection with the performance of certain activities.

National banks are presently authorized by either OCC decision or regulation to engage in the following activities:

- purchasing, on the order of customers, the shares of mutual funds for which the bank acts as investment adviser
- private placement, as agent, of a customer's commercial paper, as well as advising the customer with respect to the structure and terms of the transaction
- selling, on commission, notes of its parent BHC to the bank's institutional customers
- maintaining (through a subsidiary) memberships and seats on national and regional securities exchanges
- engaging in securities lending (margin lending) and borrowing as part of its brokerage business
- purchasing and selling shares of mutual funds or UITs as agent for a customer
- offering sweep services in connection with brokerage, in which idle deposits exceeding a predetermined amount are swept into money market mutual funds or other investments
- engaging in riskless principal transactions whereby the broker, after receiving a customer's order to buy or sell a security, buys or sells that security to offset a contemporaneous sale to or purchase from the customer

Although the regulators now accept a brokerage operation within the bank, many banks have chosen to form a registered broker/dealer as a subsidiary of the bank or the holding company. Banks see this as providing legal protection in two ways. First, as a licensed, registered broker/dealer using licensed personnel, the bank gains a more professional standing in the securities market.

This indicates to customers a more serious attitude toward the brokerage market. Furthermore, the NASD compliance rules and regulations protect all participants in the securities markets, including the firm and the registered rep as well as the customer. Following proper compliance procedures makes excellent business sense. Second, many banks choose to form a subsidiary to house the securities business because this provides some insulation—however thin—from the vagaries of the securities business and whatever hazards bank management thinks it might pose for the bank itself. As soon as bank management decides to form a brokerage subsidiary, it has to be registered.

New OCC Guidelines for National Banks

In July 1993, the OCC issued guidelines applicable to bank-related sales of "nondeposit investment products." (We have reproduced these guidelines as an appendix to Chapter 13.) The guidelines apply to the sales of both securities and insurance products. These include sales made by bank employees, sales made by employees of affiliated or unaffiliated entities occurring on bank premises (including telephone sales and sales initiated by mail from bank premises), and sales resulting from customer referrals when the bank receives a benefit for the referral.

The guidelines indicate that the NASD's Rules of Fair Practices are an appropriate reference in constructing a compliance program. The guidelines also set forth standards for (1) program management, (2) the setting and circumstances of retail nondeposit investment sales, (3) disclosure and advertising, (4) determination of investment suitability, (5) qualifications and training of the sales and supervisory personnel, (6) compensation of sales personnel, (7) treatment of fiduciary accounts, and (8) implementation of the compliance program. The bank's board of directors is required to adopt policies and procedures in this area.

There has been much discussion among those in the bank brokerage business about *exactly* what these guidelines mean and what actions banks should take in order to follow them. Some banks have curtailed further development of their platform programs because they think the guidelines call for a complete separation of deposit-taking and investment activities. Other banks have decided that these regulations are only general guidelines and as long as they are followed in spirit, activities that have long been practiced can continue. There is little question that the controversy will continue until the regulators clarify some of the issues raised by these guidelines.

State Member Banks

Sections 16 through 21 of Glass-Steagall, as well as certain state banking and securities laws, apply to state member banks.

In June 1993, the Federal Reserve Board issued guidelines for state member banks selling mutual funds. (These guidelines have been reproduced as an appendix to Chapter 13.) Unlike the OCC, the Fed's guidelines apply only to the sale of mutual funds. They establish measures for separating the bank and mutual fund activities. They are intended to ensure that mutual fund purchasers do not have the impression that the mutual funds are federally-insured deposits or obligations of the bank. The guidelines also require disclosure to investors that mutual fund investments are subject to risk and may fluctuate in value.

State Nonmember Banks

State nonmember banks must first look to state banking and securities laws to authorize bank brokerage activities. The FDIC has also adopted regulations that set forth the conditions under which state nonmember banks can engage in a broad range of securities activities through subsidiaries (12 C.F.R. 337.4). These regulations, however, do not apply to most third-party brokerage activities. In addition, state nonmember banks may not engage in activities not permissible for national banks without the prior consent of the FDIC (12 U.S.C. §1831, 12 C.F.R. Part 362). Customers must also be advised that there is a risk as to loss of principal.

The FDIC has recently issued a supervisory statement for state nonmember banks governing sales of mutual funds and annuities. This statement requires banks to take an active role in supervising sales of these two products, and is similar in tone to the guidelines issued by the OCC. Banks are expected to develop policies and implement control procedures to guard against the risks of potential customer confusion about these products and the potential for mismanagement of sales programs that could expose a bank to liability under the antifraud provisions of the securities laws.

Bank Holding Companies

In *Securities Industry Association v. Board of Governors*, 468 U.S. 207 (1984), the Supreme Court upheld the Fed authorization of a bank holding company to acquire Charles Schwab & Co., a discount broker. The Court held that the mere execution of orders, as agent, for the purchase and sale of securities did not violate Section 20 of Glass-Steagall.

In Regulation Y, the board specifies those nonbank activities that are closely related to banking and therefore permissible for bank holding companies. Regulation Y specifically authorizes BHCs and their subsidiaries to provide securities brokerage services and incidental activities (as NASD member firms) if the brokerage services are restricted to buying and selling securities solely as agent for the account of customers and do not include securities underwriting, dealing, investment advice, or research services (12 C.F.R. §225.25(b)(15).

The FRB has, by a series of orders, expanded the scope of permissible brokerage activities set forth in Regulation Y. The FRB permits bank holding companies to offer combined investment advisory and securities brokerage activities to retail customers as well as institutional customers. It also allows them to exercise limited investment discretion with respect to client accounts as well as to transfer client information to a lending affiliate, both at the client's request only. Such subsidiaries are generally required to register as broker/dealers and investment advisers under federal securities laws and are subject to fiduciary standards and certain director interlock prohibitions.

An application or notice for the FRB's prior approval is generally required before a BHC can engage in a nonbanking activity. Again, performance of the above activities may be subject to certain conditions imposed by the FRB as well as to federal securities law requirements.

The FRB's Regulation Y currently permits BHC affiliates to provide investment advice, discount securities brokerage, or a combination of the two (12 C.F.R. §§225(b) (4), (b) (15) (i) and (b) (15) (ii), respectively) on a "pre-approval" basis.

The affiliate is required to disclose prominently in writing to each customer before providing any brokerage and/or advisory services, and again in any customer account statements, that:

- The brokerage company is solely responsible for its contractual obligations and commitments.
- The brokerage company is not a bank and is separate from any affiliated bank.
- The securities sold, offered, or recommended by the brokerage company are not deposits, are not insured by the FDIC, do not constitute obligations of any bank, and (unless otherwise the case) are not endorsed or guaranteed by any bank.

Recently, bank holding companies with section 20 subsidiaries have begun to consolidate their securities operations by moving their brokerage activities within their section 20 subsidiaries. This simply means that full-service brokerage, which was separate and legal before, is combined operationally under the auspices of section 20 for organizational efficiency. The section 20 is of course a member of the NASD. In addition to that provision in Regulation Y, the FRB has revised an interpretive rule clarifying that a bank holding company and its nonbank subsidiaries may act as agent for customers in the brokerage of shares of an investment company advised by the holding company or any of its subsidiaries. That is, the holding company and its nonbank subsidiaries may sell its own proprietary funds through its own brokerage subsidiary. They may also provide investment advice to customers regarding the purchase and sale of shares of investment companies advised by a holding company affiliate.

Bank Insurance Activities

Historically, insurance activities of banks and thrifts have been regulated by state law. In some states, banks and thrifts have largely been prohibited from engaging in insurance activities. Although many state laws have been liberalized in recent years (and the OCC has allowed national banks to sell fixed- and variable-rate annuities), many restrictions still apply. Check state law before engaging in insurance activities in your particular jurisdiction.

There is an ongoing dispute between the banking industry and the insurance industry. Banks are eager to enter the insurance industry, seeing that as one more way to increase fee income. Furthermore, annuities (investment-like insurance products) and mainstream insurance products make a good fit with retail investment services programs to provide a complete financial program for customers. The insurance industry and its regulators would like to keep the banks out. This issue has yet to be resolved.

National Banks

The OCC has permitted national banks to engage, as agents on behalf of their customers, in the sale of fixed and variable annuity products. *See* OCC Interpretive Letter No. 475 [1989-90 Transfer Binder] Fed. Banking L. Rep. (CCH) ¶83,012 (March 22, 1989) (authority to sell variable-rate annuities) and OCC Interpretive Letter No. 499, [1989-90 Transfer Binder] Fed. Banking L. Rep (CCH) ¶83,090 (February 12, 1990) (authority to sell fixed-rate annuities). In granting this approval, the OCC has determined that annuities are essentially financial investments and not traditional "insurance" products.

The authority to sell annuities was challenged in the courts by the Variable Annuity Life Insurance Company, which had argued that section 92 of the NBA (12 U.S.C. §92) prohibited the sale of annuities by national banks. *Variable Annuity Life Insurance Co. v. Clarke*, 786 F. Supp. 639 (S.D. Tex. 1991). The district court upheld the Comptroller's ruling but the Court of Appeals for the Fifth Circuit reversed. The court held that fixed and variable annuities are insurance products and section 92 continues to prohibit national banks, except in towns with 5,000 or fewer people, from acting as agents for fire, life, or other general insurance companies.

The Comptroller has permitted a national bank, on a percentage lease basis, to lease space on bank premises to insurance agents, who in turn offered a full range of insurance products to the bank's customers and to the general public. See OCC Interpretive Letter No. 274, [1983-84 Transfer Binder] Fed. Banking L. Rep (CCH) ¶85,438 (December 2, 1983). Pursuant to its approval, the OCC required that the lease arrangement be at arm's length, that the insurance agency be appropriately and separately identified through signs and other labeling, and that bank advertising and literature that mentions the insurance agency make clear the agency's independent ownership and operation. The leased space may be adjacent to the retail banking area or lobby so as to be accessible to customers and does not need to be separated from the bank by a wall. However, the approval letter stressed that "some effective differentiat[ion] between the two must be made so that the public will understand it is not buying insurance from the bank." The OCC's recent guidelines should also be followed.

The Supreme Court in June, 1993, reversed a ruling of the D.C. Circuit Court of Appeals that section 92 of the NBA no longer existed as a part of the United States Code, thus affirming the authority of national banks located in communities of fewer than 5,000 inhabitants to sell insurance. *U.S. National Bank of Oregon v. Independent Insurance Agents of America*, U. S. Sup. Ct. No. 92-494 and 92-507 (1993)). The court remanded the case for a determination of whether banks in small towns may sell insurance to customers outside those communities. On remand, the D. C. Circuit Court upheld the OCC's interpretation of section 92 allowing such sales.

"On July 16, the Circuit Court ruled that section 92 imposes no geographic limit on the insurance market so that, as along as it is located in a small town, a bank is free to solicit and serve insurance customers everywhere. In upholding the Comptroller of the Currency's interpretation of section 92, the court stated that 'when time and technology open up a loophole, it is up to Congress to decide whether it should be plugged, and how' (Ct. Opin., p.7). The Independent Insurance Agents will likely seek Supreme Court review of this latest ruling of the D.C. Circuit."[2]

This decision dramatically expands national banks' insurance powers. In over half the states, state banks can take advantage of this ruling through "wild card" statutes. (A wild card statute allows state banks to exercise the powers of nation-

---

2   Ronald R. Glancz, "Bank Insurance powers Still Up in the Air in the Courts,", *Bank Investment Representative,* Sept. 1993, p. 39.

al banks. This power is granted by the state authority.) The court's ruling is not limited to any particular insurance products; it allows banks to sell all types of insurance products. However, many issues are left unresolved by the court's ruling, such as whether the activity is limited to mail order or telemarketing.

"Adding to the uncertainty is the fact that the Supreme Court declined to review *American Land Title Association v. Clarke.* In that case, the Second Circuit Court of Appeals ruled that section 92 bars national banks from selling title insurance under section 24 (Seventh), and held that Section 92 prohibited that activity except for national banks located in small towns. The Second Circuit also indicated that section 92 impliedly bars national banks in towns with more than 5,000 inhabitants from engaging in insurance activities generally.

"These are important issues to banks that want to engage in insurance activities. Unfortunately, it is unlikely that a clear resolution will be forthcoming from either Congress or the Supreme Court in the near future."[3]

All this means that, more than ever, third-party providers will continue to play a role in marketing insurance products through financial institutions, except in some states that have anti-affiliation statutes. Bank customers will continue to find annuities an attractive investment vehicle as tax rates creep up, and third-party providers will continue to be eager to structure programs to offer through financial institutions.

State Banks

State banks that are not direct or indirect subsidiaries of a bank holding company may generally sell insurance subject to the following limitations. The FDIC prohibits state banks it insures from engaging in a surety business, insuring titles to real estate, or guaranteeing the obligations of others (12 C.F.R. §332.1 (1990)). In addition, section 303 of the Federal Deposit Insurance Corporation Improvement Act of 1991 and 12 C.F.R. §§62 prohibit state-chartered banks and their subsidiaries from engaging in a number of activities, including insurance underwriting, except to the extent such underwriting is permitted for national banks. National banks are currently prohibited from underwriting insurance. The only exception provided in the statute is for those few state-chartered banks and their subsidiaries that provided insurance before September 30, 1991 (in the case of banks), or November 21, 1991 (in the case of bank subsidiaries).

Certain states permit banks to engage in insurance activities. Other states are currently considering authorizing such activities. Several states restrict the relations between insurers and banks.

---

3   Glancz, "Bank Insurance," p.39.

BHCs and Their Subsidiaries

Section 4(c)(8) was amended in 1982 by the Garn-St Germain Act to prohibit bank holding companies from selling or underwriting insurance. Section 4(c)(8) does contain several limited exemptions from the prohibitions on insurance activities.

In *Merchants National Corporation, 75* Fed. Res. Bull. 388 (1989), the FRB held that it lacked jurisdiction over a bank holding company's state bank subsidiary. This was affirmed by the Second Circuit of Appeals. *See Independent Insurance Agents of America v. Board of Governors,* 890 F. 2d 1275 (2d Cir. 1989), *cert. denied,* 111 S. Ct. 44 (1990). The FRB's *Merchants National* order authorized the state bank to conduct insurance activities permissible for state-chartered banks. The Court of Appeals noted the apparently inconsistent FRB position that the FRB possesses jurisdiction over the state bank's subsidiary but not the state bank itself.

In *Citicorp v. Board of Governors,* 936 F. 2d 66, (2d Cir. 1991), *cert denied,* 112 S.Ct. 869 (1992), the Court of Appeals concluded that the FRB position constituted not merely a "tolerable inconsistency" but rather an "entirely untenable construction." The court vacated an FRB order requiring an insurance subsidiary of one of Citicorp's bank subsidiaries to terminate insurance activities that the bank subsidiary was conducting through its operating subsidiary, reasoning that "once the BHCA has been construed to leave the regulation of a holding company's subsidiary banks to their chartering authorities, the Act cannot sensibly be interpreted to reimpose the authority of the Fed . . . to regulate the subsidiary's subsidiary."

Bank and Brokerage Firm Networking Arrangements

Banks

Third-party providers and financial institutions have developed a number of legal ways to organize themselves to do business together. It's one thing for a third-party provider to offer a service as a separate company in the bank's lobby, but there is even further business involvement when a bank's employees report to the TPP as well as to the bank. Networking is the term the regulators use to refer to this arrangement (although that is not a word we otherwise use in this book).

Joint ventures are often set up so that the securities firm provides securities services at the "wholesale" level as the clearing member (execution of customer transactions, account maintenance, general advisory services, etc.) and the bank serves as a "retail" outlet for these services. The bank is then acting in an introducing broker/dealer role, regardless of its licensing status. Another increasingly popular arrangement, percentage leasing, involves the leasing of physical space in a bank by a securities firm that interacts directly with the bank's customers and pays rent to the bank for the leased space based on a percentage of gross revenues. For example, the FRB has indicated that it would not object to lobby lease arrangements in which an unaffiliated nonbanking entity would make available securities and/or insurance products to bank customers on bank premises. The OCC has authorized national banks to participate in INVEST-type arrangements under which a third party broker/dealer leased space in the national bank to provide, through dual employees of the bank and the TPP, brokerage and investment advisory services. FRB staffers have indicated orally that they would not object if state-chartered member banks participated in INVEST-type arrangements.

The Fed clearly permits state member banks to operate either a managed program using a TPP or an in-house program using a broker/dealer subsidiary of the bank or holding company. However, there seems to be some ambiguity in the Fed position on permissible networking arrangements. There is possibly a difference of opinion within the Fed. We know of cases where the Fed has prohibited a bank and a third-party provider from having common employees, citing the 1986 Baikie case as precedent. There is currently an application pending with the Fed under Regulation H for permission to run a dual-employee program, and a ruling is expected soon.

Nonmember Banks

The FDIC has approved the joint venture activities of an insured nonmember bank and an insurance agency in connection with the sale of annuities. In a letter dated April 23, 1991, the FDIC approved a proposal by the bank to sell the fixed- and variable-rate annuities of an insurance agency (FDIC Advisory Opinion No. 91-32, [Current Developments] Fed. Banking L. Rep. (CCH) ¶81,410 (April 23, 1991)). The bank proposed that the annuities would be sold by dual employees of the bank and the insurance agency and that the bank would receive a commission for each annuity sold.

In approving the bank's request, the FDIC recognized that some of the employees would sell annuities only part time and would otherwise engage in deposit-taking activities for the bank. However, the letter also recognized that although the sale of annuities would take place at the bank, this activity would occur "in a separate and distinct area of the [b]ank's premises," and that "[n]o deposit taking activity [would] occur in this separate area." The letter noted several additional FDIC concerns, including that there be adequate disclosure regarding the sale of annuities (both to purchasers of annuities and to bank shareholders) and that any third-party leasing arrangements conform to safe and sound banking practices. These concerns are echoed in the OCC's most recent guidelines.

Thrifts

The OTS, in a letter dated May 23, 1991, summarized its position regarding the sharing of office space between thrifts and other business entities (OTS General Counsel Opinion No. 91/CC-17, [Current Developments] Fed. Banking L. Rep. (CCH) ¶82,545 (May 23, 1991)). The letter explained that approval of such arrangements required the thrift to maintain office quarters separate from the other entity. The letter required that there be no commingling of the thrift's records with those of the other entity, no access to the thrift's restricted areas by the personnel of the other entity, separate operational areas and equipment, and adequate controls in place to assure the integrity of the records, computers, currency, checks, safes, and vaults of the thrift.

The letter attached a memorandum to OTS regional directors explaining the OTS's position with respect to thrifts sharing office quarters with banks and other financial institutions, regardless of whether or not such other entities are affiliated with the thrift. In addition to the requirements in the OTS letter, the memorandum stated that the responsibilities of the employees of the thrift and the other entity generally should not overlap, but that exceptions would be considered where appropriate safeguards, consistent with the OTS separateness policy, were imposed. Restricted areas such as vaults, teller counters, and records or equipment for which no security controls have been provided should be accessible only to the thrift's employees. Finally, the memorandum instructed that both entities sharing space should have a plan to avoid conflicts of interest and usurpation of corporate opportunity.

Exchange Act Broker/Dealer Registration Requirements

Banks

Many banks and bank holding companies perform brokerage services through nonbank subsidiaries. These subsidiaries are registered under the 1934 Act as broker/dealers and are subject to full SEC regulation in this regard. If brokerage services are provided directly by a *bank,* however, no federal broker/dealer registration or regulation has been required, since banks are excluded from the definitions of broker and dealer in the 1934 Act. *See* Sections 3(a), (4), and (5) of the Exchange Act. Banks should consult with counsel regarding the application of state broker/dealer regulations.

In 1985, the SEC adopted Rule 3b-9, which required banks engaging in certain securities activities to register as broker/dealers. However, this rule was invalidated by the courts, so no such registration requirement is now in effect. The SEC staff has not taken a position on the applicability of Rule 3b-9 to savings banks.

Thrifts

Savings and loan associations are not exempt from broker/dealer registration. However, various thrift brokerage programs, which limit the roles of participating institutions, have been structured to avoid such registration. Nonbank affiliates are required to register.

Networking Arrangements[4]

The SEC staff has said repeatedly in no-action letters that it would not recommend enforcement action against a financial institution or brokerage firm involved in a networking arrangement (where the employee of the financial institution is also a dual employee of the third-party provider) without registration as a broker/dealer. It is important to note that the statutory exclusion for banks does not extend to savings and loans, savings banks, credit unions or service corporations (subsidiaries that might be required due to some other regulation) set up by banks, savings and loans, savings banks or credit unions. Nevertheless, the SEC has taken no-action positions with respect to networking arrangements for all of these types of institutions.

Generally, the conditions for obtaining a no-action letter are as follows:

- The broker-dealer must exercise supervisory responsibility over the dual employee.
- Investment recommendations are made only by financial institution personnel who are also registered representatives associated with a broker/dealer.
- Customer communications, confirmation, account statements are sent by the broker/dealer and indicate brokerage services are provided by the broker/dealer.
- Unregistered employees of the financial institution provide only ministerial or clerical services and do not handle securities matters.
- No securities of the financial institution or its affiliate are sold on the premises of the financial institution.

Typically, the networking arrangements call for the lease or license of space for use by the broker/dealer on the premises of the financial institution. Banking and thrift regulations require that broker/dealer space be clearly delin-

---

4 The following section "Networking Arrangements," is quoted, with permission, from Ronald R. Glanz and Elizabeth R. Hughs, "Networking Arrangements: The Regulatory Maze," *Bank Investment Representative*, Winter 1991, pp. 28-39. This entire section reprinted by permission of *Bank Investment Representative*.

eated from the financial institution's business in order to avoid customer confusion of the deposit-taking business of the financial institution with the brokerage business. The lease or license arrangement generally calls for revenue sharing between the financial institution and the broker/dealer, with a percentage of the fees and commissions earned by the broker/dealer from the networking arrangement being remitted to the financial institution.

The dual employee may be paid a salary by the financial institution and receive transaction-based compensation from the broker/dealer. Employees of the financial institution who are not also registered representatives may receive referral fees as long as these fees are not transaction- or volume-related and these employees do not engage in securities-related activities.

There are several words of caution for financial institutions proposing to set up a networking arrangement. Recent no-action letters indicate that the SEC will permit the use of a service subsidiary only if the banking, thrift, or similar regulator of the financial institution requires such as intermediary. The state securities law in each state in which the networking arrangement is to operate may impose additional limitations. The regulator of a financial institution will have to approve the structure. With respect to a thrift, thrift regulations will require, among other things, that the financial institution obtain an SEC no-action letter with respect to its particular networking arrangement. Finally, the broker/dealer participating in the networking arrangement will be required by the NASD to seek a SEC no-action letter.

Conclusion

Financial institutions are permitted to engage in a wide variety of brokerage activities. This is an area, however, that is constantly changing, with new rulings and interpretations issued by the regulators almost monthly. Before undertaking any of these activities, you should consult with counsel experienced in this area of practice.

13

Compliance

Many people have an attitude about compliance. Some people see the compliance officer as Big Brother, and rules and regulations as business inhibitors; others think that customer complaints represent the essence of compliance. Nothing could be further from the truth. Good compliance is good business practice. The rules and regulations that have come to be referred to collectively as compliance were originally designed to protect widows, orphans, and other investors from abusive business practices. A few sections of compliance are different for "sophisticated investors" (as defined in the regulations) or other exempt organizations (such as banks and insurance companies) that are supposed to be professional investors who can watch out for their own best interests.

Compliance should be built in to your business practice. That means that all sales and processing procedures should be established in light of compliance principles and regulations. When you establish and follow appropriate compliance procedures from the start, you dramatically reduce customer complaints and enhance your reputation for conscientious service as well as the relationship of trust that your institution has with its customers.

Financial institutions that have formed their own NASD broker/dealer must follow all NASD compliance procedures. Use of a third-party provider makes no fundamental difference to the compliance procedures required. Whether a registered rep is a dual employee of a bank and a broker/dealer or the employee of a managed program, there must always be a straight line of reporting responsibility to the broker/dealer. All licensed persons engaged in securities sales are subject to the same set of rules, regulations, and procedures, regardless of the creativity of the employment arrangement. The NASD insists on this in order to retain control of the sales process and securities regulation. Furthermore, the OCC guidelines (BC-274, 7/19/93) suggest that bank personnel must also be actively involved in compliance issues and not depend completely upon nonbank personnel to ensure that adequate compliance standards are met.

The NASD and its Regulations

A large part of the body of information referred to collectively as compliance concerns securities activities that only a few banks or financial institutions engage in. Section 20 banks are allowed to underwrite securities, but there are only a handful of those banks. NASD regulations cover the full range of activities that could possibly affect securities sales and processing, from mark-ups to trading practices to settlement procedures to fraud. The NASD has stringent financial reporting requirements for every broker/dealer so it can verify the financial health of all its member firms at all times.

Both the six-hour Series 7 exam for registered reps and the three-hour Series 24 exam for principals (those who supervise registered reps) test whether registered reps and firm management have mastered this body of knowledge; there is no way we can convey the full breadth of NASD regulations in only a few pages. Our intent here is to concentrate on the compliance concepts most likely to affect your financial institution. By the time your institution is ready to sell securities, your organization will itself be a broker/dealer or will be associated with a broker/dealer, so you will have a compliance manual to follow and licensed personnel to operate your business. At the end of this chapter in Appendix 13A, some forms are included to deal with a number of different disclosure situations.

The NASD is a voluntary association of over-the-counter broker/dealers. Any firm joining the NASD agrees to abide by all its rules and regulations, including any penalties for violating those rules and regulations. Aside from the prestige of belonging to the NASD, commissions and compensation are available only member to member. It is imperative that your broker/dealer be a member in good standing with the NASD. The NASD's bylaws define its powers and list the registration and membership requirements for member firms (broker/dealers), their principals, and their registered reps.

The *NASD Manual* outlines the four sets of rules and codes the NASD uses to regulate its markets and members:

1. Rules of Fair Practice govern NASD members' dealing with the public; these are the fair and ethical trade practices that member firms and registered reps must follow.
2. Uniform Practice Code establishes trading conventions for settlements and good delivery for broker/dealers doing business with other broker/dealers.
3. Code of Procedure is how the NASD deals with member violations of the Rules of Fair Practice.
4. Code of Arbitration governs resolution of disagreements between and among members, registered reps and the public; this part of the code deals with disputes, claims, and controversies, not violations of regulations.

Our purpose here is to summarize the basic structure of the NASD and its codes. We do need to mention one aspect of the Code of Arbitration, because it has such an important bearing on a broker/dealer's relationship with retail customers.

The Code of Arbitration handles disputes between and among members, registered reps, and the public. When a dispute concerns a member of the public, the customer's written consent is necessary to bring the matter to arbitration. (No written consent is necessary to arbitrate between member firms or personnel.) Many broker/dealers require customers to sign an arbitration agreement stating that if a disagreement arises between the customer and the member firm or its registered rep(s), the customer will take the disagreement to arbitration, not to court. We recommend that all financial institutions use such a form. In fact, most broker/dealers will not accept a new account unless the customer signs an arbitration agreement.

Supervising Reps

The NASD has published a pamphlet called, "Understanding Your Role and Responsibilities as a Registered Representative,"[1] which lays out some of the NASD rules and regulations that most affect an individual registered rep in his or her day-to-day performance of duties. The pamphlet lists practices that violate NASD regulations:

- Spreading rumors, particularly while trying to induce a customer to buy on a "hot tip."

---

1   NASD, "Understanding Your Role," pp. 5-6.

- Using any kind of insider information for personal gain or for the gain of favored customers (insider trading), or placing orders based on nonpublic information that will soon affect the market (front running).
- Mixing customer funds with the registered rep's personal funds (commingling).
- Trying to get a customer to buy and sell more frequently than prudent investment practice warrants (churning).
- Making unsuitable recommendations for customer investments.
- Buying hot new issues for your own account (free riding), or holding back from the public a certain amount of new issue securities (withholding).
- Selling securities through some other mechanism than your own firm or without your firm's permission or knowledge (selling away).
- Sharing in the proceeds or profits of a customer account.
- Engaging in any activity that might be construed as a conflict of interest, such as recommending that customers purchase thinly traded stock that you own for your own account.
- Persuading your customer to switch out of a mutual fund on which he or she has already paid a load to buy a load fund from you that you will get paid a commission on (switching).
- Recommending a breakpoint sale, a solicited sale at a dollar amount just below the point where a reduced sales charge would occur.[2]
- Entering an unauthorized trade for a customer.
- Using fictitious accounts or hiding your investments in accounts belonging to someone else.
- Failing to cooperate with any request of the NASD.
- Cheating on exams.

Supervising your registered rep and/or other licensed personnel is likely to be the realm of compliance that most concerns a bank program. Most broker/dealers do not allow their registered reps to have accounts with other broker/dealers; if they do, they must notify the compliance officer and have a duplicate confirm of all trades sent to the compliance officer.

If you read the NASD's discipline list (which is sent to all NASD members and is published periodically in *The Wall Street Journal*), you will be struck by the diversity of things for which NASD members are disciplined: everything

---

2   Front-end-load mutual fund investments typically have breakpoints, points at which the load is significantly reduced. For example, the load on $2,000-50,000 might be 4%, but on $50,000 or more it might be 3%. If a registered rep persuades a customer to invest $50,000 in several different mutual funds in order to maximize the amount of commission he or she receives, rather than putting the entire amount into one fund or one fund family, that registered rep has violated the principle of breakpoint sales.

from small checks taken by registered reps for personal use to broad-based reporting fraud by member firms. We strongly recommend that anyone in any way concerned with the securities business read these listings. The cases of fraud are obvious; firms work hard to develop procedures for processing checks and securities that protect against unscrupulous registered reps. However, one can be truly taken aback by cases where a member is fined for *failing to supervise* a registered rep or a rep *and a firm* are disciplined for the rep's failure to tell the truth on a registration form.

Advertising

The NASD has strict guidelines for advertising, customer letters, and other sales literature that comes under the heading of communications with the public. The NASD distinguishes between mass communications (which could be seen by anyone), and directed communications (whose distribution is controlled by the broker/dealer). All communications with the public must be approved by a principal of the firm and kept in a special file for NASD review, including all registered rep correspondence with customers, to guard against statements that might be misleading, exaggerated, or based on rumor. New broker/dealers are required to file such items with the NASD for the first year. What this tells the financial institution is that it must cooperate with its broker/dealer in any advertising that is undertaken for the retail investment services program.

Compliance Audits

The NASD conducts periodic audits of all its members. A program using a third-party provider is unlikely to be affected by this audit (unless there are unfavorable results), which will take place at corporate headquarters. You should, however, ask your broker/dealer to talk to you about its compliance audits: what the NASD found and what actions are being taken as a result.

Every NASD firm must conduct at least a yearly on-premise compliance audit of every branch office to ensure that every branch and every rep follow proper compliance procedures. This audit will most likely be conducted by the compliance officer or general securities principal of the NASD firm. The member firm must have procedures for making this inspection and remedying any deficiencies. Every registered rep must attend at least one annual compliance meeting with the compliance officer or general securities principal of the firm. Carrying out these audits and meetings is a routine part of the securities business and is part of day-to-day business practice.

Suitability

One issue above all others concerns banks who offer retail investment programs: suitability, or making sure you know your customer well enough to recommend an investment that is appropriate for that customer. The NASD says, "The foundation of the securities industry is fair dealing with customers."[3] This issue is at the heart of delivering alternative investment products in banks. The essence of suitability is protecting the relationship of trust between a bank and its customers. Suitability is much more than a regulation, it is a moral obligation to the customer. It also happens to be by far the best sales method in the long run.

As far as the NASD is concerned, the first step in properly serving customers is obtaining a clear understanding of their financial condition. A rep must show due diligence by making a reasonable effort to obtain a customer's name, address, occupation, financial status, tax status, annual income, net worth, other brokerage relationships, and other securities holdings. Most programs have new account forms that require this information to be filled in, which helps the rep remember what to ask. In addition to financial information, a rep might perform a credit check or verify information with other financial institutions; this particular step is easy in a bank program, because the majority of new investment customers will already have financial records with the bank. A registered rep should keep customers' account records up to date.

The second part of the process is for the registered rep and the customer to come to a clear understanding of the customer's investment objectives. The registered rep is expected to be a professional trained to understand investments and investment risks and to educate the customer in such investing. The rep's recommendations must be limited to securities or investments that are suitable for that customer. The rep should review a customer's investment objectives periodically and make a written record of any changes.[4]

Strictly speaking, the NASD says suitability means selling a customer a product that is appropriate for that customer. Some houses push products in an obvious way and think suitability has been satisfied. But in a bank, the best business practice goes considerably beyond this bare-bones approach.

Suitability means identifying the customer's objectives and then choosing appropriate products to meet them. Taken as a whole, suitability asks about the customer's ability to live with the investment and the risk inherent in it; can the customer afford the product? Does it meet his or her objectives and needs? The single best approach to the question of suitability is education. Programs that follow the needs-based, consultative selling process we recommend should not

---

3   NASD, "Understanding Your Role," p.5.
4   Ibid., p.6.

have any problem with the question of suitability, because satisfying customer needs is part of the day-to-day sales process.

While it would clearly be unsuitable to sell an elderly person whose objective is income a portfolio composed of only aggressive growth funds, it is less obvious that advising young people to invest retirement funds in short-term, fixed-income investments may not be suitable. When young people want to invest in this fashion, the registered rep should be sure he or she understands their objectives clearly. The rep should ensure that customers understand the nature of long-term investing and the investments that will best help them reach their goals.

Registered reps may complain about the paperwork connected with opening an account, but the paperwork isn't very different from that necessary to open a new bank account. Opening a new account usually involves completing the following forms:

- New account form containing detailed customer information.
- W-9.
- Cash account agreement.
- Arbitration agreement, in which a customer agrees to go to arbitration in the event of a disagreement.
- New account disclosure statement for alternative investment products. (See the sample form in Appendix A at the end of this chapter.)
- Product disclosure statement, if necessary (stating that an equity transaction was unsolicited, for example).
- Trade ticket.

IRA or other tax-qualified accounts, margin accounts, or options accounts require additional paperwork. The customer's signature is needed on all of these documents except the new account form (which the registered rep signs).

Mutual Fund Disclosure

We have found it helpful to design a special mutual fund disclosure form that both reiterates the nature of mutual funds (principal is not guaranteed, etc.) and specifies the breakpoints for the mutual fund the customer is investing in. (See the sample form in Appendix A at the end of this chapter.) A significant amount of walk-in business is done with customers who have nowhere near the breakpoint amount (typically $50,000 to 100,000) to put into any one mutual fund. However, it is good compliance procedure to have all reps routinely fill in these forms with the breakpoint information. This makes compliance part of your procedures. Proper documentation ensures clean selling and protects all parties involved in the transaction from later claims or misunderstandings.

Unsolicited Transactions

Throughout this book we have stressed the importance of recommending good products that are suitable for your customer. Sometimes customers want to buy products (such as equities) that you don't perform due diligence on; sometimes customers need to liquidate securities obtained through another broker/dealer. If you can do the trade there is no reason to have the customer establish a relationship with someone else, but you need to protect yourself against the potential accusation that you recommended a penny or poorly performing stock. Have the customer sign an "unsolicited transaction" agreement stating that the broker/dealer or the registered rep did not solicit the transaction and that the customer takes full responsibility for the investment. It is in the best interest of all parties to execute these trades on an "as agent" basis for the customer, not as principal. It reinforces the broker/dealer's position of not having recommended this product. (See the sample form in Appendix A at the end of this chapter.)

Customer Complaints

Customer complaints, written and oral, are taken very seriously by the NASD. All member firms must keep a file for written complaints and a log of oral complaints. The member firm must adequately investigate all such complaints. If an individual firm does not resolve a complaint to the customer's satisfaction, the customer can file with the NASD under the Code of Procedure.

Other Compliance Procedures

- The member firm must exercise special supervision over any employee who has been permitted by the NASD to continue in employment only under prescribed conditions.
- All member firms must respond promptly and completely to NASD requests for information.
- All member firms must keep a file of internal disciplinary actions taken against registered reps or other member personnel.
- The NASD expects all member firms to investigate the background of everyone it is planning to hire. Member firms must have a copy of a registered rep's most recent U-5 (the document that terminates a rep's relationship with a member firm).

Complying With Bank Regulators

The OCC, the Fed, and the FDIC

In the last chapter we discussed the various regulators involved with retail investment services programs in banks. When these programs began, bank regulators typically tried to prohibit them, but times have already changed. What we see now from the Fed, the OCC, and the FDIC are regulations concerned with making sure customers understand how alternative investment products differ from bank liabilities or any other products that they may have bought on bank premises. The Fed guidelines apply only to mutual fund sales activities. The OCC guidelines are considerably more fleshed out than the Fed guidelines. It is well worth the time of anyone involved with AIPs to read the OCC, the Fed, and the FDIC guidelines. These guidelines are included at the end of this chapter as Appendixes B, C, and D.

The heart of this disclosure process involves informing customers of the following facts:

- Alternative investment products are not liabilities of the bank.
- AIPs are not in any way guaranteed by the bank.
- AIPs are not insured by the FDIC or any other government agency.
- AIPs may fluctuate in principal and return, possibly involving loss of principal.

These disclosures should be displayed prominently in all advertising, sales literature, and signage of the program. Confirmations and mutual fund account statements should also make them clear.

Ensuring that customers truly understand these principles is not easy, especially since they are buying alternative investment products in the bank where they have always bought their CDs; in some dual-employee programs, even the salesperson is the same. The best programs use disclosure forms, which serve two purposes. First, using the forms guarantees that the rep will follow the proper sales process and remember to mention every item. Second, the customer will initial each separate item, indicating that it has been explained and he or she understands it. This protects the institution against a customer claiming at some future time that he or she did not really understand what he or she was buying. These forms protect the financial institution, the customer, and the registered rep. We have included sample forms in Appendix A at the end of this chapter.

The OCC, Fed, and FDIC guidelines for retail investment services programs quite closely track NASD requirements. The OCC guidelines state that even when the NASD Rules of Fair Practice do not expressly apply to a given program, they "are an appropriate reference in constructing a compliance program for safe and sound retail sales of all nondeposit investment products."[5]

The OCC guidelines recommend, and the Fed and FDIC guidelines mandate, that a retail investment services program be in a physical location separate from the area where bank deposit and liability products are sold. The bank may not use its own name for its own proprietary funds and should try to minimize customer confusion when names are similar. The relationship between the bank and a proprietary mutual fund should be made clear to the customer, including the fact that investments in the mutual fund are not guaranteed by the bank. The OCC further adds that the bank should disclose any early withdrawal penalties, surrender charge penalties, and deferred sales charges.

The FDIC expresses a particular concern about certain marketing practices. "Bank management should be mindful of the potential for confusion when developing policies governing the permissibility of the use of bank customer information for marketing purposes. Marketing efforts which have targeted customers with maturing certificates of deposit can lead to abuse and therefore are of special concern to the FDIC. Banks allowing such targeted marketing should take precautions to ensure that customers are fully informed about, and understand the nature of, mutual fund and annuity investments as opposed to insured deposits."[6]

All three regulators prohibit tellers or employees who take retail deposits from offering investment advice, but the Fed specifies that bank employees should direct customers seeking investment advice to an employee of either the bank or a third-party provider who has been "specifically designated and trained as an investment adviser."[7] The OCC "strongly discourages" platform programs where the same employee both takes retail deposits and sells retail nondeposit investment products, although it does not outright prohibit them. The OCC encourages programs to employ full-time, licensed professionals with both securities training and experience. They may be employees of either the broker/dealer or the bank, as long as they have the professional qualifications.

The Fed guidelines state that Federal Reserve examiners will assess whether "the bank has adequate written policies and procedures in place to ensure that its practices are not misleading, and that mutual fund sales activities are sepa-

---

5   "Retail Nondeposit," U.S. Comptroller of Currency, p.6.
6   "FDIC Supervisory Statement Regarding State Nonmember Bank Sales of Mutual Funds and Annuities," FIL-71-93, FDIC, October 8, 1993.
7   "Separation of Mutual Fund Sales Activities from Insured Deposit-Taking Activities," Chicago: Federal Reserve Bank, 1993, p.3.

rate and distinct from routine retail deposit-taking activities."[8] The policy further states that, "In assessing the adequacy and effectiveness of the bank's policies, examiners will evaluate whether . . . the bank has a policy to ensure that a third party conducting mutual fund sales on its premises is issuing disclosures and following procedures comparable to those required for a state member bank conducting this activity."[9]

Bank Compliance

The OCC guidelines conclude by stating that "banks must maintain compliance programs capable of verifying compliance with the guidelines specified in this circular and with any other applicable requirements. The compliance function should be performed independently of investment products' sales and management. At a minimum, the compliance function should include a system to monitor customer complaints and to review periodically customer accounts to detect and prevent abusive practices."[10] This seems to recommend a bank compliance person even for those institutions using third-party providers. Although this person is not NASD-licensed, he or she must understand the securities business. This person should review the TPP's procedures and compliance manuals, as well as the flow of cash and trade tickets.

Financial institutions offering retail investment services programs must of course also continue to comply with any other regulations that affect them and their programs.

The Municipal Securities Rulemaking Board

The MSRB has a much longer history with banks than the NASD, as explained in the last chapter. Many regional institutions have been regular members of the MSRB for years and fully understand their roles and responsibilities within that organization. Institutions beginning a retail investment services program without that institutional history will find that selling municipal securities is not greatly different from selling other securities. There are separate reporting requirements for underwriting municipal securities or participating in a syndicate in any way, but your retail investment services program is not likely to be involved with those activities. Confirms must contain certain information, but this is the kind of technical information you will have to acquire if you issue

---

8 Ibid., p.4.
9 Ibid.
10 "Retail Nondeposit," U.S. Comptroller of Currency, p. 6.

your own confirmations—and that is a different book. Your clearing agent or the clearance software system you buy will do this for you.

Licensing

Securities Licensing

All those who sell securities must be appropriately licensed by the NASD. Individuals can take exams only under the auspices of a broker/dealer; they cannot contact the NASD directly and register for an exam. Exams take place at a number of different centers throughout the country. Most exams are given directly on a computer, under strictly supervised circumstances. The questions on any particular exam are drawn from a large pool of questions, so no two exams are identical.

The tests can be very demanding. They all represent a body of knowledge that must be studied; rarely would a person learn enough on the job to pass one of these exams. Study materials are available through any number of organizations, as are classes of various intensity. Study methods, materials, and classes are completely at the discretion of the individual (or his or her broker/dealer); the person needs only to pass the exam. (This is different for insurance exams.)

There are a number of different licenses; we will discuss the ones most commonly required by a bank retail investment services program.

Series 6. Investment Company/Variable Contract Products Limited Representative. This license entitles a representative to sell only mutual funds and variable annuities and is used by many firms that engage primarily in the sale of insurance-related products. The material covered by this exam is only a small portion of that covered by the Series 7, and this exam is considered much less onerous than the Series 7.

Series 7. General Securities Representative. This license allows a registered rep to sell all types of securities products, including corporate stocks and bonds, government and municipal securities, options, direct participation programs, investment company products (such as mutual funds), variable annuities (if the rep also holds an insurance license), and most other types of securities. The Series 7 exam is a rigorous, thorough exam that lasts six hours. Study time is at least 120 hours.

Series 24. General Securities Principal. Every registered rep must be supervised by a person with a principal's license. A Series 6 or Series 7 rep will be supervised by a general securities principal who has passed the Series 24. Every broker/dealer must have at least two general securities principals, no matter how few reps it has; NASD guidelines suggest one general securities principal for every ten registered reps. The general securities principal can be any person actively involved in the member's management or training activities. A general securities principal must obtain separate qualifications to function as a municipal securities principal (Series 53), a registered options principal (Series 4) or financial operations principal (Series 27).

Series 27. Financial Operations Principal (FinOp). The FinOp is responsible for supervising the financial administration of the firm, including preparing, maintaining, approving, and filing the reports required of member firms.

Series 52. MSRB Municipal Securities Rep. This license entitles a rep to sell municipal securities. It is often used for bank bond departments that are not NASD members or for individuals who sell nothing besides municipal securities. A person who wants to sell municipal securities must serve a 90-day apprenticeship before doing business with the public. A rep with a Series 7 license does not need this separate qualification.

Series 53. Municipal Securities Principal. Every member firm doing municipal securities business with the public must have at least one municipal securities principal who manages the municipal securities business of the member. This qualification is also necessary for bank bond departments that sell municipal debt products but are not members of the NASD.

Series 63. Uniform Securities Agent State Law Exam. A Series 63 license is required by most states in addition to the Series 6 or 7. The exam covers state securities law and regulation. The Series 63 is a one-hour, 50-question exam administered by the NASD.

GSA. (Government Securities Association). U.S. government securities are totally exempt from NASD registration. However, the GSA keeps track of those individuals who sell only U.S. government securities. Currently there are no testing requirements, but anyone who deals in these securities or makes recommendations about them must be registered and fingerprinted. This applies particularly to individuals working in a bank or a brokerage house that specializes in U.S. government securities. Those individuals who have a Series 7 are exempt from this separate registration.

Series 3. Commodities Futures. A Series 7 license allows a registered rep to sell financial futures, but a Series 3 license is necessary to sell commodities futures such as oil or pork bellies. If you intend to offer these products, you will need to employ a rep with this license, although such programs are rare.

Series 4. Registered Options Principal (ROP). If you have any Series 3 reps selling commodities or any Series 7 reps selling options, you must have a ROP. In addition, you must have a compliance registered options principal (CROP) and a supervisory registered options principal (SROP). These principals have also passed the Series 4, but they are registered separately with the NASD.

Insurance Licensing

Insurance activities are regulated at the state level, and all insurance exams are state exams. Most states require proof of a certain number of credit hours of class before one can take the insurance producers' exam or obtain a license. Requirements vary from a few hours to a full week's worth of classes. A rep can be licensed in (1) life, (2) accident and health, and (3) property and casualty. Individuals usually take life and accident and health together, although they are separate exams (generally taken in the same testing period). Some states require an individual to be sponsored by an insurance company. Many states require some individuals to carry small bonds (perhaps $2,500, depending on the kind of business they write).

To sell insurance in a state other than one's home state, the requirements vary from easily obtained reciprocity to virtual hostility between states. Sometimes requirements are not easily satisfied.

Variable Contracts

An individual selling variable annuities, variable life insurance, or variable universal life must have both a securities license (Series 6 or 7) and an insurance producers' license. To have variable contracts (which include these three products) added to one's insurance license, state insurance departments require proof of the appropriate NASD license. Some states merely record that a person is so licensed; other states write "variable contracts" on the license. Variable contracts are sold through insurance companies, which all require proof of appropriate licensing for both the company and the individual before allowing their products to be sold.

Note: *The NASD Compliance Check List* is available from the NASD for $35. (Call NASD MediaSource^SM at 301-590-6578.) This booklet gives a good overview of NASD compliance regulations and procedures.

Appendix A
Sample Disclosure Statements

Sample Bank

NEW ACCOUNT DISCLOSURE STATEMENT

_____ I understand that LCL Investments, Inc. is not a bank and the products it offers are not backed or guaranteed by a bank, nor are they insured by the Federal Deposit Insurance Corporation (FDIC.).

_____ As a client of LCL Investments, Inc., I acknowledge that all transactions will be considered the sole responsibility of LCL Investments. All confirmations, account statements, and correspondence resulting from a transaction are the responsibility of LCL Investments, and not of the bank.

_____ I understand that LCL Investments is not affiliated with Sample Bank.

_____ I understand that the investment and insurance products that I purchase or may purchase are not issued or guaranteed by LCL Investments and are not insured by the FDIC or any other governmental agency.

_____ I understand that I am making an investment, and that the principal value of my investment may be higher or lower in the future, depending upon market conditions, and that my principal may be subject to loss.

_____ I understand that my investment will have either a sales charge which will be included in the yield quoted or a service fee (or load) which will be added at the time of the transaction.

This document has been fully explained to me. I have initialed each section to show that I have read each statement and my registered representative has explained each statement to me, and I understand them.

_____   _____   _____
Name (please print)   Signature   Date

For joint accounts:

_____   _____   _____
Name (please print)   Signature   Date

Asset Manager' Signature_____

_____

Asset Manager

DISCLOSURE STATEMENT FOR DIRECT EQUITY TRANSACTIONS

- This product is direct equity. By definition, direct equity is an ownership investment in a company. Direct equity products include, but are not limited to, common stock, preferred stock, and warrants. The rate of return and market value of the shares will fluctuate with changes in market conditions.

- This product is not a certificate of deposit, and it is not insured by the FDIC or by any federal agency. Banks and savings institutions offer a number of products that are federally insured. By signing this letter, you are acknowledging that you have determined that this product is a more suitable purchase for your financial needs and objectives.

- I acknowledge that this direct equity transaction was not solicited by LCL Investments and that I have chosen this security on my own. I have done the research and have determined that it is a suitable investment for my portfolio.

- I understand that, due to equity price fluctuation, the principal value of my investment may be higher or lower in the future, depending upon market conditions, and the principal may be subject to loss.

- By signing this disclosure statement, I acknowledge that it applies to every direct equity transaction I do.

I acknowledge that I have read each of the above items. My registered representative has explained each statement to me, and I understand them.

_____   _____   _____

Name (please print)   Signature   Date

For joint accounts:

_____   _____   _____

Name (please print)   Signature   Date

_____
Asset Manager

DISCLOSURE STATEMENT FOR MUTUAL FUNDS

_____
Fund Name

- This product is a mutual fund. By definition, a mutual fund invests the money it receives from shareholders such as yourself in securities, as outlined in the prospectus. The rate of return and market value of the fund shares will fluctuate with changes in market conditions.

- This product is not a certificate of deposit, and it is not insured by the FDIC or by any federal agency. Banks and savings institutions offer a number of products that are federally insured. By signing this letter, you are acknowledging that you have determined that this product is a more suitable purchase for your financial needs and objectives.

- It may take ten business days or longer before the funds will be available when you choose to redeem your fund shares.

Service Fees (Load Charges)

- This mutual fund has an initial sales charge of _____ %. This charge is represented by the difference between the public offering price and the net asset value on the date of purchase. It is incurred at the time you make your initial investment and each time you make an additional investment in the fund.

  This mutual fund has a breakpoint (reduced sales charge for a minimum dollar investment). Your current contribution of $_____ carries a load of_____ . The next breakpoint for this mutual fund is $_____ . An additional contribution of $_____ will reduce the load charge to_____ .

No-Load Funds

- If this mutual fund does not have an initial sales charge, it may contain a contingent deferred back-end sales charge of __% which you will be required to pay each time that you redeem shares.

I acknowledge that I have read and understand each of the above items. I have initialed each section to show that my registered representative has explained each statement to me, and I understand them. **I ACKNOWLEDGE THAT I HAVE RECEIVED A PROSPECTUS THAT CONTAINS COMPLETE DETAILS OF THE FUND.**

_____   _____   _____
Name (please print)   Signature   Date

For joint accounts:

_____   _____   _____
Name (please print)   Signature   Date

Appendix B
OCC Guidelines to Retail Nondeposit Investment Sales

BANKING ISSUANCE

Comptroller of the Currency
Administrator of National Banks

Type: Banking Circular   Subject: Retail Nondeposit Investment Sales

TO: Chief Executive Officers of National Banks, Deputy Comptrollers, Department
and Division Heads, and Examining Personnel

BACKGROUND

National banks are offering mutual funds, annuities and other nondeposit investments for sale
to retail customers through various types of arrangements. Banks must develop programs
and procedures addressing their investment sales activities to apprise customers fully of the
nature of these investments. The Office of the Comptroller of the Currency (OCC) is issuing
this circular to provide general guidance to national banks engaging in such activities.

Banks should view customers' interests as critical to all aspects of their sales programs.
Banks that do not operate their programs safely and soundly risk potential liability from
customer actions. The OCC will take appropriate actions to address unsafe and unsound
banking practices and violations of law and regulations associated with bank-related sales of
nondeposit investment products.

SCOPE

The guidelines in this circular apply to bank-related retail sales (including marketing and
promotional activities) of nondeposit investment products. Such sales include:

- sales made by bank employees,

- sales made by employees of affiliated or unaffiliated entities occurring on bank
premises (including telephone sales from bank premises and sales initiated by
mail from bank premises), and

- sales resulting from customer referrals when the bank receives a benefit for the
referral.

BANK RESPONSIBILITIES

The OCC expects national banks to comply with all applicable laws, rules, regulations, and
regulatory conditions in any bank-related sale of mutual funds, annuities or other retail

BANKING ISSUANCE

Comptroller of the Currency
Administrator of National Banks

Type: Banking Circular   **Subject:** Retail Nondeposit Investment Sales

nondeposit investment products. Bank directors are responsible for evaluating the risks posed by bank-related nondeposit investment sales. Bank directors must adopt self-regulatory policies and procedures to ensure compliance with those requirements and to ensure consistency with the guidelines in this circular. A bank's policies and procedures must address bank-related retail sales made directly by a bank, through an operating subsidiary or affiliate, or by an unaffiliated entity.

The OCC's examination authority covers all bank-related retail sales operations, including sales by other entities. Bank management should enter into a clear agreement with any entity involved in bank-related sales that outlines the duties and responsibilities of each party. The agreement should specify that such entities will comply with all applicable requirements, including those in this circular. The bank should make it clear to other entities that bank management and the OCC will be verifying such compliance. The governing agreement should include provisions regarding bank oversight and examiner access to appropriate records.

MINIMUM STANDARDS

The antifraud provisions of the federal securities laws and regulations prohibit materially misleading or inaccurate representations in connection with offers and sales of securities. If customers are misled about the nature of nondeposit investment products, including their uninsured status, sellers could face potential liability under these antifraud provisions. Safe and sound banking also requires that bank-related sales programs be operated to avoid customer confusion about the products being offered. Use of nonbank employees to sell these products does not relieve bank management of the responsibility to take reasonable steps to ensure that the investment sales program meets these requirements.

The Rules of Fair Practice of the National Association of Securities Dealers expressly govern sales of securities by broker/dealers who are members of the NASD. These rules apply to bank-related securities sales by banking subsidiaries registered as broker/dealers, affiliated broker/dealers, and unaffiliated broker/dealers operating under agreements with banks. These rules apply whether such sales are made on bank premises or at separate locations. Even for bank-related sales where such rules do not expressly apply, the Rules of Fair Practice are an appropriate reference in constructing a compliance program for safe and sound retail sales of all nondeposit investment products.

Date: July 19, 1993   Page 2 of 7

BANKING ISSUANCE

Comptroller of the Currency
Administrator of National Banks

Type: Banking Circular   Subject: Retail Nondeposit Investment Sales

GENERAL GUIDELINES

Bank-related sales of nondeposit investment products should follow the guidelines listed below. Although these guidelines are generally consistent with the requirements of the Rules of Fair Practice, they may vary to accommodate the particular circumstances surrounding bank-related sales of nondeposit investment products.

A.   Program Management

Banks should adopt a statement describing the features of the sales program, the roles of bank employees, and the roles of third party entities. At a minimum, this statement should address the following issues:

- **Supervision of personnel involved in nondeposit investment sales programs.** Senior bank managers will be expected to ensure that specific individuals employed by the bank, an affiliated broker/dealer, or a third party vender are responsible for each activity outlined in the bank's investment sales policy.

- **The roles of other entities selling on bank premises, including supervision of selling employees.** Bank management must plan to monitor compliance by other entities on an ongoing basis. The degree of bank management's involvement should be dictated by the nature and extent of nondeposit investment product sales, the effectiveness of customer protection systems, and customers' responses.

- **The types of products that the bank will sell.** For each type of product sold by bank employees, the bank should identify specific laws, regulations, regulatory conditions and any other limitations or requirements, including qualitative considerations, that will expressly govern the selection and marketing of products the bank will offer.

- **Policies governing the permissible uses of bank customer information.** Such policies should address the use of bank customer information for any purpose in connection with a bank-related retail investment sales activity.

BANKING ISSUANCE

Comptroller of the Currency
Administrator of National Banks

Type: Banking Circular   Subject: Retail Nondeposit Investment Sales

B.   Setting and Circumstances of Retail Nondeposit Investment Sales

Banks should market nondeposit products in a manner that does not mislead or confuse customers as to the nature of the products or the risks. To avoid customer confusion about these products, bank policies should specifically address the locations at which sales will take place. To the extent permitted by space and personnel considerations, bank management should take steps to separate the retail deposit-taking and retail nondeposit sales functions.

Banks should prohibit tellers from offering investment advice. In addition, the OCC strongly discourages employees who accept retail deposits from selling retail nondeposit investment products. Due to the potential for customer confusion if the bank permits an employee to perform both functions, the bank should disclose this dual role to customers in addition to the disclosures outlined below.

Banks should avoid the possibility of customer confusion by following the guidelines set forth below. In addition, banks may not offer uninsured retail investment products with a product name identical to the bank's name. Banks also should recognize that the potential for customer confusion may be increased where the bank uses uninsured product names that are similar to the bank's own and should design their sales training to minimize this risk.

C.   Disclosures and Advertising

Complete and accurate disclosure must be provided to avoid customer confusion as to whether a bank-related product is an investment product or an insured bank deposit. When selling, advertising or otherwise marketing uninsured investment products to retail customers, the following product disclosures should be made conspicuously: The products offered (1) **are not FDIC insured**; (2) are not obligations of the bank; (3) are not guaranteed by the bank; and (4) involve investment risks, including the possible **loss of principal.**

The OCC believes it is appropriate to obtain a signed statement acknowledging such disclosures from customers at the time a retail nondeposit investment account is opened. For accounts established prior to the issuance of this circular, the bank should consider obtaining such a signed statement prior to the next sale. These disclosures also should be featured conspicuously in all written or oral sales presentations, advertising and promotional

BC -274

BANKING ISSUANCE

Comptroller of the Currency
Administrator of National Banks

Type: **Banking Circular**   Subject: Retail Nondeposit Investment Sales

materials, prospectuses, and periodic statements that include information on both deposit and nondeposit products.

The bank should review bank-related sales advertisements to ensure that they are accurate, do not mislead customers about the nature of the product, and include required disclosures.

Where applicable, the bank should disclose:

- The existence of an advisory or other relationship between the bank and any affiliate involved in providing the nondeposit investment product, and

- The existence of any early withdrawal penalties, surrender charge penalties, and deferred sales charges.

D.   Suitability

Consistent with the Rules of Fair Practice, the OCC expects banks to determine whether a product being recommended is an appropriate investment for the customer. Banks should ensure that any salespeople involved in bank-related sales obtain sufficient information from customers to enable the salesperson to make a judgment about the suitability of recommendations for particular customers. At a minimum, suitability inquiries should be made and responses documented consistent with the Rules of Fair Practice concerning the customer's financial status, tax status, investment objectives and other factors that may be relevant, prior to making recommendations to the customer.

E.   Qualifications and Training

Banks should ensure that sales personnel are properly qualified and adequately trained to sell all bank-related nondeposit investment products. Bank management should consider securities industry or other professional qualification training as an appropriate reference. Banks should implement training programs to ensure that sales personnel have thorough product knowledge (as opposed to simple sales training for a product) and understand customer protection requirements. Background inquiries about new bank sales employees with previous securities industry experience should include a check of possible disciplinary

BANKING ISSUANCE

Comptroller of the Currency
Administrator of National Banks

Type: Banking Circular   Subject: Retail Nondeposit Investment Sales

history with securities regulators. Audit and compliance personnel should be properly qualified and trained as well.

F.   Compensation

Bank management should ensure that compensation programs do not operate as an incentive for salespeople to sell retail nondeposit investment products over a more suitable option. If tellers participate in referral programs that include compensation features, banks should not base such compensation on the success of the sale.

G.   Fiduciary Accounts

Banks must comply with all applicable state and federal restrictions on transactions involving the bank's fiduciary accounts. For example, pursuant to 12 CFR 9.12, national bank fiduciaries are restricted from using the bank's own brokerage service, or any other entity with which the bank has a conflict of interest, to conduct fiduciary transactions without express authorization in the governing trust documents, under local law, a court order, or without informed consents from all beneficiaries. Similar restrictions govern purchases of a bank's proprietary and other products for fiduciary accounts where a conflict of interest arises. If so authorized, bank trust departments are reminded that they must conduct a regular and reasonable periodic review of the continuing prudence of holding the product for a fiduciary account. Banks also should comply with any applicable provisions of the Employee Retirement Income Security Act of 1974, including its prohibited transaction provisions.

H.   Compliance Program

Banks must maintain compliance programs capable of verifying compliance with the guidelines specified in this circular and with any other applicable requirements. The compliance function should be performed independently of investment product sales and management. At a minimum, the compliance function should include a system to monitor customer complaints and to review periodically customer accounts to detect and prevent abusive practices.

BANKING ISSUANCE

Comptroller of the Currency
Administrator of National Banks

Type: **Banking Circular**   Subject: Retail Nondeposit Investment Sales

SUPERVISION

The OCC will continue to include a review of compliance with all applicable requirements, including those in this circular, in its supervision of national banks involved in retail sales of investment products. The guidelines take effect immediately. Questions on the content of this circular may be submitted to the Office of the Chief National Bank Examiner, Capital Markets Group, Washington, DC 20219.

[signature]

Susan F. Krause
Senior Deputy Comptroller for Bank Supervision Policy

Appendix C
Federal Reserve Guidelines on Mutual Fund Sales

FEDERAL RESERVE BANK
OF CHICAGO

Supervisory Policy

July 2, 1993
CSC No. 93-98

ATTENTION: Chief Executive Officer

SUBJECT: Separation of Mutual Fund Sales Activities from Insured Deposit-Taking Activities

EFFECTIVE DATE: Immediately

HIGHLIGHTS: The Federal Reserve System offers the following supervisory policy as guidance for state member banks selling mutual fund shares, directly or through a subsidiary. The supervisory policy outlines the responsibility of the bank for ensuring that their customers are made aware of the differences between mutual funds and insured deposit instruments. Further, measures should be taken by state member banks to ensure that the sale of mutual funds poses minimal risk to the safety and soundness of the bank.

The supervisory policy is intended to be used as general guidance on an interim basis, while a general review is conducted, in conjunction with the other regulatory agencies, on the sale of all uninsured investment products on bank premises.

Please refer to the attachment for further details.

**FURTHER
INFORMATION:**   <u>Supervision and Regulation Department</u>

William Barouski
Assistant Vice President
(312) 322-8178

Kathleen Benson
Examining Officer
(312) 322-8179

ATTACHMENT: Mutual Fund Sales Activities Guidance Letter

P.O. BOX 834
CHICAGO, ILLINOIS 60690-0834

SUBJECT: Separation of Mutual Fund Sales Activities from Insured
           Deposit-Taking Activities

Banks have become increasingly involved in offering mutual
funds to their retail customers, prompting a renewed focus on the
role of a bank in the sale of mutual funds including a bank's
responsibility for ensuring customers are made aware of the
differences between mutual funds and insured deposit instruments.
In some cases, the mutual funds offered by a bank are third-party
funds that the bank simply makes available for purchase directly
from a distributor. In other cases, the mutual funds offered are
private-label or proprietary funds, which may be advised by the
bank or an affiliate. In these instances, the banking
organization receives some sales-related compensation, and when
it is employed by the mutual fund as an investment adviser, it
also receives compensation for this service.

State member banks selling mutual fund shares, directly or
through a subsidiary, must conduct that activity in compliance
with principles of prudent and safe banking. State member banks
should take sufficient measures to ensure that their customers
understand the nature of mutual fund investments. Prudent
measures should also be taken by state member banks to ensure
that the sale of mutual funds poses minimal risk to the safety
and soundness of the bank.

A state member bank that sells shares of a mutual fund
advised by the bank's parent holding company or by a nonbank
subsidiary of the parent holding company is subject to additional
requirements as set forth in the Board's interpretative rule
under the Bank Holding Company Act (12 CFR 225.125(h), as amended
8/92). A state member bank must meet the requirements contained
in the Board's interpretive rule as well as the requirements in
this letter.

The information presented in this letter is intended to be
used as general guidance on an interim basis while a general
review is conducted, in conjunction with the other regulatory
agencies, of the sale of all uninsured investment products on
bank premises. It is expected that, as a result of this review,

a more extensive policy statement will be released at a later date and will contain more detailed guidance on the sale of mutual funds for use by examiners and the banking organizations supervised by the Federal Reserve System.

Location of Mutual Fund Sales

When mutual funds are sold by bank employees, or are sold in a retail banking area, measures should be taken to ensure that purchasers do not have the impression that the mutual funds are federally-insured deposits or that they are obligations of the banking organization. To lessen the potential for confusion between mutual fund investments and insured bank deposits, mutual funds should be sold in a physical location separate from the area where business involving insured bank deposits is conducted. This area should be distinguished from the routine retail deposit-taking area through the use of signs and other means of identifying the sales area for mutual funds. Bank tellers should not offer any investment advice to any customer. Bank employees should direct customers seeking investment advice to the employee of either the bank or a third-party specifically designated and trained as an investment adviser.

Disclosure

Uninsured Nature of Mutual Funds/Investment Risk

It is important that sales programs targeting retail customers not employ practices that could mislead the bank's customers with respect to the uninsured nature of mutual funds and the investment risk associated with mutual funds. When reviewing the adequacy of mutual fund disclosures, examiners consider whether a bank's disclosures appear to inform investors adequately of the risks associated with the products they are purchasing. To help ensure that retail customers are able to understand the uninsured nature of mutual funds, state member banks should not sell shares of any mutual fund, or allow third parties to sell shares of mutual funds on depository institution premises, in a manner that conveys the impression or suggestion that such instruments are either: 1) federally-insured deposits, or 2) are obligations of, or guaranteed by, an insured depository institution.

Disclosure that mutual funds are not federally-insured and are not obligations of the bank should be displayed prominently in all mutual fund advertising, promotional and sales material issued by the bank. Mutual fund sales confirmations and periodic account statements issued by the bank should also disclose that mutual funds are not guaranteed by the bank, the Federal Deposit Insurance Corporation, or any other government agency.

At the time any account for the purchase of mutual fund shares is established, customers must be informed, in writing, that mutual fund shares are not deposits or any other type of

obligation of the depository institution, the FDIC, or any other
government agency. Additionally, the disclosure statement should
indicate that the investment is subject to risk that may cause
the value of the investment to fluctuate, and that when the
investment is sold, the value may be higher or lower than the
amount originally paid by the customer. A verbal disclosure can
be made but must be followed by written disclosure. To promote
customer knowledge of mutual funds, state member banks are
encouraged to obtain a statement, signed by the customer,
indicating that the customer has been informed and understands
that his or her investment is not insured or guaranteed, and that
the investment is subject to fluctuation in value.

<u>Bank as Adviser to a Mutual Fund</u>

In instances where a state member bank is selling shares of
a mutual fund advised by the bank or an affiliate, the bank
should take precautions to ensure that the customer understands
the nature of the advisory relationship and understands that,
although the mutual fund is advised by the bank or an affiliate,
investments in the fund are not guaranteed by the bank. In
addition to the insurance and investment risk disclosures
discussed above, if a bank sells shares of a mutual fund advised
by the bank or an affiliate, the bank must disclose, in writing,
at the time the account is opened, the role of the bank or
affiliated company as an adviser to the mutual fund.

Examination of Mutual Fund Activities

In their review of on-premise sales of mutual fund shares
during the regular examination of a state member bank, Federal
Reserve examiners will assess whether the bank has adequate
written policies and procedures in place to ensure that its
practices are not misleading, and that mutual fund sales
activities are separate and distinct from routine retail deposit-
taking activities.

In assessing the adequacy and effectiveness of the bank's
policies, examiners will evaluate whether:

1)   Disclosure is effective in conveying that mutual funds are
       not obligations of, or guaranteed by, the bank, the FDIC, or
       any other agency;

2)   disclosure is effective in conveying that mutual fund
       investments are subject to risk and may fluctuate in value;

3)   disclosure of a bank or affiliate's advisory role is made
       when applicable, and whether disclosure is effective;

4)   disclosure on periodic mutual fund account statements,
       confirmations, and promotional material issued by the bank
       is adequate in conveying that mutual fund investments are
       not insured by the FDIC or guaranteed by the bank;

5)   retail deposit-taking employees of the insured depository institution are prohibited from offering investment advice;

6)   the sales area for mutual funds is separate and distinct from the retail deposit area;

7)   the bank has a policy to ensure that a third-party conducting mutual fund sales on its premises is issuing disclosures and following procedures comparable to those required for a state member bank conducting this activity.

Examiners will be using the information presented in this letter as general guidance for the review of mutual fund sales activities on the premises of a state member bank. An additional effort is currently underway to coordinate with other agencies to ensure consistency in the supervision of mutual fund sales by banks. It is expected that a detailed policy statement will be issued at a later date which will address these activities more comprehensively.

Appendix D
FDIC Guidelines to Sales of Nondeposit Investments

FDIC
Federal Deposit Insurance Corporation
Washington, DC 20429

Office of the Director
Division of Supervision

FIL-71-93
October 8, 1993

SALES OF NONDEPOSIT INVESTMENTS

TO: CHIEF EXECUTIVE OFFICER

SUBJECT: Supervisory Statement Regarding State Nonmember Bank
             Sales of Mutual Funds and Annuities

The FDIC's Division of Supervision has developed the attached supervisory statement to alert state nonmember banks to concerns and issues raised by bank sales of mutual funds and annuities, which are investment products not covered by federal deposit insurance or other guarantees against loss. One such concern is the potential for customer confusion if a bank offers nondeposit investments at the same location where FDIC-insured deposits are solicited. Another is the potential for mismanagement of the sales program, which could expose the bank to liability under the anti-fraud provisions of federal securities laws.

For further information, please contact Curtis L. Vaughn, an Examination Specialist in the FDIC's Division of Supervision (202-898-6759) or Ann Loikow, a Counsel in the FDIC's Legal Division (202-898-3796).

Stanley J. Poling
Director

Attachment

Distribution: FDIC-Supervised Banks (Commercial and Savings)

FDIC Supervisory Statement on
State Nonmember Bank Sales of Mutual Funds and Annuities

Background

Banks increasingly are involved in the sales of mutual funds and annuities in response to changing customer needs and in an attempt to retain customer relationships while increasing noninterest income. Such activities include sales made directly by a bank, through a bank subsidiary or affiliate, or by an unaffiliated entity whether located on bank premises or located off-site but dependent on customer referrals from which the bank receives a benefit. Securities activities of subsidiaries or affiliates of insured state nonmember banks are governed by section 337.4 of the FDIC's Rules and Regulations.

The purpose of this statement is to alert state nonmember banks of prominent safety and soundness concerns and other possible issues from the sales of these two products. Two principal concerns are: (1) potential customer confusion over the nature of products offered and (2) the potential for mismanagement of the sales programs for these alternative investment products, which could expose a bank to liability under the anti-fraud provisions of federal securities laws.

Adoption of Control Procedures

Bank management should implement control procedures to guard against these risks, including development of written policies and procedures governing the bank's involvement in these activities.

Every state nonmember bank engaging in mutual fund and annuity sales should develop policies that at a minimum address the concerns highlighted in this statement. The policies should be reviewed and approved by the bank's board of directors prior to the bank's engaging in a sales program for these investment products. Senior bank management should closely supervise the operation of the bank's mutual fund and annuity sales program to ensure compliance with the bank's policies and procedures.

The bank also should have a compliance and audit program, independent of the sales program, to monitor the bank's mutual funds and annuity sales activities. Consistent with any audit or compliance function, findings should be periodically reported directly to the bank's board of directors, or a designated committee of the board. The bank should ensure that applicable laws, rules and regulations governing the sales of securities, annuities and other nondeposit investments are observed to minimize the risk of possible liability of the bank. Therefore, banks are encouraged to consult with legal counsel when designing and implementing sales programs for mutual funds and annuities.

-2-

Customer Confusion

Customer confusion may result if a bank offers nondeposit investments on bank premises in a manner similar to that in which deposits are solicited. Therefore, mutual funds and annuities should be promoted and sold, and the bank's sales activities administered, in a manner that clearly distinguishes such instruments from FDIC-insured deposits.

Banks also should recognize the potential for customer confusion if nondeposit investments are offered at the same physical locations where deposits are accepted, or if such investments are offered by bank employees who also accept deposits.

The FDIC addressed this concern in section 337.4 of the FDIC's rules and regulations in the context of securities activities conducted by subsidiaries or affiliates of state nonmember banks. Section 337.4 requires that securities activities of insured nonmember bank subsidiaries and bank transactions with affiliated securities companies be conducted in physically separate and distinct locations to minimize the potential for customer confusion. The area in which mutual funds and annuities are sold should be clearly and prominently identified to distinguish such activities from traditional deposit-taking activities of the bank.

Tellers or other bank employees involved in deposit-taking activities generally should be prohibited from selling investment products and from offering investment advice. Good practice would suggest that their involvement be limited to informing customers of the availability of investment alternatives through bank-offered mutual funds or annuities and directing interested customers to qualified personnel for more specific information. If bank employees are also representing third-party vendors, they should clearly inform customers when they are also acting on behalf of the third party.

Disclosure

Appropriate disclosures to customers interested in nondeposit investment alternatives are necessary to prevent misleading customers about the nature of the investments. The disclosures should specify that mutual funds and annuities are not bank deposits, are not insured by the FDIC, and are not guaranteed by, or obligations of, the bank.

The investment risks of the instruments also should be disclosed, including the potential for fluctuations in investment return and the possibility of loss of some or all of the principal investment. Disclosures should be made in oral sales presentations and in writing before any investment decision is made and an account is opened. Banks should consider requiring customers to sign an acknowledgement when a mutual fund or annuity account is opened to confirm that the customer received and understands the disclosures.

-3-

Banks should take appropriate steps to ensure that all advertisements and promotions for mutual funds and annuities are accurate and not misleading, and include the disclosures described above. In particular, confusion may arise from jointly advertising or marketing deposits and nondeposit investments, or from including information about the nondeposit investments in customer deposit account statements. Therefore, any joint advertising or combined account information should clearly segregate information regarding FDIC-insured deposits from information on nondeposit investments, and should include a prominently displayed disclosure statement as described above.

Customer confusion also may arise from the use of names for nondeposit investments that are similar to the bank's name. In most instances, the disclosures described above should be sufficient to permit customers to distinguish between bank deposits and investment products such as mutual funds and annuities.

If a bank or its affiliate serves as adviser to mutual funds offered by the bank, written disclosures should be made to customers of the bank's advisory role. The disclosures should reemphasize that the bank does not guarantee the fund, nor do mutual fund shares constitute obligations of the bank.

Management and Administration of Sales Programs

Apart from potential liability arising from customer confusion over the differences between insured deposits and mutual fund or annuity investments, banks that participate in sales of nondeposit investments may be liable to customers, shareholders, or others for the management of these activities. The FDIC is concerned that banks properly administer these activities to protect themselves from liability that may affect the bank's overall safety and soundness.

Written policies and procedures should address the selection criteria for nondeposit investments to be offered, the use of bank customer information for marketing purposes, and the administration and supervision of the sales program, including review procedures for ensuring compliance with these policies and procedures by third parties offering nondeposit investments on bank premises.

Customers purchasing mutual funds and annuities from banks are likely to assume that the bank has exercised some degree of financial expertise in choosing products to offer. Bank policies should establish qualitative standards for the selection and marketing of products the bank will offer. Part of the process for selecting products to be offered should include due diligence reviews of third parties with whom the bank is considering entering into arrangements or whose products the bank may offer. Reviews should be conducted prior to entering into any agreements and periodically during the term of the bank's relationship with the third party.

-4-

Arrangements for offering investment products through third parties should be in writing and include terms regarding compensation for bank space, equipment and personnel used by the third party. The written arrangements also should impose responsibility on the third party to comply with bank policies governing the activities and identify the responsibility of bank management to review compliance by the third party. All arrangements should be reviewed and approved by the bank's board of directors prior to the bank's engaging in the activities.

Bank management should be mindful of the potential for confusion when developing policies governing the permissibility of the use of bank customer information for marketing purposes. Marketing efforts which have targeted customers with maturing certificates of deposit can lead to abuse and therefore are of special concern to the FDIC. Banks allowing such targeted marketing should take precautions to ensure that customers are fully informed about, and understand the nature of, mutual fund and annuity investments as opposed to insured deposits.

Qualifications and Training

Banks have responsibility for ensuring that sales personnel are properly qualified and trained to sell the nondeposit investments offered. This includes ensuring that sales personnel meet applicable statutory and industry requirements and standards for licensing and registration. Training should emphasize thorough product knowledge and customer protection requirements. Employees should know the difference between coverage provided through the Securities Investor Protection Corporation (SIPC) and through FDIC deposit insurance, and should help customers understand this difference, if applicable. Additionally, training should be provided to all bank employees who have direct customer contact to ensure a basic understanding of the nature of products offered by the bank, and the bank's policy for limiting the involvement of employees taking deposits in the sales of nondeposit products. Bank compliance and audit staff also should be appropriately trained.

Customer Suitability

If the bank recommends nondeposit investment products to customers, appropriate documentation should be maintained to reflect that the salesperson had reasonable grounds to believe the recommended investment was suitable for the customer at the time of the transaction. This requires that sales representatives make reasonable inquiry into a customer's financial condition and background, tax status and investment objectives in order to make the suitability determination.

Documentation of the inquiry should be maintained in customer files and based on information obtained directly from the customer. The files should be updated periodically.

-5-

Other Issues

Compensation programs based on sales volume present potential conflicts of interest. The bank's policies and procedures should address compensation arrangements and how to prevent them from operating as an incentive for salespeople to sell nondeposit investments over a more suitable alternative. Employee referral programs, if allowed by bank policy, should be based solely on the referral and not whether the referral resulted in a sale.

Potential conflicts of interest may arise from the use of bank distribution arrangements to facilitate fiduciary account investments administered by the bank's trust department. Sales of mutual funds and annuities to related trust department accounts should be allowed only if they are consistent with the bank's obligations as a fiduciary and meet the criteria of the bank's policies governing trust documents and applicable law. If sales to the bank's own trust accounts are allowed, regular reviews should be conducted to ensure that the sales do not violate the bank's fiduciary obligations and constitute permitted and suitable investments for the particular trust.

Prior to embarking on a sales program for mutual funds and annuities, banks should notify their blanket bond carriers of plans to engage in these activities and the specifics of their arrangements. Written assurance should be obtained from the carrier that the bank's insurance coverage for employees includes staff representing third-party vendors.

Supervisory Policy

As part of regular safety and soundness examinations, FDIC examiners will review bank policies and procedures governing sales of mutual funds and annuities as well as management's implementation of and compliance with them. Reviews will focus on the adequacy of measures taken to inform customers of the differences between nondeposit investment alternatives and bank deposits, and the administration of nondeposit investment sales programs to guard against possible liability stemming from bank involvement in these activities. Failure of banks to establish and observe appropriate policies and procedures for mutual fund and annuity sales programs will be subject to criticism and required corrective action.

(September 29, 1993)

14

Recruiting and Compensating Reps

There is an enormous diversity in the financial institutions that are providing investment products. Programs are offered by institutions ranging from the largest holding companies in the United States to community banks with $25 million in assets, and we have discussed the several different ways that a program can be structured. Many issues about these programs are common to institutions of all sizes, but other aspects of this business refer to institutions in one part of the range.

Size- and structure-related issues are particularly evident in discussions of recruiting and compensating reps. Programs that are run in-house might have access to a much wider range of benefits to use in compensating reps, for example, and programs using a third-party provider might have a freer hand in hiring a rep who is new to the institution. We have tried to clarify which issues relate to which programs and which issues are common to almost all programs.

Recruiting

Some of the key areas to consider include defining job responsibilities, selling ability, finding the sales rep, growing the help you need, hiring the help you need, platform personnel, hiring a CFP, hiring locally, and the interview process.

Defining Job Responsibilities

Before you go looking for a registered rep to hire for your program, you need to think carefully about what that person's job responsibilities will be. In our view, the prototypical bank program includes a registered rep who can perform the following job functions:

- Proactively market to customers
- Educate customers about products and personal investing
- Give seminars
- Do financial planning for customers
- Provide training and encouragement for bank employees at all levels
- Actively build both formal and informal referral networks within the organization
- Offer public speaking to various organizations
- Coordinate with other bank programs to offer seamless service to the customer

In terms of personal characteristics, we look for a rep who:

- Has selling ability
- Is empathetic and personable
- Is articulate and able to communicate clearly with customers and bank employees at all levels
- Is outgoing but not aggressive
- Is honest
- Has integrity

Of course, the rep should also have the following:

- Thorough and complete product knowledge
- Understanding of financial planning
- Several years of the relevant experience necessary to build these skills and characteristics

Additional desirable characteristics include a knowledge of banking and the bank environment, an understanding of your customer base, and residence in the community.

Selling Ability

A certain ineffable quality that securities professionals call selling ability is essential to success in this industry. It isn't easy to convey the meaning of this term to traditional bankers. You know when you meet someone with too much of it, from the fabulously successful door-to-door salesman who can sell vacuum cleaners to anyone to the successful Wall Street guy who sells limited partnerships. You know when you see too little of it: a rep says to the customer who is holding a $100,000 maturing CD, "Let's do a financial plan and revisit the situation in a month."

Part of selling ability in the securities and insurance industry is believing in the products you offer and feeling comfortable with them. In our experience, it's a bad sign when a registered rep does not have personal investments. How can you inculcate in your customers the importance of systematic saving and investing in alternative products if you don't follow your own advice?

Although selling ability is hard to define precisely, it is a basic concept in this industry. Securities professionals will ask each other about a registered rep, "Can he sell?" This quality is hard to describe, but they know when they see it. It means giving the customer enough background to make a decision and then closing the sale. Needs-based or consultative selling is one way of approaching the issue; the solution to the customer's concerns and problems becomes obvious as the sales process is followed. Getting the customer to commit is also sometimes referred to as closing ability.

A Sales Rep to Match Your Program

We believe the job responsibilities listed above are essential components of successful programs. Are they the components of *your* program? You may have decided to offer a defensive program, where your licensed person needs only to respond to customer requests, rather than build a program proactively. Your institution may prohibit cold calling or not want to offer financial planning.

In any event, you must first define the job responsibilities of the registered rep. If you choose to use a platform or dual-employee program, you must decide which part of the job responsibilities your employees will perform. For example, if your employees have only a Series 6 license, they will be able to sell only a limited menu of products.

Growing the Help You Need

The two ways to employ the people you need to run the programs you want are to hire them or to grow them. We have mentioned before that developing an experienced, competent rep takes time. In addition to the estimated 120 hours it takes to study for and pass the Series 7 exam, it will take a year for a new rep to begin to acquire the expertise and confidence that comes from experience. It will probably take two or three years before the rep has significant experience and expertise.

Even then, the rep will not have been able to observe firsthand how different products react in different markets; true depth of experience comes from living through entire market cycles. You have to understand that the rep will be practicing on your customer base. You can expect that person to make mistakes. You can also expect the rep to err on the side of "banking" safety and recommend fixed-income products and mutual funds most of the time (and maybe not educate customers about the need for equity products).

The rep needs to understand and be comfortable with the alternative investment products that he or she sells, and that comfort takes time to develop. This works better in a program where the inexperienced rep has access to the information and superior product knowledge of more experienced reps, or has the backing of corporate headquarters with product specialists who can help and advise. Training can make all the difference. A rep can be taught how to build a referral network, give a presentation, or work with a customer to create a financial plan. If you start with a person who communicates clearly, has the right personal qualities, and can stand up in front of a group, you will probably be able to develop the rep you need.

A financial institution often wants to license someone who is already a bank employee, either because it wants to provide a career path for someone talented or because it already has an employee serving in some quasi-investment function. We just mentioned a number of disadvantages to training a new rep, but there can be significant advantages as well. The primary one is that the new registered rep will not be an outsider to the bank or branch. Being an outsider is one of the largest problems for either the third-party provider in general or a new registered rep in particular as the branch starts up an investment program. The bank employee merely shifts job responsibilities while maintaining his or her existing network of friends and co-workers. (Make sure this person does get along well with other bank employees.) Since getting the rest of the branch on his or her side is one of the registered rep's most important tasks, the bank insider at a larger organization walks in the door with a major advantage.

But being an insider could turn out to be a disadvantage in small organizations or smaller communities, where customers and colleagues alike associate the new rep either with earlier job responsibilities or with other things he or she has done in the community. The insider can bring baggage. It is important to understand your particular institution and work within the framework of your community.

Hiring the Help You Need

Your program will get up and running much faster if you hire the help you need. We have heard everything from, "We recruit 90% of our brokers from wirehouses," to "Wirehouse brokers almost never work out in the bank." There does seem to be industry consensus on the importance of hiring people with securities sales experience and a Series 7 license. "While some programs have trained employees from the bank branches to sell alternative investment products, the majority are hiring reps from wirehouses or other investment programs."[1]

Even the regulators are in favor of hiring reps with securities experience: "The single most common recommendation from the NASD (and from bank-affiliated broker/dealers [BABD] who have been through the process already) is that BABDs hire some personnel specifically experienced in the securities industry, rather than staffing the broker/dealer entirely with bank employees. For a number of reasons, it is important for individuals undertaking securities transactions on behalf of a BABD to be constantly aware of their brokerage responsibilities and how they differ from their banking duties."[2]

However, if you hire a registered rep with experience, the nature of that prior experience will have a profound effect on his or her orientation within your program. Wirehouse reps tend to have the product knowledge you are looking for. They have experience working in a stressful environment where there was a constant emphasis on moving product—and that is the drawback most often expressed about reps with this background.

Institutions might look for registered rep candidates among the ranks of experienced insurance agents. Some of these people have experience with financial planning and would like to add securities sales to the range of products they can offer their customers, although sometimes an insurance agent's idea of financial planning is providing a full range of insurance products. The extra accreditations they may have (for example, CLU, chartered life underwriter) can provide extra background for educating and assisting customers.

However, some insurance sales reps have the same reputation as securities brokers for being excessively sales oriented. Furthermore, they are used to the generous fixed-percentage spreads available in the insurance industry, and they never get used to the floating (and sometimes narrow) spreads of some securities sales. In addition, hiring an experienced insurance agent can bring two administrative headaches, both following from the structure of the insurance industry.

---

1 Gina Lauer, "Hiring the Right Person," *Bank Investment Representative*, December 1992, p. 21.
2 Jacqueline H. Hallihan, "Regulatory Concerns for Bank-Affiliated Broker/Dealers," *Bank Investment Representative*, Apr/May, 1992, p. 34

Most noncaptive insurance agents are licensed with two to ten different insurance companies. Many insurance products are structured so that they continue to pay fees for many years. To continue to be paid fees by the organizations he or she placed the business with, the agent must continue to be licensed by those organizations. If you want to oversee and control that business and those commission dollars by acting as the insurance agency, receiving the agent's commissions and then paying him or her, your organization will have to be licensed with all those companies. If you hire three insurance people and each one has had sales with six different companies, you might be forced to carry licenses for 18 separate companies, most of whom you will otherwise not do business with. Do not underestimate the administrative burden this can cause, with no net profit to you.

The more serious problem with insurance agents is the liability that accrues to your organization from an agent doing independent sales on the side. The NASD and securities laws are very clear on the subject of "trading away," or doing trades on the side without going through the main securities firm. It's not allowed under any circumstances. However, it is perfectly legal for an insurance agent you employ to continue to write business directly for an insurance company and not through your organization. The problem is that you have thereby lost control of your employee.

You can say your organization is not liable for what your employee does independently, but the liability laws work against the entity with the deepest pockets, which is the financial institution. If your organization decides not to pick up the agent's several licenses but instead gives the insurance agent permission to be paid directly by the insurance company, you are in effect giving him or her permission to write independent business. Even if you do take on all previous insurance relationships, you will never be sure of the business the agent might do away from you. It would benefit him or her to do business on the side for a private customer, because the agent wouldn't have to go through the financial institution and give up that portion of the commission. You would have to be extremely confident of any employee to allow him or her to function in this manner.

The interviewer needs to probe to find whether the rep has the integrity and honesty that are essential to the bank program. Ask the wirehouse reps or insurance agents why they want to work in a bank. Many of them were uncomfortable with the constant push on proprietary products and look forward to a situation where the customer's best interest comes first. However, do beware of the rep looking for an easy life living off bank referrals. He or she is no doubt unaware of the work involved in integrating into the bank culture.

Even when you hire an experienced rep from the brokerage industry, in a real sense you still have to grow your own. You must work with the rep to convey the importance of customer relationships and fitting into the banking environment. Establish a probationary period with the rep and state your goals and objectives clearly. You should be able to tell within 90 days (or fewer) if the rep has the basic qualities necessary to adapt to the banking environment.

The ideal rep, in our view, is one who has learned something about products and selling from a brokerage environment and then had the opportunity to unlearn bad habits by working in someone else's bank program. But these people are very hard to come by, because once they have established a successful program in a bank, why should they leave?

Platform Personnel

The main complaint made about bank employees who have gotten licensed is that they don't know how to sell. There is a similar problem with licensing platform personnel. The platform employees who are outstanding at making referrals are not necessarily the best salespeople. Some of the best personal bankers are older, have been out of school for some time, and are afraid of computers. They recognize a customer need for financial products and are comfortable sending the customer over to the specialist. If you ask them to get a Series 6, they aren't happy about going to school, are uncomfortable with the computers they have to take the test on and, even if they do pass, do not feel confident advising customers themselves. It is important not to force a platform employee to become a securities salesperson. Bankers are not always the best spokespeople for alternative investment products and a reluctant banker is not going to perform at all.

Hiring a Certified Financial Planner

Should you look for a CFP? A CFP has completed two years of formal coursework in finance, investments, estate planning, tax planning, and related areas. The CFP training emphasizes looking at an individual's finances as part of a complete picture; each separate transaction should be part of the whole financial plan. This perspective is the exact opposite of product pushing and can fit beautifully with a bank's relationship orientation. However, this person might also go to the other extreme—all advice and no sales. A very few bank programs *require* reps to be either CFPs or CFAs (chartered financial analyst). While this accreditation is helpful to the program and you should certainly encourage reps to achieve it, it is not critical to the success of the program, nor does it guarantee success.

Hiring Locally

Many banks play an important role in the life of the community they reside in. If this is true for your financial institution, try to remain consistent to this perspective by hiring a registered rep who also lives in the community. When a registered rep is part of the bank's community, it helps to minimize his or her position as an outsider to the banking culture. Hiring locally may be difficult in some communities, but it is worth the effort to try. This difficulty is one of the reasons financial institutions decide to train their own reps.

In smaller institutions or communities, the disadvantages of the local hire parallel the disadvantages of hiring a bank insider. Susie may have been the local lifeguard, or whatever, and people have clear memories of her in this capacity. It might be to your advantage to hire an experienced registered rep who can move to the area and become local. *Local* is the important part; there is more than one way to accomplish this.

The Interview Process

Who makes the decision about hiring a registered rep, and who has input into that decision? The people and units who will be most directly affected by this person's performance should play a part in the decision. That means the third-party provider, bank management, and branch management should all interview the prospective rep. Bank or branch management will defer to the judgment of the third-party provider or, in the case of an in-house program, the sales manager or program director, but when they have been part of the process and given their personal approval, then they have bought into the program. They have put their own personal reputations on the line in approving the rep, which will lead to them giving the program help and support.

Compensation Systems

Draws and Commissions

When all things are right with a program—program structure, the registered rep, organizational support—an institution with $100 million in total assets should expect to produce $180,000 in gross commissions annually, or an average of $15,000 monthly. Our rule of thumb says approximately one-third of the gross should go to the distribution system—which is the registered rep. So you can see that many community banks should be able to support a registered rep. We have heard of much smaller financial institutions producing prodigious amounts, and there are many programs in much larger banks that don't produce nearly as much. You can use this guideline of $100 million to calculate what larger banks should produce and how many reps it makes sense to have.

Reliable comparative information about compensation is hard to come by. Financial institutions are reluctant to disclose information that might fall into the hands of their competitors, while wishing they could get such information for themselves. William F. Broderick of Human Resources Matrix (HRM) has recently completed his fifth annual compensation survey, "Productivity and Compensation Report on Bank Brokerage 1992." This report surveys 12 programs at large banks; asset size averages $14.8 billion and ranges from $2.1 to $63.0 billion. Although the study covered organizations that paid reps in a number of different ways, and rep productivity and compensation varied significantly, the average compensation across 572 reps was 33.5% of average gross commissions per rep. This accords with our basic guideline.

There are four basic ways that registered reps have traditionally been compensated: all commission, draw plus commission, salary plus bonus, or all salary.[3] Commission payouts traditionally are tiered so that a registered rep receives a higher commission percentage as gross commissions produced increase. The rationale is twofold. First, you want to provide as strong an incentive as possible for a registered rep to produce more. Second, that marginal production doesn't cost you any more in underlying expense of the program (the basic cost of the rep in terms of physical cost and benefits, entertainment expense, or licensing fees, remains constant), so you can afford to pay out a higher percentage of the higher production. The reps who achieve the higher production amounts will almost certainly be writing larger tickets, which will minimize the clearing cost.[4]

---

3   The difference between a draw and a salary is that a salary is simply paid out to the rep no matter what production results are. A draw is paid monthly as though it were a salary, but the rep is expected to produce high enough gross commissions so that his or her percentage of gross commissions at least equals the draw. For instance, if a rep is paid a straight percentage of 25% of gross commissions and has a draw of $2,000, then each month he or she must produce at least $8,000 in gross commissions (25% of $8,000 equals the draw of $2,000). If the rep produces more, he or she gets paid more; if he or she produces $12,000 in gross commissions, his or her total compensation for the month would be 25% of $12,000, or $3,000. However, if a rep in this situation produced only $5,000 in gross commissions, he or she would earn only $1,250, which would not cover the draw. The financial institution would expect the rep to earn enough next month to cover both that month's draw and the deficit from the prior month.

4   For example, say it costs $25 to clear a mutual fund trade. If I write 10 tickets for $1,000 each for a mutual fund with a 4% load, my gross commission will be $400 and my clearing cost will be $250 (ticket charges are 62.5% of gross commission). If I write one ticket for $10,000, my gross commission will still be $400, but my clearing cost will be only $25 (ticket charges are 6.25% of gross commission). If I write one ticket for $50,000, gross commission is $2,000 and ticket charge is $25 (1.25%).

Many programs in large institutions using an all-commission system have breakpoints at monthly production of $10,000, $20,000, and $30,000, and pay out 25%, 30%, and 35%. Many programs have a top payout of 40%, usually for commissions over $40,000 or $50,000 in a month. Community banks might want to put their tiers at monthly production of $5,000, $10,000 and $15,000. Tiers encourage registered reps to strive for higher productivity, but they need to be adjusted for the size of the program and what a rep can realistically achieve. We have heard of programs where there are only two tiers and everyone reaches the top tier. We wonder if reps might be more challenged if the tiers were adjusted, or another tier added.

Many programs that pay all commission incorporate a draw within that system. There are different issues concerning draws, depending on the size and kind of financial institution and retail investment services program. Startups of any size can take a while to become profitable, and a registered rep needs something to live on. Some of the larger bank programs pay full benefits to registered reps but base those benefits (including pension or 401(k) plan) on the dollar amount of the draw, not on the full commission amount.

Draws are often used as the discipline amount; whatever formula is used to set the draw, registered reps will typically be required to meet that amount every month. If they do not meet that amount for three months in a row, they might be put on probation or subject to other procedures. Banks vary on how seriously they take this. Many banks or third-party providers take quite protective attitudes and try to work with the rep, especially if there are mitigating circumstances. Other managers we have talked to take a hardline approach.

The design of these all-commission programs is based on the brokerage house model. Dual-employee programs, on the other hand, use compensation systems more like those of the financial institutions they are part of. A dual employee might get something like a bank salary, plus a bonus of 10% of gross commissions. The salary of the dual employee needs to fit within the context of the institution.

Although it is theoretically possible for a registered rep to be paid salary only, with no incentive or commission pay whatsoever, we have never encountered such a person in actual life. Some unlicensed employees who work with a discount brokerage operation receive no incentive pay. But since the biggest complaint we hear from program managers is the difficulty of finding excellent registered reps, we have to think that any rep in a program that provided no incentive pay would either not stay with that program for long or would not try very hard to write more business.

We add one last caveat about paying incentives to motivate behavior. A compensation system that provides greater financial incentives for one particular part of the program will get results accordingly; don't do this by accident. If you pay out a greater percentage on one kind of product or one particular product carries a much higher load, you will find your salespeople very favorably disposed to selling of product. This can wreak havoc with a program that is designed to be product neutral and will undoubtedly create suitability problems down the road.

Study Results

The HRM study included data for four institutions that paid either full commission or draw versus commission. Only one plan in the study paid full commission. It covered 151 reps. The average total annual compensation was $60,400, with a range of $24,800 to $360,000. The three plans using draw versus commissions (covering 93 reps) paid average annual compensation of $76,318, with a range of $493 to $220,000. For the eight plans (covering 328 reps) using salary plus incentives, the average total annual compensation was $51,834, of which $22,882 was average base salary.

These compensation numbers allow for considerable variation in the achievements of individual reps. However, the most interesting part of the study concerns pay versus the total dollars of annual gross commissions produced by each rep.

	Representative Pay	Production	Percentage
Base salary	$51,834	$109,239	47.4
Full Commission	60,400	258,033	23.4
Draw v. Commission	76,318	262,752	22.9

Reps who are paid base salaries receive far more than a one-third share of gross commissions and produce, per rep, about half as much as those who are paid on an incentive basis. Clearly the most productive people are paid largely on incentives. This has been true for all five years of the study, although the gap has become more pronounced over the past two years. Broderick points out that less highly motivated people tend to seek out salaries and then get comfortable. Not only does having a salary serve as less motivation, but it also draws less motivated salespeople. More entrepreneurial salespeople welcome the opportunity to earn high compensation on full commission.

Some programs report that salaries on a continuing basis seem to have a detrimental effect on production. Bette B. Daniels, chairman of First Colonial Investment Services, has already been quoted about this effect. "First Colonial ... found out that the way brokers are compensated makes a difference in the way they sell investment products. 'Brokers were very comfortable with the base salary we initially paid them, and productivity wasn't increasing at all,'

Ms. Daniels said. Now, brokers are compensated solely on their production, a change that has helped step up product sales, Ms. Daniels said."[5]

We heard a similar story from another institution that does not wish to be named. The program had been in place for two years, so it was well established. The reps were paid salary plus commission bonus. Management thought the situation was entirely too comfortable for many reps, who did not need to exert themselves very much. Many of them were happy with salary alone and didn't worry about trying to earn much bonus. The whole program was changed to draw plus commission, and production tripled within a very short of time.

Since the HRM study included only large programs that are run as separate organizations within the financial institution, it did not include data on new or small programs whose dual employees are paid a banker's salary and a small commission. We will be very interested as new studies are done to see how these programs measure up in terms of productivity. We have to think that programs of this sort either fit well within their own bank environment and community or will soon be forced to change by market pressures.

New Program Structures from Larger Banks

Some larger bank programs have begun to experiment with using more than one level of reps. The reps with little experience are given most of the referrals and receive a lower commission payout. They are expected to serve the customers who walk in the door and to learn as much as they can about the business. There might be two or three levels of reps. Second level reps get technology and a sales assistant and are expected to "work their book," i.e., go for those second sales. Because they do not receive referrals, payouts are higher. If there is a third level, those reps are the most experienced and knowledgeable and work with the private banking market, receiving more technological support (programs supporting the rep's activities and access to research, all in the interest of reaching and satisfying more sophisticated customers), and writing much larger tickets.

The New Program

When a new rep from whatever source starts employment in an established program, that person will probably receive referrals from an ongoing referral program and in general get a step up to the possibility of success. Be aware of the needs of a rep who is starting out in a new program. In our experience, programs can take six months to a year to produce at anything like full capacity.

---

5   Karen Talley, "First Colonial Helps Small Banks Sell Funds," *American Banker,* August 25, 1993, p. 12.

Your rep is going to give his or her all to the program and could end up being very hungry for some time if gross production in the first few months starts slowly. You have spent a great deal of time and effort structuring a program that is right for the sales philosophy of your financial institution, and then you end up with a salesperson who is desperate, or at least edgy and unhappy, and overeager to make a sale. You need to give your registered rep a chance to settle in and grow the program. The way to do that is with a guaranteed draw or base salary. Many programs offer that security for the first six months or a year before switching to the permanent compensation program. Later on, many reps are comfortable with pure commission, because they know they have what it takes personally plus a book of continuing relationships and business that they know will continue to produce for them.

Compensating for Relationship Building

Bank retail investment services programs are struggling to find ways to compensate reps that include incentives for the kind of behavior banks want to encourage. So important are personal relationships that a bank program suffers every time a registered rep leaves the institution. Ways to keep the rep at the financial institution include the following:

- Holding back a small percentage of commissions every year, to be paid out at the end of three years if the rep is still in place
- Adding one to two percentage points commission to the commission schedule after a certain period of time (paying 27% instead of 25%)
- Paying out a percentage of the 12b-1 fees so that the rep would be leaving a significant income stream to start again somewhere else
- Increasing payouts for repeat business
- Providing reps with more technology (laptop computers and smart programs) to help them become still more productive
- Compensating the rep through bank stock-option plans

This is one place where the structure of the program makes a big difference in the method that can be used. Most of these suggestions come from the in-house programs of large banks. Compensating the rep through bank stock options almost demands an in-house program, where such a plan should be in effect for officers throughout the organization. Offering bank options to the registered rep would be out of the third-party marketer's control. However, even in a third-party situation it makes sense for the financial institution to offer the rep stock options, because that transforms the employee into an owner and can effect a major change in outlook.

The relationship selling most bank programs want to encourage can be measured in part by trailer fees, because assets under management is one key to long-term success. Selling wrap programs accomplishes a similar goal.[6] Many bank programs either pay incentive fees or use a different payout scale to recognize the difference between domestic and foreign invested funds, to encourage reps to gather assets from outside the institution.

Who Pays Expenses

Questions arise about who pays a number of expenses incidental to the registered rep's position. These include the following:

- Ticket charges
- Referral incentives
- Other marketing expenses (birthday cards, notecards, pizza for branch employees, prizes, customer appreciation nights, etc.)
- Entertainment (internal or external)
- Seminar materials and expenses
- Branch visits
- Training/conferences
- Licensing fees and continuing credit hours

The cost of processing transactions (ticket charges) is second only to compensation. Ticket charges are part of the cost of a retail investment services program and, in our view, should be subtracted from gross commissions before any payouts are calculated. However, the total cost of processing transactions includes more than just the basic charge for a ticket (such as the basic $25 it costs to process a mutual fund trade or $22 to process a stock transaction). Processing costs include separate costs incurred for special customer transactions, such as a legal transfer, a wire charge, or a securities processing fee. Such charges are incurred only if the customer has a separate need, so the customer should be charged for such costs.

Training, seminars, marketing materials, and referral incentives should be provided without direct charges to the registered rep. These are important to the success of the program, but when the rep has a choice of keeping $500 or spending $500 for a training course, it may be hard to focus on the long-term benefit. As we mentioned before, when reps are asked to pay for training out of their own pocket, it tends to punish the reps who need it most, because those are the people least able to afford it.

---

6   See Chapter 4 on products. In a wrap program, the customer has a manager handle a large portion of his or her assets through a single account that is charged an annual percentage of assets under management, such as 2%-3%. The customer pays no other charges.

This is one place where it makes sense to bundle fees, paying parties to the agreement a slightly lower percentage and including necessities like training as part of the program (which are as important to the success of the program as paying the electric bill). We have heard the argument that since some of these items increase the rep's income, the rep should pick up the cost. Referral incentives and seminars increase revenue to *all* parties and should be split among all of them. Even a training course for the rep should result in a more successful program for all concerned.

Many registered reps have learned the importance of the personal touch, the extra that really shows they care, such as flowers for a new customer or a flower for a teller. Tellers and CSRs are particularly touched when they know a rep has paid for pizza out of his or her own pocket. To many people, paying for something yourself is the ultimate in personal sacrifice. We encourage reps to do this. Many reps also earn significantly more in total compensation than their fellow bank employees and should be able to afford it.

Since dual-employee programs are often set up with much lower payouts than managed programs, some financial institutions give the dual employee an allowance for such extras. However, that takes away the personal touch. While we recognize that some dual employees receive compensation that is quite low by industry standards, what makes certain gestures special is the fact that they are not funded by the financial institution.

In fact, an allowance or allocation is an idea we like. Who should pay to take a customer for lunch, especially if the branch manager is invited? Each program has to work this out for itself. If the rep thinks it's appropriate, probably the rep should pay. If the rep thinks the organization should pay, the program will certainly require advance permission.

For a program using a third-party provider, the contract will usually specify who pays what part of these various expenses. The same principle applies to this as to most other parts of a program: it's not all that important who pays for what as long as all parties to the agreement understand exactly what kind of expense is involved and who is going to pay it. These expenses should not be optional; they are essential to the program's success.

Compensating Other Personnel

Sales Managers

Sales managers, or managers who oversee the sales function of registered reps and report to the president or COO of an organization, have as many different titles, job structures, and ways of being compensated as there are different sales organizations.

There is a certain amount of consternation in the industry about how to pay these people and how to define their function most effectively. The heads of retail investment services organizations, however those organizations are structured, hate paying nonproducing employees, especially those in the high-bracket range. If you use producing managers, it cuts away at their effectiveness in supervising and you have to hire twice as many employees in this function. If you have nonproducing managers, they represent pure overhead, which eats away at commission profits. Salespeople do need day-to-day supervision from a functional as well as the compliance point of view, but the industry has not been able to produce an answer about how best to provide it.

Sales managers at the larger banks are often paid a base salary plus an override. In our experience, overrides fall generally into the 35 to 150 basis point range, and total compensation can reach six figures.[7] One bank pays sales managers a 75 basis point override on production up to the level achieved the previous year, then 150 basis points on everything more than that. Another bank we know pays sales managers nothing extra at all except the honor of being first among equals and getting first pick of all new accounts. This is an unusual bank where internal recognition is very important, and we are told this system works extremely well. Another bank puts sales managers on the bank's executive compensation system, but with incentive bonuses of up to 50% available.

The HRM study shows five institutions using regional managers and five using sales managers, although some organizations used both. Organizations vary widely in how they define these positions, with base salaries of $45,333 and $41,875, respectively. Both positions show an average bonus of approximately $37,500. Since the number of branches in the organizations surveyed ranged from 45 to 942, obviously the different institutions would have different requirements for the number and kind of sales managers required. Only three of these organizations use producing managers, with an average base salary of approximately $54,000 and average total compensation of $99,000.

The job responsibilities of a sales manager will probably continue to evolve. We return to our basic principle of providing an incentive only for behavior you can influence. How much effect does a sales manager really have on the productivity of a registered rep? The answer is unclear, which means the answer to the question, "How much of an override is it justifiable to pay?" is also unclear. A sales manager's position might be seen as a career path, and the need to provide career paths for the many young reps who are currently gaining experience may influence the development of this job function.

---

7   One basis point (bp) is equal to one one-hundredth of a percentage point; therefore 10 bp equal one-tenth of a percentage point and 100 bp equal one percentage point. To calculate a 40 bp override on $50,000 of gross commissions, multiply $50,000 by .004 to equal $200. If a manager supervised 14 registered reps and each rep produced $200,000 in commissions, and the manager's override was 40 bp, the manager would earn $12,000 in override compensation.

Branch Managers

Although it makes sense to us for a highly productive registered rep to earn more in dollar compensation than the president of a bank, we think it is unlikely that a branch manager will find it acceptable to have a registered rep earning twice the dollar amount the branch manager earns. Branch managers need to be compensated for contributing to the success of the retail investment services program, but they should also be part of a senior management incentive system and should be compensated on "big picture" results. Registered reps are compensated only on the dollars they themselves bring in the door. Since a branch manager is not licensed, it is illegal to split commissions or give some kind of override on commissions produced.

In Chapter 10 on referrals, we suggest paying the branch manager a small amount for each referral generated. We also suggest that the best method for compensating the branch manager is formally incorporating goals for retail investment services into the strategic plan of the branch. The branch manager should be paid the same kind of incentive for achieving these goals as for achieving other goals of the organization, such as levels of core deposits attained, accounts opened, and mortgages made—and we think incentives should be paid for each one.

Sales Assistants

A registered rep must do much more than simply sell product. The rep has to process all paperwork correctly, which is crucial from a compliance point of view; fill out and submit trade tickets; deal with customer monies (however the particular program does this); carry out constant marketing campaigns, whether sending out statement stuffers, getting new customer lists to invite to seminars, or other tactics; organize and give seminars; organize and give training sessions to bank employees and more. With this long list of time-consuming activities, it would be easy for a rep never to spend any time actually selling! If the amount of time the rep spends on these various associated activities can be reduced, the rep will be able to spend more time dealing with customers. Many institutions use a sales assistant to assist the registered rep with almost every aspect of his or her job except actually selling to customers.

Sales assistants are most often encountered at the larger in-house programs that are well established and have healthy revenue streams; these institutions can afford to pay sales assistants. The usual structure is to pay sales assistants salaries from the bank or broker/dealer and then pay bonuses on top of that, taken as a small percentage of gross commissions. The ratio varies from one sales assistant per two reps to one to ten or more. Banks might have a lower ratio in the branches, where there is a definite need for a sales assistant but only one or two or three reps. Sales assistants at corporate headquarters usually play a significant role in processing tickets; when they're located in branches, they are likely to have more responsibilities connected to servicing customers (making appointments, checking on accounts, sending out mailings). A sales assistant is almost by definition excluded from playing a role in a dual-employee program, because the registered rep is an employee of the bank and will be assisted by another bank employee as needed.

A sales assistant can make an enormous difference in the productivity of a rep. The HRM study reports that 83% of the institutions surveyed for this study use sales assistants compared to 67% last year. This is part of the trend among successful programs to become even more successful and increase the productivity of reps. The ratio of sales assistants to reps in this survey was one to four.

The most striking comparison is the difference in productivity between programs with sales assistants and those without: average commissions per rep on a program with sales assistants were $177,606; in a program without sales assistants, they were $95,125. That's an 86% increase in commissions for the use of a sales assistant whose job responsibilities are split among four reps! Considering that the average salary of a sales assistant was $17,634 and that no sales assistants in this survey received any incentive or commission pay, that is a remarkable accomplishment. However, the two programs that do not use sales assistants are the youngest programs in the survey and would normally be expected to produce lesser amounts per rep.

Institutions vary in the qualifications they require from sales assistants, but the most conservative view—since a sales assistant will probably talk to customers—is to require a Series 7 license. However, sales assistants are not necessarily sales people in training. Many are happy with lesser responsibility for the customer relationship and don't want to take on the selling function. Managers of bank programs report indifferent success with sales assistants moving into registered rep slots; many find it too demanding.

If sales assistants are to be paid any kind of incentive based on sales, NASD regulations state that they have to be licensed. Commissions cannot be split with nonlicensed people. It would be illegal to pay incentives based on commissions to processing personnel or employees in the branch. This is why it is important to design and maintain a referral system that allows additional compensation (although not *commission-based*) compensation to go to other bank employees.

It is rare to find sales assistants outside of in-house programs; third-party providers do not usually use them, and many dual-employee programs simply utilize available bank personnel for assistance with some of the administrative responsibilities involved in a retail program. Based on informal evidence, it seems to us that a few of the larger and most securities-oriented organizations are starting to pay a small percentage of commissions to sales assistants. These employees compare in bank grade level, experience, and education with CSRs. The Broderick study reports that pay ranges from $14,183 to $32,200. It would be easily possible for a successful sales assistant working with busy reps to add thousands of dollars to his or her total compensation, which brings us back to the banker's abhorrence for the kind of incentive-based pay that upsets strict hierarchies. Most institutions still retain that view.

Sales assistants will add value to a program whenever they make a larger contribution to overall profitability than they take out in pay, although we qualify this statement by saying that, so far, only certain kinds of programs use sales assistants. (They are unlikely to be located in a community bank.) If adding a sales assistant (who might be paid $25,000) allows a registered rep (who earns six figures) to increase production by more than the sales assistant's pay, then it makes sense to add a sales assistant. More programs than ever are finding this to be the case.

Product Providers

A product provider is the person who gets the product and executes the trade for the sales force. A registered rep in any program is not likely to be the person who has actual contact with a trading desk. The rep calls the product provider, who takes the customer's criteria and shops for the requested product. When the product provider has located the instrument, he or she will contact the rep, who calls the customer. The product provider may place equity or mutual fund orders as well, depending completely on the structure of the program.

A large bank program or traditional bond department might call this person a trader. The difference is that a trader buys and sell instruments for the institution's proprietary position, in the hope of making a profit, but a product provider buys only on customer orders. The transaction can be done on a riskless principal basis, meaning that the product provider buys the bond for his or her own account and then resells it to the customer after the customer places the order. Or it can be done on an agency basis, whereby the product provider executes the transaction directly in the name of the customer. (See Chapter 3 for definitions.) In these institutions, the product provider can either generate incentive-based pay based on the markups in products, or receive a percentage of the gross commissions paid into a pool to be split among such staff.

A financial institution using a third-party provider will not get involved with the question of product providers, because anything the financial institution needs in the way of product is at the other end of the phone line to the third-party provider. If the clearing broker/dealer uses an automated system, then most equity orders will be filled automatically (usually within one minute). Broker/dealers that are not on-line to an automated system call in equity orders to the floor of the exchange for execution.

Whichever system is used, very large equity orders or those in obscure stocks always need intervention by a human trader to "work the order." Introducing broker/dealers fill these orders by a call to their clearing firm, which has the equity trading desk take care of the order. If a registered rep in a financial institution using a third-party provider needs a municipal or corporate bond, the rep calls corporate headquarters to ask the product provider there to look for the bond.

Related Issues

When to Compensate

Although some insurance and securities firms pay out commissions quickly, we think it makes the accounting simpler if you pay off of the settlement date only, with a 30-day lag from the end of the current month. Settlement date is the date when the money actually changes hands so that the security is paid for and is usually five business days after the trade date. If a trade settles April 12, the payment to the financial institution and/or the registered rep should be made May 31. This allows most adjustments to be made before the commissions are paid out.

Occasionally there may be either a canceled trade for a securities transaction or a chargeback on an insurance policy. The laws governing insurance state that a customer has a ten-day "free look" at an insurance policy. The customer can cancel without penalty during that time. If the commission had already been paid out, the company would have to ask the agent to give it back. There is also the possibility of fraud in an insurance policy. If a customer says he or she has no heart condition and then dies of a heart condition within two years of the policy issuance, the insurance company will not pay out on the policy. Instead it will refund to the customer's estate all premiums paid. Again, the agent would have to surrender the commission paid on the policy.

Employees writing insurance business need to understand that they will be charged for commissions on any business that gets reversed, for whatever reason. Most agents will experience a customer change of mind at some point. But if it happens repeatedly, management should realize that an appropriate sales process is not being followed and customers aren't being properly sold. If employees know the chargeback policy, they will be motivated to write cleaner business to begin with. (Employees who think they get to keep all commissions, no matter what happens with the policy or annuity, will be motivated to write sloppy business or take a chance with a customer who is not really sold.)

Prizes and Contests

Although holding contests and offering sales prizes are recognized business practices, we are wary of an excessive emphasis on such sales techniques. Offering extra incentives to sales reps to work a little harder and try to make a few more sales is laudable, but encouraging a rep to sell a customer an unsuitable product in order to make the points necessary for the trip is not.

Many organizations prohibit reps from participating in sales contests or require management approval beforehand, but many do allow participation. Preliminary data from one study reported that about 80% of the programs allowed such incentive awards for reps and managers.[8] The manager of a retail investment services program at a larger financial institution we know (with dozens of reps) asked several mutual fund families to contribute prizes for a combined contest within the institution.

Reporting Relationships

Every registered rep, no matter what the program, should have a direct reporting relationship to a sales manager and the broker/dealer, regardless of the rep's relationship with the third-party provider or the financial institution. This direct report is required by the regulators.

There is a greater variety of direct and dotted lines when you figure in the insurance authority. Sometimes one third-party provider offers insurance as well as securities. Some TPPs specialize in securities but have teamed up with an insurance provider, so there are reporting lines running in several directions. There are a few programs in larger banks where the third-party provider of insurance is there for legal reasons only and hardly exists except as a paper trail. There is virtually no reporting authority in that case.

We have stressed throughout this book that successful registered reps practice their own profession within the banking context and must fit in with the bank's functions and sales philosophy. Most reps have at least a dotted line reporting relationship to the bank, and some dual employees have a fully matrixed situation with the bank and the TPP. Specifying the reporting relationships only formalizes what we know to be true about the importance of both parts of a rep's job.

---

08 Jeffrey H. Champlin and Gina Lauer, "Payday at Bank Investment Programs," *Bank Investment Representative*, July/August 1993, p. 14. The study is the K^2 (Kehrer/Kreuter) 1992 Bank Securities & Insurance Program Compensation Study.

Titles

Titles of every kind are used for registered reps, from the usual banking title, investment officer, to asset manager, investment specialist, etc. Each bank has its own orientation about how to title these people, and that is how it should be. Each financial institution needs to decide for itself how best to integrate the program. One bank decided not to use certain titles for its reps because if it ever had to go to court, it didn't want a senior investment officer on the stand.

Bankers Versus Commissions: The Long-Term Perspective

We have suggested that banks and other financial institutions would be well served by the introduction of incentive-based pay for all bank employees. We know that many bankers are grappling instead with the issue of how to tame the pay levels that very productive registered reps achieve. Bankers are already unhappy when the referral fees paid out to tellers result in large percentage increases in base pay. What are these bankers going to do with the soaring incomes of successful reps?

If you tell bankers that the registered reps in their lobbies could make more than the bank president, most of them are appalled. On the other hand, managers of the most successful bank broker/dealers all have reps who make more than they do, and they think it's great; they universally express the hope those reps will do even better next year. These people understand that a highly paid rep is a highly productive person, and the high level of pay his or her productivity generates results in more profit for the institution. They do not take the moral high ground of banking and insist that a certain hierarchy of pay is necessary to maintain discipline. The most productive people who bring in high levels of revenue should be compensated accordingly; an incentive-based system accomplishes this automatically. Employees who do not do well in an incentive-based environment should either become more productive or change careers.

There will continue to be a clash of cultures within the banking community for the next few years. In our view, this clash will resolve itself with the demise of the financial institutions that have not adopted a sales culture or adapted to the proactive marketing necessary in a highly competitive marketplace. The financial institutions remaining will have embraced the sales culture necessary to the survival of retail banking.

The banking community would be well served by trying to utilize the compensation methods coming from the securities' side rather than superimposing bank salary levels on registered reps. Until that time, productive registered reps will leave institutions where they are not adequately compensated and seek out programs that recognize their achievements with cash. Programs that do not fully utilize the personnel they have will suffer. Programs that can provide appropriate incentives, goals, and objectives will continue to thrive.

15

The Future of Retail Banking

Why does the retail bank have to be reinvented? Is there something wrong? There are three issues we want to focus on:

- Customer relationships
- Marketing
- Systems

We believe these are the key points to reinventing the retail bank and survival of the banking industry.

The retail bank has a cancer that is eating away at the core customer base. The banking industry is mortally ill, although many bankers haven't realized it yet. The major symptoms are the dwindling of core deposits and the loss of the lending business. The amount of money invested in mutual funds will soon surpass the amount invested in banks. The lending business has slowed dramatically and the competition has made heavy inroads into bank lending. If bankers are not lenders or deposit takers, what are they? But beyond the symptoms, the disease itself is the loss of the customer relationship that has sustained banks.

Banks have old products, obsolete systems, and antiquated service policies. The industry is unresponsive to change and engulfed in regulations. Yet in spite of all of this, customers still trust their banker and believe in the banking franchise. There is reason to hope. If bankers can reinvent their business and build on the foundation of this relationship between banker and customer, then the banking industry can survive.

Banks took a beating from the high interest rates and tight credit of the early 1980s but benefited greatly from the introduction of IRAs when interest rates were at 16%. It was easy for everyone to open a bank IRA account with a CD; only the most educated or aggressive investors opened self-directed IRAs for stocks or mutual funds. As interest rates dropped during the late 1980s and early 1990s, the banking industry flourished—but at a price. As interest rates dropped, the cost associated with those higher earnings was the shift of long-term investing dollars out of the banking industry to higher-yielding, riskier investments.

The reason banks are thriving is not because their core business of lending is prospering; banks are doing well because interest rates have dropped so low. As loan demand continues to decline, banks are forced to find additional sources of revenue to improve the bottom line and stay competitive. As rates continued to drop, bank profit margins continued to increase. However, traditional savers have begun to leave traditional bank savings products for alternative investments in order to maintain yield. The cost of the current prosperity has become even greater; it is no longer the disintermediation of investable funds (that used to be thought of as core deposits) that should worry bankers, but the loss of the customer relationship and the bank's core customer base.

Banks are not unique as financial intermediaries. Retailers and manufacturers provide their own financial intermediation services as an extension of their day-to-day business. When interest rates are high and credit is tight, financing their own products becomes necessary to keep business flowing. But today everyone is in the business of extending credit. Mortgage banking has become its own industry, check printing is now a mail-order business, and asset securitization has become a household term. These quasi-banking services by non-banks demonstrates that although the world needs a banking system, it doesn't need banks.

We have mentioned in this book the many financial or near-financial intermediaries that also provide financial services, including banks, the financial corporations of manufacturing companies, brokerage houses, credit-card companies, and mortgage companies. Once upon a time, these didn't even exist. As they came into being, it was clear what role each individual institution played in which markets. Banks provided insured savings for widows and orphans and lending to commercial and retail customers. Savings and loans did mortgage lending. Investment bankers provided capital and insurance companies provided protection. Long-term uninsured investing was done through securities firms. All of this has changed: insurance companies provide capital; banks want to be investment bankers and sell insurance; the brokerage industry is selling insured deposits; the savings and loan industry is reinventing itself after having virtually gone bankrupt, and the investment banking firms want to do it all.

But banks have a secret weapon: they have earned the trust of their customers since the banking industry started in the Middle Ages with gold safekeeping. Lords and commoners both left their gold with the safekeeper, who issued receipts showing ownership. When gold owners needed their gold, they showed their receipt to the safekeeper, who returned their gold. The banking industry developed because it became much easier to trade the receipts given out for gold than to withdraw and deposit the gold itself. This new method made life easier for all concerned, and the trust of the safekeeper was created.

The banking industry evolved when goldkeepers expanded their business by lending gold. A certain amount of gold would always stay on deposit, and the goldkeeper could issue receipts without having all of the gold on deposit. The goldkeeper had created a new business by creating receipts that would be accepted by any merchant just as if gold were backing those receipts. As long as the goldkeeper did not get greedy and could sufficiently predict deposits and withdrawals of gold, clients would continue to trust him. Thus financial intermediation was born. Add to this story government regulation and federal depository insurance and you have created modern-day banking.

The trust between the bank and customers is how the bank can distinguish itself from other financial intermediaries. This competitive advantage is enjoyed only by banks, but the banking industry has only a short time to exploit this niche. The window of opportunity is closing much faster than most bankers realize. The current core customer base of banks comprises the generation age 55 and older. We call this group the "savers," and they are still very loyal to the bank and to traditional banking products. Since this market segment currently has the majority of investable dollars, it is being bombarded with information from other financial intermediaries regarding investment products. We believe the bank is in the best position to educate savers as they start to shift to higher-yielding investment products. Whoever educates the customer earns the customer relationship.

Over the next decade, the largest transfer of wealth in the history of the nation is going to take place. Trillions of dollars in assets will flow from the savers to the next generation, the baby boomers, and they are not savers like their parents. Boomers do not have the same loyalty or trust in the banking system that their parents did. If the banking franchise is going to survive, it must offer products and services to satisfy the financial needs of the next generation.

Alternative investment products are no longer truly alternative products; they are additional investment products. Additional investment products are no longer a luxury for an investor's portfolio but a necessity. We have discussed the changing economic scene that makes it imperative for individuals to learn to manage their investments. A portfolio that consists of 100% CDs is no longer a suitable investment strategy; it will never grow enough to provide for retirement needs, let alone allow the individual to pay for children, medical bills, and education along the way. Asset allocation is the way of the 1990s, and the baby boomers are asset allocators. They will need checking and savings accounts, but they will also look to long-term, higher-yielding investment products to satisfy their retirement and wealth-accumulation needs.

A banker friend recently told us of an individual who came into the bank with $85,000 to invest in an IRA. Our banker admitted that he no longer felt comfortable recommending that this customer put the entire investment in a bank CD. We have stressed the importance of focused investment objectives leading to portfolio diversification as well as suitability. The institution needs to be concerned with giving customers the products and services that will meet their changing needs.

Beyond the question of how the banking industry will compete is the question of how the community bank will compete in the 1990s. Every day the newspapers are filled with stories about larger regional or superregional banks buying community banks. It won't be long before most of today's community banks will be branches of larger institutions. Changing regulations are making it easier and economies of scale are making it a reality. Not only have alternative investment products been the answer to banks' need for increased earnings, but they have also provided a way of competing with other financial intermediaries. While we would not claim that offering a retail investment services program is going to keep any given bank from being purchased or going bankrupt, we can say that offering these products will give you a chance against the competition, however your institution defines competition.

Banks have been offering alternative investment products for years; they have had the capital, the customers, and the expertise. Many banks have quietly been selling insurance for so long they were grandfathered with their own insurance agencies when the regulation was passed prohibiting banks from doing this. Term insurance, mortgage insurance, and credit life insurance have been legal in some states and offered through banks for a long time. Many banks have been selling a variety of securities products for years, first through the capital markets area and later through discount brokerage units. The problem with all these programs and products is that they have not been actively offered. They have merely been made available, and that's not enough to help reinvent and reinvigorate the banking industry.

As usual, the larger banks are leading the way with innovation. Proprietary funds were the first innovation, giving banks one more rung on the ladder of vertical integration. Some money center banks with their own proprietary mutual funds allow customers to switch from one fund to another in the same family at any local ATM machine. It should not be too long before you will be able to make a deposit to an existing mutual fund account through the same machine. These banks are taking an existing product and using technology to add ultimate convenience for the customer.

We have discussed the reasons banks have had such little experience with the proactive, state-of-the-art marketing that so many other industries have mastered. Twenty years ago bankers talked of a banking charter as a license to print money. With that kind of tradition, it is understandable that banks have resisted the self-analysis necessary to go forward. If banks are to survive, they must add marketing skills to their portfolio of competencies.

Proactive marketing begins with information and the systems to track and manage the results of marketing programs. This process includes obtaining and utilizing both the marketing information and customer information to maximize the bank's bottom line. Banks must institute cost accounting systems to figure out the marginal cost of a new checking account, or a mortgage loan, or a CD. Until banks know that, they can't assign the appropriate incentive pay to the employee who brings in that new relationship. Customer information is the other new frontier for banks—serious, demographic, analyzed, formatted customer information necessary to conduct target marketing campaigns and reach out to prospective customers.

This is a good start. Other aspects of a sales culture must also be introduced, such as recognizing that customers don't just come to you, you have to reach out for them with systematic, organized target marketing campaigns. Sales goals, incentive-based pay, and referral systems are other aspects of a sales culture that banks have long resisted.

Additional investment products are part of every citizen's future because of the changing demographics and economic situation. Banks must offer these products to keep their customers. Beyond that, additional investment products and a retail investment services program offers banks the opportunity to tune in to the various proactive marketing programs and increase their customer base.

Resources

Richard A. Ayotte (CPA)
Senior Partner
American Brokerage Consultants, Inc.
405 Central Avenue, 7th floor
St. Petersburg, FL 33701
813-898-5551
813-895-1192 (fax)

ABC provides management consulting and strategic planning services to the various participants in the bank-brokerage industry. ABC also publishes the *Bankers Guide Series,* a three-volume resource covering third-party firms, mutual fund companies and insurance companies that distribute investment products through banks. ABC is the oldest consulting firm in the U.S. that focuses its entire efforts on the bank-brokerage industry.

William F. Broderick
Human Resources Matrix
355 North Williams
Palatine, IL 60067
708-202-9144

Since 1986 HRM has worked with dozens of bank-brokerage programs on the sales and marketing dimensions of performance. Projects have included business development, account management, compensation, sales management, and bank relationships.

Ronald R. Glancz, Esq.
Venable, Baetjer, Howard & Civiletti
1201 New York Avenue, NY, Suite 1000
Washington, D.C. 20005
202-962-4947
202-962-8300 (fax)

Ronald R. Glancz is a partner and head of the securities and insurance brokerage practice of Venable, Baetjer, Howard & Civiletti in Washington, D.C. For many years Glancz has advised banks, thrifts and third-party firms on regulatory issues related to securities and insurance brokerage activities.

Jon Higgins
National Regulatory Service
323A Main Street
Lakeville, CT 06039
203-435-2541
203-435-0031 (fax)
NRS is the nation's leader in investment advisory and broker/dealer registration and compliance services. NRS is devoted exclusively to providing registration and compliance-related services to both investment advisors and broker/dealers. It is all they do, and they pride themselves on the breadth and quality of the services offered.

Joy P. Montgomery
President, Money Marketing Initiatives, Inc.
55 Madison Avenue, Suite 200
Morristown, New Jersey 07960-1905
201-984-3850
201-984-3853 (fax)
Money Marketing Initiatives, Inc. (MMI) is a nationally-recognized expert in bank mutual funds and investment products. MMI specializes in custom-designed marketing and business development consulting to improve the profitability of banks, mutual funds, trusts and investment management firms.

Bank Investment Representative
632 North Main, Suite 1C
P. O. Box 4364
Logan, UT 84323-4364
801-752-1173
801-752-1193 (fax)
Bank Investment Representative is the magazine of investment marketing and investment program management. Now in its fourth year of publication, it is the bank-brokerage and insurance industry's forum for exchanging management, sales, marketing, service and motivational strategies, in addition to industry, legislative and regulatory news. For a free subscription, call 801-752-1173.

Bank Securities Journal
1000 Westlakes Drive, Suite 310
Berwyn, PA 19312
215-640-2087
215-640-2089 (fax)
The *Bank Securities Journal* is the official publication of the Bank Securities Association (BSA). The journal is positioned to directly reach the key decision makers at all levels and in virtually all areas of the bank securities industry.

Pershing
Division of Donaldson, Lufkin & Jenrette
Securities Corporation
One Pershing Plaza
Jersey City, New Jersey 07399-0002
201-413-2000
Pershing executes and clears equity, fixed-income, mutual fund and option transactions for more than 650 independent brokerage firms and banks and provides account administration, management information and investment-related services to the securities industry. It is the nation's largest provider of correspondent brokerage services.

Lasalle Consultants, Ltd.
203 N. LaSalle Street
Suite 2100
Chicago, IL 60601
312-558-1589
708-343-2669 (fax)
Suburban office: 708-343-2668

LCL Investments, Inc.
1440 W. North Avenue, Suite 400
Melrose Park, IL 60160
708-343-4450
708-343-4460 (fax)

Index

About the Authors

Lawrence E. Harb is the President and Founder of Lasalle Consultants and LCL Investments, Inc. Mr. Harb was previously Senior Vice President and Manager of the Bond Department of the Exchange National Bank of Chicago. Mr. Harb holds a Master of Management degree from Northwestern University's Kellogg School of Management. He holds a degree in management from Northern Illinois University and currently serves as Adjunct Professor in the Illinois Institute of Technology financial markets and trading program offered through the Stuart School of Business.

Sarah E. Sleight is a Vice President with Lasalle Consultants and Customer Service Manager with LCL Investments. Previously, Ms. Sleight was a vice president and fixed-income salesperson for First Chicago Capital Markets. She also worked in the Asset-Backed Securities Division where her responsibilities included producing the *Asset-Backed Securities Commentary*, a weekly newsletter widely quoted in the financial press. Ms. Sleight has a Master of Management degree from Northwestern University's Kellogg School of Management and a BA in history from Bucknell University.

That's the academic background, but the background we wrote this book out of is our practical experience.

When Larry Harb worked for a major Chicago bank managing an institutional capital markets department, he wrote a business plan detailing how his department should enter into the business of selling retail investment products. At that time, banks were even more suspicious of the securities industry, its personnel and practices, than they are now. What he thought was needed was an investment program offered through a bank by bankers—an entire program planned and executed from a banker's perspective.

Larry was a little ahead of his time with that project. As it turned out, he founded Lasalle Consultants, Ltd. in 1990 to work with money center and regional banks at developing and fine-tuning both the capital markets and retail investment areas. Lasalle Consultants realized that community bankers needed to offer alternative investment products and had few means to receive the help or service they needed. They were, for the most part, too small to start their own broker/dealers, and the third-party providers available to them were owned by either insurance companies or brokerage houses. Community bankers were leery of both those sources. They sought programs that were run by people who understood banking, but they had few alternatives.

That's when LCL Investments became Lasalle Consultants' best customer. LCL Investments was founded in 1992 by a group of ex-bankers who wanted to meet the needs of community bankers for programs offering alternative investment products. We spent the first year analyzing structures, building the program, and bringing up our test banks, trying to discover optimal ways of offering alternative investment products in banks. We are now ready to launch ourselves in 1994. Our goal is not to become the largest third-party provider because, as we stress in the book, bigger is not always better; our goal is simply to become the best at what we do.

We have learned an enormous amount as our business has evolved. We wrote this book out of our experiences both as consultants and in founding our own broker/dealer. This book is not written out of theory, but from the theory applied to hands-on practice. In every circumstance, we have been there.